"Joe is an emotionally intelligent leader, and an insightful holistic systems thinker. Both qualities come alive in his writing."
—Yosi Amram, CEO Coach, and former Founder and CEO, Individual Inc. and Valicert Inc.

"Joe Marasco has assembled a smorgasbord of thought-provoking material that will appeal to anyone who deals with software projects and software developers. Dip into the book at any place and savor new ideas about the nature of software, how to motivate professionals, or one of many other topics that will make you stop and think about your current notions. You may not agree with everything Joe says, but you will respect his position and probably change many of your ideas. Many of the chapters will be required reading for my software engineering students."
—Gary Pollice, Professor of Practice, Computer Science, Worcester Polytechnic Institute

"A unique and passionate philosophical work, with wisdom distilled from both academic and business careers…. A down-to-earth, subversive, and witty guide for managing the software of machines and of the human soul. Joe shows how the foremost ingredient for success and happiness, in business and in life, is integrity."
—Kate Jones, President, Kadon Enterprises, Inc. (www.gamepuzzles.com)

"Joe Marasco's new book is not only a solid introduction in project management discipline, but is also entertaining reading. Using very simple, easy-to-understand-and-relate-to examples, he manages to uncover and describe the most fundamental issues of successful team building and people and project management. His book is a must-read for everyone who wants to get a deeper insight and understanding of this discipline."
—Boris Lublinsky, Enterprise Architect, CNA Insurance

"There isn't a manager worth his salt who is going to look for salvation in a 'how to' book. What he is going to look for, however, is a nugget or two that will help him out of a specific dilemma or, given time for reflection, provide him with reinforcement that he is on the right track, or trigger thought processes about new ways to solve stubborn, recurrent problems. Well, Marasco provides a mother lode of nuggets for a manager to mine."
—Bill Irwin, Retired Executive, High Technology Industry

Praise for The Software Development Edge

"This set of articles captures decades of 'in-the-trenches' experience across a broad spectrum of software topics. Joe Marasco has the scars and the smarts to articulate patterns of success that can satisfy a broad audience. He uses mathematics, physics, common sense, and storytelling along with a no-candy-coating style to provide unique perspectives on significant problems in delivering software results as a business. Whether you are a computer science theoretician, a frustrated software project manager, a successful businessman, or a skeptical programmer, you will learn a lot from this compilation."
—*Walker Royce, author of* Software Project Management:
A Unified Framework *(Addison-Wesley), and Vice President, IBM Software Services-Rational*

"Joe Marasco's readable essays on managing successful projects shows that software development managers——no different from all managers——must embrace the fundamentals of management if they are to succeed: working through people and process to be decisive, dealing with politics, keeping on schedule, and, yes, shipping a well-developed product. Marasco uses plain English to explain many integrated skills, ranging from estimating the time it will take to really do things, to negotiating effectively, even to eloquently describing three distinct phases of our personal development. He frequently uses a "can we talk?" conversation with a fictional colleague, Roscoe Leroy, in a Socratic dialogue to illustrate the two sides to a point in many areas (reminiscent of Galileo's writings to explain his then-heretical views); in this case, Marasco's advice will help technology professionals escape the clutches of pervasive Dilbertian incompetence, and enable readers to be more effective in our ever-changing world."
—*Carl Selinger, author of* Stuff You Don't Learn in Engineering School:
Skills for Success in the Real World *(Wiley-IEEE Press), and Contributing Editor,* IEEE Spectrum *magazine.*

"This is a book loaded with practical experience distilled into insights useful for every software manager, and for thoughtful software engineers. Joe brings his keen observations on engineering, physics, software, and management to bear on managing software projects, and the real-world practices and problem-solving techniques required to be successful."
—John Lovitt, Senior VP, Rational Software (retired)

"You don't have to be in the software business to benefit from this book. This is a book that any manager at any level can pick up at any point and enjoy at any time. Highly recommended reading."
—R. Max Wideman, Fellow, Project Management Institute, AEW Services, Vancouver, Canada

"Marasco's book makes for fascinating reading for anyone concerned with management problems in general. The reader is introduced to simple quantitative models, based on the author's experience, that help in assessing performance and choosing a roadmap to successful completion of a complex project. In addition, the author's use of anecdotes and his writing style make for both an entertaining and informative read."
—Professor Martin Lesser, Department of Mechanics, Royal Institute of Technology (KTH), Stockholm

"Individually, each chapter is articulate, engaging, thought- provoking, informative, and well informed. Collectively, much as a compilation of short stories from a skilled, mature author, these chapters invite and help train the reader to see into and to understand what is often only observed in passing or scarcely noticed. Seeing the big picture in little things and identifying critical components of the large landscape, Marasco's analytic and synthetic skills both impress and enlighten."
—Stephen D. Franklin, University of California, Irvine

"Practical advice on project management expressed in an erudite and entertaining style. The insights are an impressive synthesis of management principles and practical experience that should contribute to improved project management in any organizational activity."
—Steven Globerman, Kaiser Professor of International Business, Western Washington University

The Software
Development Edge

The Software Development Edge

Essays on Managing Successful Projects

Joe Marasco

Addison-Wesley

Upper Saddle River, NJ • Boston • Indianapolis • San Francisco
New York • Toronto • Montreal • London • Munich • Paris • Madrid
Capetown • Sydney • Tokyo • Singapore • Mexico City

The publisher offers excellent discounts on this book when ordered in quantity for bulk purchases or special sales, which may include electronic versions and/or custom covers and content particular to your business, training goals, marketing focus, and branding interests. For more information, please contact:

U. S. Corporate and Government Sales
(800) 382-3419
corpsales@pearsontechgroup.com

For sales outside the U. S., please contact:

International Sales
international@pearsoned.com

Visit us on the Web: www.awprofessional.com

Library of Congress Catalog Number: 204118158

ISBN 0-32-132131-6

Text printed in the United States on recycled paper at R. R. Donnelley in Crawfordsville, Indiana.

First printing, April 2005

To Wini, the light of my life.

Contents

About the Author	**xvii**
Foreword	**xix**
Preface	**xxi**

PART 1. GENERAL MANAGEMENT	**1**

Chapter 1. Beginning at the Beginning	**3**
The Importance of Good Software	4
Hard Rocks in the Swamp	5
Audience	6
The Iterative Problem-Solving Clock	6
Recap	10

Chapter 2. Computational Roots	**11**
The Precipitator	11
The Answer	12
How This Program Worked	13
Why Was This Generation of Engineers Special?	15
Computation	16
Getting to Know the Numbers by Their First Names	17
So How About Those Computers?	18
Our Computational Heritage	20
Recap	20

Chapter 3. Mountaineering   23
On Climbing Big Mountains   24
Common Causes of Failure   30
Ingredients for Success   31
The Human Factor   32
Recap   32

Chapter 4. Managing   33
Managing Teams   34
Recap   40

PART 2. SOFTWARE DIFFERENCES   41

Chapter 5. The Most Important Thing   43
Iterative Development   43
Roscoe Leroy   44
Going Over the Waterfall   45
The Other Extreme   47
Roscoe's First Picture   47
Roscoe's Second Picture   48
Wait a Minute!   49
Keeping the Vectors Short   49
The Application to Software Development   50
Applied Learning and Short-Vector Direction   51
Risk Targeting   51
Have You Heard This One Before?   52
More on Applied Learning   53
Business Implications   54
The Staffing Effect   55
Just Plain Horse (shoe) Sense   57
Recap   58

Chapter 6. Modeling   59
How to Explain the UML   60
What Is the UML, and Why Is It Important?   61
A Second, Less Trivial Example   61
The Third Example   63
And Now for the Relevance to Software…   65
Raising the Level of Abstraction   66
Recap   66

Chapter 7. Coding   69
How Managers Can Learn a New Programming Language   70
The Problem, Better Defined   71
What Should the Standard Problem Contain?   71
The Animal Game   72
Does the Animal Game Fit the Criteria?   73
Does It Pass the "So What?" Test?   74
It's Your Game   76
Recap   76

PART 5. THINKING LATERALLY   **195**

Chapter 17. History Lesson   **197**
Don't Let the King Be Your Architect   198
Things Aren't Always as They Seem   198
Checking the Design   198
Knowing What You Don't Know   198
Continuity of Leadership   199
In a Hurry, As Usual   199
Focusing on the Wrong Features   199
When the Design Is Bad…   199
The Relevance of Testing   200
Prototype Versus Product   200
The Inquest   200
Recap   200

Chapter 18. Bad Analogies   **201**
Houston, We Have a Problem   201
Fig Newtons   203
Everything's Relative   205
Quantum Nonsense   207
Heat Death   211
Other Examples   213
Good Science   213
Recap   214

Chapter 19. The Refresh Problem   **215**
Refreshing Embedded Software   216
The Current Situation   217
The Software Upgrade Game   218
A Modest Proposal   218
Software Upgrades, Revisited   219
Some Nice Things Come for Free   220
Why This Will Work   221
Refinement   222
What About Software Piracy?   223
Until the Sun Takes Over   223
Recap   224

Chapter 20. Not So Random Numbers   **225**
Roscoe Sets the Stage   226
Simulating the Batter   226
First Steps   228
Second Steps   230
Generating More Probabilities   230
Of Course, We've Already Left the World of Baseball   232
Reality Is Ugly   233
Monday's Solution   234
Lessons Learned   239
Recap   240

PART 6. ADVANCED TOPICS   **241**

Chapter 21. Crisis   **243**
   The Five Days of the Fish   244
   The Fish Market   244
   Day 1: Unaware   244
   Day 2: Avoiding the Issue   244
   Day 3: Enter "The Fixer"   245
   Day 4: The Turning Point   245
   Day 5: Two Critical Paths   246
   Moral of the Story   246
   Recap   247

Chapter 22. Growth   **249**
   Growth Issues   249
   The Naïve Model   251
   Consequences of the Model   253
   An Illustrative Example   259
   Non-Linearity   260
   Call to Action   261
   Conclusions   263
   Nomograph   264
   Spreadsheet   265
   Recap   267

Chapter 23. Culture   **269**
   What Is a Culture?   270
   Strong and Weak Cultures   271
   Defining Corporate Values   271
   And the Applicability to Software Is…   274
   Building a Strong Culture   275
   When You're Looking for a Job…   279
   The Bottom Line   280
   Recap   280

Chapter 24. Putting It All Together   **281**
   Schlepper   282
   Macher   284
   Mensch   286
   More on Mensches   287
   Population Distribution   288
   Some Final Thoughts on the Model   289
   Recap   290
Acknowledgments   **293**
Index   **297**

About the Author

Joe Marasco is a retired senior vice-president and business-unit manager for Rational Software, now one of the five brands of the IBM Corporation. He held numerous positions of responsibility in product development, marketing, and the field sales organization, overseeing initiatives for the Rational Apex product and Visual Modeler for Microsoft Visual Studio. In 1998, he served as Senior VP of Operations. He retired from Rational in 2003. He holds a bachelor's degree in chemical engineering from The Cooper Union, a Ph.D. in physics from the University of Geneva, Switzerland, and an M.S.A. from the University of California, Irvine Graduate School of Management. When not writing, he barbecues and plays golf; his ribs are much tastier than his scores.

Foreword

Why should anyone listen to what Joe Marasco has to say about software development and the people who do it?

In the spring of 1991, we awarded Joe his five-year service award. Back then, Rational Software was small enough to individualize these awards, and Joe's was quite unusual. We obtained the hood ornament from a Mack truck—the classic bulldog—and mounted it on a plaque. Everyone agreed that this award symbolized Joe's dedication and tenacity when it came to getting the job done.

So it wasn't too surprising when, later that year, we selected Joe to lead a watershed development effort at Rational. At the time, our flagship product, the Rational Environment, ran on proprietary hardware, and we realized the importance of moving it to the UNIX platform. While this move was inevitable, it was fraught with risk; in fact, many other companies suffered fatal damage trying to move their software solution from proprietary hardware to industry standard platforms—among the carcasses littering the side of the road were electronic design automation (EDA) companies such as Daisy and language-specific companies such as Symbolics. The task was known to be difficult, the result uncertain, and the need essential.

Joe, on the other hand, was positively ancient by Silicon Valley standards: he was 46. But we believed that Joe's experience and "steady hand at the tiller" would see this project through. We also knew that Joe would do whatever it took to get the project done.

The record speaks for itself. In September 1991, Joe took on the leadership of the new team with a plan to deliver "Rational II" in two years on two UNIX platforms. After seven months, a limited-function subset prototype was up and running. After 16 months, the development team was "self-hosted," which meant that it was able to complete the development of the product using the partially-completed product itself. And, to the minute, the team delivered what became known as Rational Apex on two UNIX platforms—IBM and Sun—in the two years that had been promised.

Apex was an extremely successful product, one that is still delivering value to customers today. Joe was the Business Unit Manager through releases 2.0 and 3.0 and also oversaw its porting to every significant UNIX platform and to the Windows platform as well. More important, for the 10 years following the release of Apex 1.0 in 1993, Joe was the "go-to" guy whenever we had a difficult product delivery problem in the company. As the company grew through merger and acquisition, Joe assumed the role of troubleshooter, helping out wherever the need was greatest, wherever the pressure was most intense.

One of the reasons Joe was so successful in delivering products is that he spent a lot of time with his developers understanding the details of the products and the development problems. But he also spent a lot of time with Rational's customers, developing a keen understanding of their needs. As every product delivery is the result of many compromises, Joe was always well informed to make good judgments when it came to product decisions.

Near the end of his career at Rational, Joe began to write about software development in a series of articles in Rational's e-zine, *The Rational Edge.* Unlike the articles written by our "Three Amigos," these were much more down in the trenches, reflecting his experiences both at Rational and in his previous environments. What we discovered was that Joe was able to cogently articulate his experience and act as a "virtual mentor" for budding software development managers worldwide. The response to these articles was extremely positive, and it is a pleasure to see them all collected here in one place.

This is not a theoretical treatise on software development. That's not what Joe was all about. Joe was about having his teams ship products we could all be proud of, products that were easy to maintain and offered real value to customers. If you want to develop products that you can be proud of, that lend value to your customers, this book is a "must-read."

Mike Devlin
General Manager
Rational software, IBM

Preface

This book draws heavily on a series of columns called Franklin's Kite that appeared in Rational Software's e-zine, *The Rational Edge,* in the early 2000's. These articles were aimed at software development managers, and their goal was to help readers avoid many of the common pitfalls that await software development projects and teams. More than 20 appeared, and we—my editor, Mike Perrow, and I—noticed that readers often began their monthly perusal of *The Edge* with *The Kite.*

My intention here is to not only to collect these articles but to sew them together in a form that makes them even more useful for software development managers *and their managers.* I have done that by reorganizing them thematically, instead of presenting them in the order they originally appeared. This has caused me to do some light editing in places where "forward-referencing" would otherwise take place. I have also paid attention to the footnotes, many of which appeared in the original as URLs and appear here as more formal citations where appropriate. Finally, I have added material at the beginning and end of each chapter so that the context of each article as part of the whole becomes clearer.

The reader will quickly note that the chapters have several different styles. Some of them are expository, some are fairly analytical, and some are folksy "Socratic dialogs" between the author and his avatar, one Roscoe Leroy. Roscoe is an invented character, a good technical general manager who initially knows little about software development. I use him as a foil, allowing his "naïveté" to force me to explain things without using technical jargon. My approach is ecumenical and subversive: I will use any technique that permits me to get the message across. Some of these chapters will appeal to some readers, and others will appeal to others. Whatever works is, by definition, good. I take my cue from Horace, who wrote in *The Art of Poetry,* "He has won every vote who has blended profit and pleasure, at once delighting and instructing the reader."[1]

I divide the work into six parts of four chapters each. Briefly:

- **General Management:** These chapters deal with topics that are useful to managers in general and also expose the reader to my background and biases. I include them so that we have a common baseline for what follows.

- **Software Differences:** In this section, we take a look at those things that distinguish software development from other management challenges.

- **The Project-Management View:** I take the perspective that a software-development project is a variant of the generic project and, as such, amenable to classical project-management techniques. On the other hand, I strive to point out what *is* different about software development.

- **The Human Element:** I turn around in this section and look at software development from the perspective of the people who do it. Once again, I try to compare and contrast that which is similar to that which is different for software-development projects.

- **Thinking Laterally:** Software people come at problems from many different points of view. In this section, I expose the reader to some of the more speculative and original ideas that he or she may not have seen before.

- **Advanced Topics:** The successful software-development manager is like a really good pinball player: His reward for high scoring is given in free games. This additional "stick time" leads to his becoming even more proficient. In this section, I talk about some of the challenges that come with success.

This book has 24 chapters.[2] You can read it serially, or pick out a chapter at a time; they can stand on their own. This is a good "airplane book"; read a chapter and then think about it for the rest of the flight. If you get just one new idea from one of the chapters that covers the price of the book, I will have been successful.

With these prefatory remarks out of the way, let's get down to it.

---

[1] Horace, Satires, Epistles, and Ars Poetica (Cambridge, Massachusetts: Harvard University Press, 1999). The original Latin text is "Omne tulit punctum qui miscuit utile dulci, lectorem delectando pariterque monenendo." It can be found at line 343 of Ars Poetica.

[2] Coincidentally, so does *The Iliad.*

PART 1

GENERAL MANAGEMENT

The first section of this book deals with generally useful stuff.

Chapter 1, "Beginning at the Beginning," introduces the subject of software development and my particular view of managing it. I include some thoughts on general management problem-solving.

This perspective is colored by my education and experience, so in Chapter 2, "Computational Roots," I take some time to further introduce myself. One of the themes of this chapter is that my roots in software development are deep in "computation"—that is, I started out as a scientific programmer at a time when computer science was in its infancy, and my "basic training" was as an engineer.

In Chapter 3, "Mountaineering," I use a mountaineering metaphor for the software development project; I did some mountaineering as a young man and discovered that there were a lot of parallels between the two activities and the teams that undertake them.

In Chapter 4, "Managing," I talk about what a good manager does and does not do.

CHAPTER 1

Beginning at the Beginning

Several years ago, my cardiologist told me I needed an implanted cardioverter defibrillator (ICD) installed in my chest. I have a condition known as ventricular tachycardia, which means my heart occasionally beats too fast. This can lead to fibrillation, which is usually fatal; the deck-of-cards-sized ICD monitors heart rate and triggers an electric shock if it detects an aberrant rhythm that persists too long. The shock is about the same as you'd get from those well-known electric paddles in the emergency room.

The installation of an ICD is not something you take lightly. So, as a veteran project manager, I quickly did a risk analysis. The question was binary: install, or not install? If not, my best hope was that there would never be a fibrillation, in which case not installing would be the right solution. But if a fibrillation occurred, not having the ICD would most likely lead to a wrong and fatal "solution." This branch of the decision tree favored going ahead with the surgery.

But there was more to consider. While the risk in the surgical procedure itself was fairly small, there was still the possibility that the device could fail—but that turns out to be no worse than not having the device at all! The more interesting question was, what happens if I got a classic "false-positive?" That is, the device fires when there is *no* imminent fibrillation.

One thing was certain: When the device fires, the recipient experiences what my doctor described as "inconvenience." Certainly, dying without a necessary shock would be

3

more inconvenient, but you can imagine scenarios where an unnecessary firing of the device could put you at risk. I needed to think about this branch of the decision tree.

What could go wrong? The device is pretty simple. It has a long-life battery, a big capacitor, and a software-driven microprocessor. The battery and capacitor are stock hardware items that can be subjected to the usual quality control metrics; the same can be said for the microprocessor. But what about the software?

Most of my career has been in software development project management. Knowing perhaps too much about how software is developed, I was concerned about trusting my life 24 × 7 to the performance of a piece of software. For the rest of my existence, electrodes implanted in my heart muscle could deliver a significant shock based on the commands processed by the software monitoring its cadence.

I went ahead with the procedure and, so far, the device and I have successfully coexisted for seven years. The data we can read from the device's memory shows that it has gotten ready to fire several times, but only once has the software logic made the decision to pull the trigger. Yes, it was "inconvenient," but not overly so. And I'm glad it worked when I needed it.

The Importance of Good Software

This example goes right to the heart of why software development is important. For me and thousands of others, this is a "mission-critical" application. In most embedded applications we can really ignore the details. If software in a microwave oven occasionally malfunctions, at worst we might overcook something. But we really want the software that manages the ABS braking in our cars to work all the time, along with all the other software systems in our vehicles to control engine performance, traction, ventilation, instrumentation, and so on. Getting interdependent systems like these to function properly isn't easy. And as the number of interacting, distributed software systems increases, the probability of unforeseen error rises.

We want to trust the software that increasingly runs the world we live in, but unless you work within the software development industry, you probably know little about how software is created, tested, or fielded. Software quality varies widely. We hope that higher-quality software resides in the more mission-critical applications; otherwise, disaster awaits.

During the past 20 years, software professionals have made considerable progress toward getting "engineering discipline" into software development. Usually this means a better, more consistently practiced "process." This is a good thing, but it is far from the total solution. While lack of process can often derail a project, good process never created good software.

To make good software, you need good people. And, just as important, you have to manage them intelligently. Software developers, or programmers as we used to call them, get a bum rap: Everything that goes wrong is assumed to be their fault. In fact, most bad software results from less-than-inspired programming coupled with sloppy management. That combination causes software that works most of the time but not always, and that's not good enough.

Hard Rocks in the Swamp

I draw on an experience base that spans a 30-year career in software development management, and 10 years in the trenches before that. During that time, almost everything in our industry has seen pervasive change: hardware, operating systems, networking, languages, tools, and so on. It might legitimately be claimed that software development is the most rapidly changing technical field in existence today. It is for this reason that I have tried to identify the things that have not changed in the past 40 years. For, if some things have remained constant during the past 40 years of tumult, it is likely that these same things will remain constant for the next 40. Knowing where these "hard rocks in the swamp" are located can help us navigate forward, keeping in mind that our field will continue to grow, evolve, and be subject to periodic fads and fashions. The good managers will continue to be successful by integrating the "eternal verities" with the best of the new technology, always seeking balance between the conservatism of proven practice and the risk and reward of innovation.

Fully half my management career was spent at Rational Software, which is now one of the five brands at IBM. Its influence on my thinking was profound, and I profited greatly in three regards.

First, I got to interact with many sophisticated customers all over the world, customers who were attempting some of the largest and most difficult software development projects in a variety of different application domains. These customers gave me insight into key determinants of project success and failure; it was an invaluable database.

Second, I got to manage some of the finest teams of people in my experience, and any success I may have had as a software development manager needs to be ascribed in large part to the talent of the teams I got to manage. A good manager can enhance the performance of a great team, but as a savvy horse player once said to me, "I've never yet seen a jockey carry a horse across the finish line."

And third, I got to interact with some truly great thinkers, people who not only understood what was working and not working, but who took the time to carefully integrate and articulate their experience. There was a constant buzz within the company, a whirlpool of sometimes competing philosophies as the theoreticians, methodologists, and practical, pragmatic managers engaged in a real marketplace of ideas. I have to admit that never once did one of my colleagues say, "Well, Joe, that may work in practice, but what does the theory have to say?" No, rather I like to believe that we got to the right place by successfully tempering new theoretical approaches with hard-earned field experience.

That is not to say that I was a novice when I first came to Rational in 1986. I had already accumulated lots of scar tissue from the software development wars. I had opinions based on seeing the good, the bad, and the ugly. Rational held out the promise of a bunch of talented individuals who had formed a true team and were dedicated to making things better for their customers. It was very exciting to be part of that adventure for more than 16 years.

Audience

This book is not only for software development managers but also for *their* managers, who often know little about software. This can be a dangerous thing if the senior manager (unknowingly) makes unreasonable demands and the software development manager (all too willingly) accedes when he shouldn't. A year later, a flaky product ships. A year after that, everyone is pointing fingers, and the programmers get blamed for doing a poor job. Wrong answer!

So let me state my position simply. To be a good software development manager, you first must be a good manager. Most of the general principles of managing teams apply to software development teams. In a similar vein, most of the normal, standard, project management principles apply as well. If you know a lot about software but are a terrible manager or violate basic project management principles, you will fail. That is why a lot of what you will find in this book is suspiciously close to "general management." You need these basic ideas as a foundation.

Then you need to know what is different about software engineering. If the last paragraph is addressed to the new software development manager, this paragraph is addressed to his boss. Yes, boss, you are a good general manager; that is how you got to be the boss. But what you need to know is that some things *are* different in software. These differences have to do with a variety of things, some of which are connected to the relative immaturity of the discipline. The more you know about these legitimate differences, the more you can have intelligent conversations with the software development manager who is reporting to you. And that means together you can make more well-informed decisions for the team. So your reading this book will help you learn what is different about software development. Without snowing you with a lot of technical jargon, we seek to make you a more understanding collaborator in the process. If you will invest the time and the energy, it will pay big dividends.

The Iterative Problem-Solving Clock

Whether you are a software development manager or his manager, you are going to have a variety of real-world problems to solve day in and day out. How do you go about solving problems? Is this a random process that sometimes works and sometimes fails miserably? Do you get "stuck?" Do you have trouble directing your creative energy, and do you have difficulty achieving closure?

We all do. However, there is a way to get control of this very important process. I solve problems by going around the circle in Figure 1.1 at least twice, and more than that if required. In the real world, it is possible to begin the process at almost any point on the circle, but for convenience I begin my explanation at the most "logical" place, nine o'clock. And I'll switch from "I" to "we" because we are going to do this *together*!

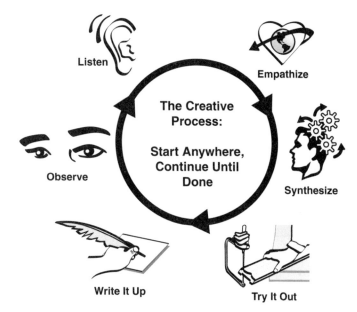

Figure 1.1   The iterative problem-solving clock.

The First Time Through the Loop

The first time we go through the loop, the steps are a little different from those on subsequent trips:

- **Nine o'clock: Observe.** We need to be *aware*. We need to have our antennae out all the time. We aggressively watch what is going on around us, and we try to sniff out problems.

- **Eleven o'clock: Listen.** Having detected a problem, we engage with others to find out what they think. We use active listening, creating a Socratic dialog with our conversational partner, alternating teacher and student roles. We try to listen more than we talk, and we take good notes.

- **One o'clock: Empathize.** I separate this from listening to make sure that you understand the difference. One can listen to get "objective" data; *empathy* is the bridge between listening in the fact-gathering sense and the beginning of the synthesis part of the process. We listen with our ears and synthesize with our brains; empathy involves use of the heart. It requires that we step outside ourselves and truly put ourselves in the other person's shoes. This is not always easy to do when what we are hearing does not agree with our previous notions. Hence we must empathize before we can synthesize. Managers who come from engineering sometimes skip this step because they are used to solving problems that are 99.44 percent technical in nature; unfortunately, this is not the case with most general management problems.

- **Three o'clock: Synthesize.** Here we bring together all the pieces:
  - The data we have gathered through observing and listening
  - The affective elements discovered by seeing it from other people's perspective
  - All our previous experience in dealing with problems of this type
  - Other "lateral" experience that may be relevant
  - Our "tool bag" of methods, processes, strategies, tactics, techniques, and tricks
  - We fabricate a trial solution to the problem, using everything we know

- **Five o'clock: Try It Out.** In this crucial step, we perform tests and do experiments to see if our solution is workable. Here is where we weed out those ideas that looked good on paper but are unimplementable in the real world. We can't discover this until we try it. Be especially hard on yourself in this phase; shooting down bad solutions is a vital part of the creative problem-solving process.

- **Seven o'clock: Write It Up.** Here is where you document your solution and the tests and experiments you have performed. This is how you are going to present your solution to the rest of those involved, so take the time and care to do a good job of it. If you don't write it up, you will have a harder time selling your idea, and things that are not written down tend to fade quickly.

The Second and Subsequent Times Through the Loop

We've gotten the trial solution out, and enough time has gone by for people to evaluate it. Now it is time to go through the loop again. Here is what the six steps look like this time:

- **Observe:** See how people are reacting to the trial solution. Have we made a dent?
- **Listen:** Talk with people about the pluses and minuses of the solution. Get them to tell us what they like and don't like, what works and what doesn't work.

- **Empathize:** What factors could be influencing what we are hearing? Are people just resistant to change? Is someone's personal ox being gored by the solution? Are there side effects or unintended consequences that are causing people grief? Or, is there "irrational exuberance"?

- **Synthesize:** We need to take the new data and fold it back into the synthesizing process. Can the original solution be tweaked, or does it need a major overhaul? Most of the time we can go forward by modifying or improving on the last pass. But we shouldn't be afraid to start our synthesis from scratch if we blew it the first time.

- **Try It Out:** With each pass through this station, we should become more intelligent about how to test the solution. After all, we have the tests from the previous pass, plus new data on what to look out for. Beat up the solution worse than the critics will. Anticipate objections or problems, and see how the solution performs when confronted by them.

- **Write It Up:** Using the original document as a starting point, modify what we need to, and point out what we have changed and improved.

When Are We Done?

When are we done? Closure is important; we don't want to cycle through the loop forever. A good guideline is to stop when there is very little significant new information obtained during the observing and listening phases.

The process can begin at any point on the circle. We must be opportunistic when it comes to problem-solving. Real life is "messy," and sometimes the germ of an idea may come up, for example, through some random synthesizing going on at the time. While it might seem better to stop and go back to nine o'clock, sometimes the best thing to do is to seize the moment and go forward from there. Don't forget, we will always do at least two complete cycles no matter where we start, so feedback is ensured. That's why that step at seven o'clock is so important—it's what precipitates the feedback.

Note also a very important beneficial side effect: Because we have been "writing it up" as we go through the process loop two or more times, we don't have a huge documentation chore at the end. We will have progressively built up the "final documentation" as an organic part of creating the solution in an iterative way.

Solutions obtained using this method tend to "stick." The art is to navigate through the six steps crisply and with all deliberate speed. Don't skip steps, and don't get stuck too long on any one step. Once you gain experience with the approach, you can improvise at will. But in the beginning, use the framework to add discipline to your creativity. You may be surprised and pleased with the results.

Recap

One way to think about this book is that at various points along the way I have stopped at seven o'clock and "written it up." This book is a collection of those stopping points where I was able to freeze in time the provisional solutions to the problems I was facing. When the time came to collect and integrate them into this book, I got to take one more pass. In most cases, I found that what I had put down needed little modification. The result, stabilized by several previous and subsequent iterations around the clock, had withstood the test of time.

CHAPTER 2

Computational Roots

I entered software development through the back door. When I was in high school and college, "computer science" was just getting started. Most of the software development managers my age similarly got their start in some other field: math, physics, chemistry, or engineering. We learned about computers because it was the new computational tool available to us. Some of us then replaced our passion for science or engineering with programming. This, over time, led to a desire to build better software.

What this means is that I come at the management of software development from a different perspective than someone who has been formally trained in a university computer science department. I tend to view it as an engineering management problem, first and foremost. I've had a chance to work with some really great software people, and the mix of talent and competencies we together bring to a development project can be quite powerful.

So how did I come to be an engineer in the first place? It's a long and personal story, one that you might find interesting. If not, just go on to the next chapter after reading the final section, "Recap."

The Precipitator

On October 4, 1957, the Soviet Union put into orbit a satellite called Sputnik. It was reputedly only about the size of a basketball, weighed 184 pounds, and emitted beeps that could be monitored by shortwave radio. The world was shocked, and America's preeminence in the world of science and engineering took a huge public-relations hit. And, to make matters worse, on November 3 of that year the Soviets launched the 1,121-pound Sputnik II, which contained a dog named Laika. This occurred before Sputnik I spiraled to Earth and disintegrated, and its effect was profound. Just as the Nagasaki bomb detonated so shortly after Hiroshima, Laika showed that the Russians had the capability to do this regularly, and that it was not a one-shot deal. Even if the timing was calculated precisely to have this effect, the psychological perception transcended objective reality. We were at the height of the Cold War, and the Russians had trumped us badly. For, if they could put a dog in space, was a monkey far behind? And, once a monkey was up there, well, you could figure it out. Nuclear missiles launched from space were now practically a reality. In military terms, the Russians had captured the ultimate "high ground," and our scientific, military, and political leadership figuratively and literally "went ballistic" over it.

Now Sputnik certainly was a barnburner, but it was also an event that triggered other things that turned out to be much more important for the country. Its legacy for John Kennedy included using the "missile gap" to help win the presidential election of 1960, and his subsequent engagement of the entire country in the space race of the 1960s culminated by our putting a man on the moon in 1969. In 12 short years, we caught up and surpassed the Russians, much to the awe of the rest of the world. It was a great example of American "can-do" spirit.

Of course, the physics required dated back to Newton, and the rocketry was, oddly enough, managed by veterans of Germany's V-2 days (at least if the popular myths are to be believed). But Sputnik changed a whole generation because of something more subtle—it challenged our educational system to its roots.

Basically, what came out of Sputnik was that we Americans were behind because the Russians had a better educational system and funneled more of their "best and brightest" into science and engineering. While the Americans were kings of mass-producing consumer goods and raising the middle class's standard of living, the Russians were solving the really hard problems and getting ahead of us where it really mattered. Regardless of the reality of the situation, this perception was widely disseminated and accepted as the gospel truth. For a while, it seemed the whole country was in a dither over this. Something had to be done.

The Answer

In America, there is a time-honored solution to every new crisis. If you are unclear on the concept, it is called "throwing money at the problem." That is, one can short-circuit a lot of dickering and consensus-building in a democratic society by using the free-enterprise system of rewards to influence behavior. While this method is not always the most efficient, and is almost always not pretty, it can be effective. It may attract a lot of the wrong kind of people—those interested in making a fast buck, not in solving the problem—but it will also redirect a lot of the "right" kind of people.

Now, the people who needed influencing were *not* the young people who were my age. Sure, some of us would get caught up in the glamour, mystery, and intensity of science for the right reasons. Some of us might become interested out of some patriotic streak. But by and large, hormones dictated that for most of us—I'm speaking for the adolescent males here—the main "problematic" issues for the next few years revolved around the opposite sex. For the geeks among us, this loomed much larger and more daunting than getting to the moon. Seeing those attractive young girls hanging off athletes' shoulders was a motivator at least as powerful as atomic energy, believe me. Sputnik didn't change that.

No, the people who needed to be influenced were our parents, because the late fifties and early sixties were the last time kids even pretended to listen to them. The timing was perfect; within 10 years, the rebelliousness of the sixties' generation would make parental influence *de minimus*. So the first bit of fortuitous timing was that we were literally the last generation who paid any attention when our parents spoke. It is hard to imagine the teenagers of the seventies and eighties being anything like those of the late fifties and early sixties. Think "Father Knows Best"[1] and a middle-class culture in which marijuana was something only jazz musicians smoked to get high.

Of course, we had no idea it could be any other way.

How This Program Worked

So the great public-relations campaign began. The unofficial message to the parents of America's youth ran something like this: "Science and engineering are a priority for the country." It was especially important for the campaign not to leave out the engineering part. This had (and still has) to do with the popular culture's beliefs about science and engineering. Science is hard; engineering is routine. Science is glamorous; engineering is grungy. Science is performed by aristocratic philosopher kings; engineers are closer to blue-collar people. Only brilliant people can aspire to science, whereas, with enough application, almost anyone can become an engineer. Stereotypes, each and every one. But think about it. If you were the nation's internal PR machine trying to recruit the largest technological pool of young people you could, what would you do? Pitch just to the scientists? No, to catch as many fish as possible, you cast the net as widely as you can, and point out that scientists and engineers are both needed. That way, if a potential

---

[1] "Father Knows Best" was an American television situation comedy of the day that presented a "typical American family" in which everyone was perfect and all problems were resolved in 30 minutes, less time out for commercial announcements.

scientist washes out along the way, you perhaps recapture an engineer.[2] And for every parent who worries that perhaps his son is not quite M.D. material, the notion that dentistry is an honorable (and lucrative) profession is a great source of comfort.

Now, the people who were being pitched to had lived through the Great Depression of the 1930s. Because of the subsequent intervention of WWII, and the fact that at this point in time (1957) they had school-aged children, we can infer that they had not gotten a lot of education themselves. (They couldn't go to college because of the Depression, they were taken out of action for the five war years in the early to mid-forties, and then got married and had kids as soon as the war was over. Many of them never benefited from their G.I. Bill of Rights.) So now they were lower-middle-class blue-collar workers, their kids were getting ready for high school, and they were struggling economically. The pitch was brilliant: Get your kid to be a scientist or an engineer, and he will be set for life.[3] "Economically, this is the ticket. Don't miss the boat. Make sure your kid doesn't wind up in the same bind you're in!"

The rest of the pitch was even more persuasive: "We are going to make it easy on you. We are going to pump an incredible amount of money into educating these kids for free. Scholarships and fellowships will be abundant. Don't worry about the costs. If your kid has talent, the country will educate him, and he'll never have to worry about anything again."

Let me tell you: This was a great campaign, and it worked.

What was the reality? Well, as usual, good news and bad news. The country did pour a lot of money into many science and engineering programs. There was a lot of pump priming. Sputnik went up when I was 12 years old, and I came out of the other end of this process in 1972 (oh yeah, it takes a long time if you get serious about it) with a Ph.D. in physics. My entire undergraduate and graduate studies were financed through a combination of summer and weekend earnings, scholarships, and fellowships. Aside from the opportunity cost of foregone wages during that time, I can honestly say that my entire education did not cost me (or my parents) a dime. I entered the job market entirely debt-free: Look, ma, no student loans to pay off!

The bad news is that the lifetime meal ticket, as is true of all lifetime meal tickets, was an illusion at best. It may be hard to imagine that anyone could believe getting a bachelor's degree in engineering would secure economic well-being for a lifetime. But at the time, it seemed much more plausible and practical than any of the alternatives, and a lot of young men (and later, young women) were pushed in this direction. And in one sense it worked. For example, by the early seventies, we had physicists coming out of

---

[2] The careful reader will note that this reinforces the previously mentioned stereotypes. However, it was more common for physics students, for example, to migrate into engineering than the other way around. As you will see below, I was a curious exception to this general rule.

[3] The masculine pronoun is used advisedly. We hadn't yet figured out that women could be scientists and engineers. That would take 10 more years and another revolution.

our ears and a legitimate job crisis, because supply had outstripped demand (at least in academia).[4] We forgot to stop priming the pump; as usual when the government is involved, fine-tuning is not remotely close to possible.

Of course, in 1960 we had no clue that this could possibly happen. It was as improbable as putting a man on the moon.

Why Was This Generation of Engineers Special?

After this rather long prelude, I want to talk about 10 years of engineering students, those from roughly 1960 to 1970. I entered engineering school (The Cooper Union) in 1962 and graduated with a bachelor's degree in chemical engineering in 1966, so I consider myself a representative of this group. After lots of high school preparation, I entered college almost exactly five years after Sputnik went up. I was going to be an engineer.

I also want to talk about engineers, not scientists. I did my graduate work in physics and earned my doctorate in experimental high-energy particle physics in 1972, so I can claim and consider myself both an engineer and a physicist. But while the physics and other sciences saw relatively little change during this decade, the engineering profession and engineering schools saw a lot of radical change.

I might also remark in passing that this may have been the last great wave of *American-born* engineering students. Once this group of people passed through the system, we reverted to not pushing kids into engineering. The vacuum was then filled by students from overseas.

This generation of engineering students was on the cusp. We were the last to undergo some of the classical disciplines of engineering. This may have varied from school to school (Cooper was on the conservative side), but before 1960 things were one way, and after 1970 they were another way. During the sixties it was a mix; depending on which school you attended, you got a slightly different mix.

For example, my freshman class was one of the last classes to receive formal training in engineering drafting and projective geometry. Drafting meant using dividers and straightedges to do professional-quality engineering drawings. Today, you might know one subclass of these as blueprints. We had to understand top view and side view, and how to generate views at any arbitrary angle given these two. And my own special hell: We couldn't pass the course until we had done at least one India ink drawing on vellum paper.[5] This was all part of the tradition of the engineer being just down the hall from the

---

[4] Ironically, it was this job crisis that helped me continue my progression into software development.

[5] Strictly speaking, vellum is not paper. It is not parchment, either; it is made from calfskin. But if I didn't say "vellum paper," no one would know what I was talking about.

machine shop. You needed to be able to complete drawings that communicated some-thing meaningful to a machinist. It was the part of engineering that was "sleeves rolled up, loosen your tie." To be part of the team, you had to understand and be able to do en-gineering drawings, even though you wore a white shirt and tie and the machinist wore a blue-collar shirt and apron. In some sense, you were going to be peers (at least for awhile), and learning to draw was part of the apprenticeship. The idea that you could be-come an engineer without being able to do "mechanical drawing" was a non-starter. They laugh when I tell these stories today. But it was dead serious stuff back then. Imagine be-ing able to ace calculus because you can do integration by parts to beat the band, but are in mortal fear of flunking out because that damn ink always runs underneath the straight-edge before you can finish the bloody drawing.

Computation

By far, the biggest "cusp" experience had to do with computation. We were the genera-tion that bridged the slide rule and the computer. Let me explain.

In the sixties, the pocket calculator was still Flash Gordon[6] stuff. The HP-35, the first real pocket calculator for engineers, appeared on the scene in 1972. (What a coincidence—just as I was finishing my Ph.D. Timing is everything!) The slide rule was instantly and ir-revocably dead. But up until that point, slide rules were an engineering staple. Simply put, you performed calculations on your slide rule. Using a computer to get everyday answers was simply not practical back then. Computers were batch-oriented, and to get answers, you had to write programs. In FORTRAN. It was just too much overhead for one-off work. Whereas today you might fire up Excel, back then you whipped out your slide rule.[7]

You started to learn how to use the slide rule as a freshman in college, if not sooner. It was not just a matter of learning how to do it. You had to learn how to do it reliably, accurately, and quickly. You used your slide rule to get answers on 50-minute physics, chemistry, and engineering examinations. If you couldn't use this as a real tool and if you couldn't compute quickly, you would fall off by the side of the road. It was as bad as having the ink blot under the straightedge.

The instructors didn't cut you too much slack, either. Sometimes we would receive some partial credit if we showed we understood the computation but screwed up the

---

[6] Another antiquated American reference. Flash Gordon was what we had long before we had Luke Skywalker. In an interesting twist, his villainous arch-nemesis was Ming the Merciless instead of Darth Vader. Things were much less politically correct back then.

[7] The slide rule was sometimes called a "slip stick." We joked that we did our calculations with a "s drool." We were very geeky.

result; but ultimately we found that you didn't get enough credit for good grades if you didn't get the right answer. What a novel concept—lots of credit for the right answer, not much for the wrong one. But, as one of our crusty old professors once remarked, "Engineers get paid for getting the right answers." By the way, did I mention that speed was important?

So, we practiced. Herman Bilenko, an upper-division electrical engineering student, ran a slide rule remediation club. We met at lunch, and he would give us problems and we would race to see who could get the right answer the fastest. As Dave Barry would say, I am not making this up.

Getting to Know the Numbers by Their First Names

Now, if you have never used a slide rule, I will point out that in most cases you are performing a computation with four or more factors in the numerator, divided by four or more factors in the denominator. The "answer" the slide rule gives you is something like "123." The decimal point location and the exponent (the "times ten to the sixth power," for example) are up to you. This is a crucial point. To get a correct answer, you have to do two things right. First, you have to figure out where the decimal point goes in the final three-digit result based on the eight or more factors. Second, you have to be able to figure out, using rules of scientific notation, what the exponent of the final answer is going to be based on the exponents of all the factors. It was absurdly easy in these calculations to be "off by one" in either the exponent or the placement of the decimal point. So for a correct answer of 1.23, it was almost always possible, through carelessness or misjudgment, to come up with an answer of 0.123 or 12.3. This is called in the profession "off by a factor of ten."

Consider this: A factor of ten is enormous. Apply it either way to your salary and see what I mean. Yet it is very, very easy, using a slide rule, to be off by a factor of ten. What this means is that for every calculation you did, you had to have some idea of what the answer should be *before* you did the calculation. You had to "know" that the answer should be around "one," so that if you "computed" that it was 0.123 or 12.3, you would know that you had made a mistake and go back and find it. This meant that you had to estimate the result beforehand. It was a survival skill.

The people who never mastered it flunked out of engineering school, because it was just too easy to make a mistake. If you couldn't smell out a bad result, you were in big trouble.

Of course, this knowledge led to other interesting acquired behaviors. Most computations were multistage, requiring that you plug an intermediate answer into another formula to get a secondary result, and then plug that in, and so on. So mistakes made early propagated, and if you got a completely absurd result at the end, it was a bear to backtrack all the way to the beginning. So we developed the habit of maniacally testing all of our intermediate results for reasonableness before going on. We became our own computational QC inspectors, not letting a computation proceed unless we were sure we were still in the ballpark. This was a great instinct to develop early in our careers.

Needless to say, as a by-product, we also got to be pretty good at computing things in our heads. None of us were equal to the legendary Richard Feynman[8], but we all got to be pretty good. It was sometimes enough to make a liberal-arts student's head spin. For us, it was just another acquired survival trait.

By the way, we often were asked about performing computations to only three significant digits—the "123" mentioned previously. Was that good enough? Well, it's one part in a thousand, roughly. Most experimental physical data is lucky to be within plus or minus 1 percent, or roughly ten times less accurate. So if you had three or four factors in the numerator and three or four factors in the denominator, each with at best 1 percent error, it was illusory to think that the calculated answer could be good to one part in a thousand. Ergo, slide rules could be used for most calculations with few problems.

Of course, when computers came in, it all changed. Then calculations were done by numerically iterating the equations—replacing derivatives by finite differences, as it were. Then, because the result was obtained by cycling through thousands of steps, errors could accumulate insidiously. That's why computers have to have so much higher precision; you need lots of precision at each step to guard against accumulated error. But in the end, the result can *never* be more accurate than the input data. Many people have either never understood that or lost sight of it throughout the years.

So How About Those Computers?

You can be sure that I believe we collectively lost a lot in terms of skills when we went from slide rules to pocket calculators. Years later, I was amazed at how students would punch in numbers to their pocket calculators, come up with a patently ridiculous answer, and defend the answer based on the idea that "That's what the calculator says." The notion of an input mistake was somehow not part of their equation, nor was the idea of trying in some way to judge whether the answer made sense or not. How sad.

But, you say, no matter. Computers fixed all that.

Well, the hell they did. But let's not get off on that rant. What is more interesting to talk about is how the last generation of slide rulers became the first generation of computer jocks. For during that 10 years before the pocket calculator replaced the slide rule, computers arrived on campus, and those of us who could see the future knew there was a computer in it.

---

[8] Also a graduate of Far Rockaway High School.

So we learned FORTRAN on an IBM 1620-class machine. I won't bore you with war stories. But we learned a lot about how to translate computations done by hand into computations done on a machine. And because the process was onerous, to say the least, we reserved writing programs for something that really merited it, like a computation you had to do over and over again.

Even for those of us who took to programming like a fish to water, using the computer was a big pain in the butt. We discovered that these machines were notoriously picky about misplaced punctuation marks and inadvertent intrusions into column six. (Anything punched into column six on a FORTRAN statement card meant, "Tack this statement onto the previous one." It was the "continuation" field. Naturally, if you did this by accident, the FORTRAN compiler would burp unpleasantly.) It seemed to us that most of the time our programs were rejected for the most silly of reasons.

The reality was that we were being inconvenienced by batch processing. A single error could halt the entire process, and we had to fix these serially, one at a time. If you didn't get multiple "passes" at the machine per day, debugging took a long, long time. So we learned to be precise because, like it or not, the machine was unforgiving. We also learned to put in lots of diagnostic print statements, so that, when things "went off into the weeds," we could detect when, where, and, hopefully, why. Above all, we became the original "defensive programmers." Once interactive terminals came, followed by personal computers, this style diminished in use—not in importance, mind you, but in use.

We also made a discovery that would be remade over and over again for the next 40 years—most college-level problems are "toy" problems, so your computer programs don't have to be very long or very good. But, ironically, we didn't write much code to handle errors on data input. After all, the computer was a tool to be used by professionals, meaning engineers. The idea that "civilians" would use a computer and need error-checking on input was as improbable to us as a man walking on the moon.

Were we better computer users for having been slide rule jockeys? You bet we were. We were trained to suspect the result of every calculation, whether performed by man or beast (the computer was considered a beast). So there was no hypnotic trance induced by seeing results neatly printed out in rows on forms paper that had tractor hole punches on both sides. No GIGO[9] for us. We knew that the answer was probably wrong. Only after a lot of scrutiny were we willing to accept that the computer hadn't screwed it up this time. Like their pocket calculator brethren, we marveled at how many people would blindly accept a result just because "a computer" had printed it out. We knew that a person had written a program to obtain that result, and we all knew how easy it was to make a mistake when writing a program. We had written enough of them ourselves to be painfully aware.

---

[9] GIGO is an acronym standing for "Garbage In, Garbage Out."

Our Computational Heritage

In the sixties, there was a generation of engineers trained in both slide rules and computers. Those who went before never really adopted computers, and those who went after never really learned how to compute by hand. But this group of young engineers received their most intensive engineering education working with both the tools of the previous generation and the tools of the next at a time when the tools couldn't have been more different. This, in turn, cultivated an entire behavioral culture toward engineering results. Among the tenets were the following:

- Accept no answer just because you had computed it. Question everything. By the time we had gotten to computers, this principle had morphed its way to "trust no input data."

- Break complex computations into reasonable-sized chunks, and check every intermediate result to avoid error propagation.

- For both manual and computer calculations, figure out a way to debug your computation so that when you do generate a patently ridiculous result, you have a built-in way to sort it out.

These ideas were not abstractions; they were keys to survival. And from a pragmatic point of view, they became instincts that enabled survival in a cold, ruthless world of problem-solving.

My theory is that this golden generation of engineers became the leaders of today's Silicon Valley colossus, and that we are now at risk as this generation approaches retirement age. We have bigger, faster, more powerful computers, and magnificent software running on them. But who is going to tell us when the answers are wrong?

Recap

This chapter is dedicated to Andrew Marasco (1916-2004), who just missed seeing this book in print.

There's nothing so tragic as an elegant theory assaulted by a brutal gang of facts. My friend Bob Marshall recently sent me an article from *Invention and Technology* entitled "How America Chose Not to Beat Sputnik into Space." In this article[10] T. A. Heppenheimer asserts, "We could have launched an Earth-orbiting satellite more than a year before the Soviets, but we intentionally held back. And by handing them a propaganda

---

[10] Heppenheimer, T. A. "How America Chose Not to Beat Sputnik into Space." *American Heritage of Invention and Technology,* Winter 2004 Volume 19, Number 3, p. 44.

triumph, we ensured their ultimate defeat in the Cold War." I'm just wondering if part of the defeat had to do with mobilizing a generation of scientists and engineers, and if this wasn't one of those "unintended consequences" which this time worked in the right direction.

What does all this background into engineering and computation have to do with software development and its management? Well, it has to do with an approach to problem-solving. We were taught to make estimates, then calculate, then compare. What happens when the results of your calculation turn out to be very far off your original estimate? There are three scenarios you need to examine, in the following order:

1. Check to see if you made a computational error. Everything else is right, but you screwed up the numerical part.

2. Your computation is right, but there is an error somewhere in your model. For example, you assume something varies linearly, when in fact it should be quadratic. You have focused on the right phenomenon but have modeled it incorrectly.

3. Your model is correct, but it is the wrong model. That is, there is something else at work that dominates your model. The effects your model predicts, while correct, are dwarfed by another effect that may work in the same or opposite direction, and you have overlooked this other effect.

Now this approach turns out to be quite general, and as such there are applications to software. For example, I have frequently found that debugging a bizarre result in a program *in this order* leads to enlightenment. Before questioning fundamental assumptions, check to see that you did the math right—in the case of a program, did we use the right data at the right time? Then check your model—in this case, the algorithm. If things still don't make sense, you now need to examine if something is going on that you really didn't understand. This may lead to discovering that the basic programming approach was faulty to begin with.

More fundamentally, our computational grounding led us to question almost everything. As pointed out previously, we were the original "defensive programmers." Later on, as managers we tended to be quite hard on ourselves—and our teams—in terms of using "solid engineering." That meant putting a lot of emphasis on basic architecture, on useful things like design reviews, and on testing our systems early and often.

We were sticklers for detail. We remembered that just because "things almost balance" doesn't mean the answer is right. Sometimes in draft financial statements you find that totals are off by only a little bit, and are tempted to blame "round-off error" as the culprit. Too often you find, on closer examination, that two rather large mistakes in opposite directions have coincidentally almost cancelled each other out. When the gods of computation smile on us, they leave us this clue. Don't be too lazy to follow up, remembering at all times Richard Hamming's Golden Rule: "The purpose of computing is insight, not numbers."[11]

Lastly, our engineering background taught us about complexity and scaling. I will always remember my senior engineering thesis project. A team of us had to design an entire petrochemical refinery from scratch. We had a few weeks to do it, working day and night. Here's what we learned: It is hard to coordinate multiple engineers simultaneously working on different parts of the project, because one person's output from his stage of the plant is another fellow's input. Everything changes at once! In order to get around this problem, we had to cleverly design interfaces that we could stabilize. Many years later, it turned out that this notion proved to be invaluable in the construction of large, complex software systems. Other concepts of "building big things" were similarly usefully borrowed and transplanted into software development soil.

[11] Richard W. Hamming was one of the greatest applied mathematicians of the 20th century. He had a glorious career at Bell Labs, and later taught for many years at the Naval Postgraduate School in Monterey, California. He published extensively, and his well-written books have had a great influence on me.

CHAPTER 3

Mountaineering

Back in the early 1970s when I lived and worked in Switzerland, I joined the Swiss Alpine Club and spent several glorious summers moving from novice to intermediate climber. It turned out that mountain climbing was more to my taste than rock climbing; perhaps this was because there was more variety in mountain climbing which, after all, has rock climbing as a subset. Or perhaps it was because mountain climbing placed more emphasis on stamina over peak athletic performance. In any event, I learned that to be successful in this activity required merging basic technical skills with good people skills and good judgment. I found that there were lots of climbers but few really good climbing-party leaders. So I tried to figure out what made the good leaders really good.

All the people I sought to emulate had come into their own at a point when they were definitely past the peak of their physical prowess, but had accumulated incredible judgment and people skills. While they were still technically strong enough to "climb lead"— that is, be first on the rope—it was their other leadership strengths that distinguished them.

Later on, when part of my job was to evaluate software development managers, I noticed that tremendous similarities existed between the good managers and those lead climbers I had worked with on the peaks. Perhaps, I reasoned, it was because the two activities had a lot in common. This led to thinking of a mountain climbing expedition as a metaphor for a software development project. In working out the details of this metaphor, I came to embrace it more and more, although, as with all metaphors, one needs to be careful not to carry it too far.[1]

On Climbing Big Mountains

Building a large software system is very much like climbing a big mountain. Both activities have a well-defined goal and require the coordinated efforts of a team of highly qualified people placed in circumstances they can foresee and plan for—but not control. Success in both cases is a probabilistic calculation because risk plays a role. While I will detail some of the issues in later chapters, here I'm considering the project as a directed team activity and paying particular attention to some of the key elements that come up time and time again.

Let's explore in more detail.

Understanding Scope as a Prelude to Planning

For both activities, good planning increases the chances of success. The first step in good planning is to understand the scope of the task. For a mountain climbing expedition, this consists of understanding the height of the mountain, the relative difficulty of the terrain, special weather conditions, and so on. One can hardly imagine a climbing team, when asked about the height of the mountain they are about to scale, responding, "We'll know when we get to the top!" In a similar vein, I expect a software team to understand the scope of the job they are about to undertake: How big is this mountain? How many lines of code, how many special device drivers, what fancy user interfaces, what performance characteristics, etc., will be required? In neither case can the team nor its leaders foresee every possible "gotcha," but the salient features of the problem must be identified and written down so that they are addressed in subsequent planning.

A second step in planning is to review the scope of the project and the major obstacles to success, and to identify the size and skill set of the team necessary to accomplish the objective. My experience in both domains tells me that the smallest possible team is best. All participants need to have a minimum skill level so they don't drag the team down. For example, if the expedition warrants having a medical doctor as part of the team, the doctor should be a good climber and not a burden as the team makes its way to the summit. In both domains, participants who can play multiple roles are more valuable than specialists; when things get difficult, flexibility is an incredible asset in a small-team environment.

---

[1] I should mention that James Highsmith has made extensive use of the mountain-climbing metaphor in his book *Adaptive Software Development: A Collaborative Approach to Managing Complex Systems* (New York: Dorset House Publishing Company, 1999). I developed my ideas independently throughout many years and didn't see James' treatment until a reviewer pointed it out to me.

Selecting the Team

When you are identifying potential team members, it is important to evaluate candidates along several dimensions. Clearly, you are going to recruit specialists as required: if you must traverse a difficult, crevasse-riddled glacier, you are going to need a good ice climber. In a similar vein, if you are producing a product with real-time requirements, you are going to need a runtime expert. In addition, as mentioned previously, there should be a strong effort to choose overall competent climbers and engineers; in drafting for professional sports, this is the philosophy of picking the best athletes as opposed to drafting for position players. Finally, you need to gauge character: in addition to assessing skills, you need to evaluate how each individual will work as a team member, and how each person will bear up under stress and adversity. It is important that the prospective team member be a good climber and partner in foul weather as well as in fair. Because foul weather is certain at some time or other on most climbs, one can even make the case that performance under those conditions is the most important criterion.

One factor above all else helps to factor risk: experience. The more people you can add to the team who've been up this kind of mountain before, the better. Climbers who have scaled many, many mountains are sure to have better judgment based solely on Darwinian considerations! This is known as the "Alaskan Bush Pilot Algorithm": When choosing amongst alternatives, pick the pilot who has been in business the longest. Experienced sailors have a saying: "Excellent sailors use their excellent judgment to keep them out of situations requiring the use of their excellent skills." The same applies to mountaineers and software managers. It is better to avoid problems through savvy than to solve them through heroic efforts. The single easiest discriminator for judgment is experience. Look for people who have done it before and who have been successful. All other things being equal, take those people who have survived a tough mountain over those who haven't climbed at all.

Can you imagine attempting Everest without sherpas?

Organizing the Team

Having put together a prospective pool of climbers/engineers, the team leader now needs to think about how to assemble the sub-teams. In climbing, this means allocating two, three, or four people to each rope.

It is a given that no one climbs unroped on a mountain of any significance. In addition to the great danger this would present to any climber foolish enough to try it, it also represents risk to the rest of the party. They would have to take extraordinary measures to rescue their colleague from even the smallest of missteps. Likewise, in large programming projects, lone-wolf behavior is very risky. At least two on a rope should be the rule.

For teams on which three or more engineers need to collaborate, pay attention to composing the right mix. You always need a strong lead climber, and the mix of skills and personalities needs to be distributed so that you don't wind up with one rope that is much weaker than the others. The guiding principle is balance: No one rope should be unbalanced, and the ensemble of teams should also be well-balanced. If you can't construct reasonable sub-teams from the pool, you need to analyze why, and either add to or prune the pool until you can.

The goal should always be the smallest number of small parties. Four teams of three or four players each can accomplish great things.

Remember, in software engineering as in climbing, there is an insidious logistical pyramid silently at work—the more people you attempt to put on the summit, the more people you need to support the effort organizationally. The growth tends to be exponential with the height of the mountain.

Scheduling

Another aspect of planning is scheduling. Once you sketch out the team, you can begin to figure out how much food and what kind of climbing gear you need. The software equivalent is figuring out how much development hardware and software you will need and at what time. In order to make the resources come out right, you need some idea of how the team will progress up the mountain. Remember, there are three possible ways to go wrong:

- Not enough resources

- Too many resources

- The wrong *kind* of resources, which translates to useless weight to carry

If the climb is going to take 10 people four days, that is one set of resources; if it is 15 people for two weeks, that is another matter entirely.

Now, the interesting thing is that in order to do this work, you need to know

- What route you are going to take

- What the intermediate stopping points are

- About when you plan to get to each intermediate point with a given number of people

That is all you need in order to draw up a schedule and calculate what you require to get the job done. You don't need to know every detail of how you are going to get to each stopping point. That's a good thing, because any plan that depends on that information is highly risky: Most of those details are unknowable with any certainty before you actually get on the mountain. Even if you plan them down to the gnat's eyelash, they will all change as you make progress. Barring contingencies that force a route change, however, the overall stopping points, or *milestones,* should not change much.

Milestones are useful for two things: to get a gross idea of how you are going to do the job and what resources you will need; and to monitor important progress. If you thought it was going to take you two days to get to your first base camp and it takes you six, then you had better sit down and think about the rest of the endeavor. That the team's morale is still wonderful and that the base camp is the best-designed one you have ever seen are largely irrelevant, considering that the whole project is likely to take (at least) three times as long as planned.

Milestones or Inchpebbles?

So I advocate rough, bottoms-up planning with consensus from the team about how long it is going to take to achieve significant milestones. And I believe in taking very seriously the time it takes to actually get there. For this to be useful, the milestones cannot be too close together nor too far apart. On a climb of a day or two, the milestones are typically on the order of a few hours apart. For a climb in the Himalayas with a duration of weeks, my guess is that significant milestones are days apart. For a software project that has a duration of 18 to 24 months, somewhere on the order of three to four months between milestones feels right. This translates to about six significant milestones for the project, give or take a few. If you are using an iterative development approach, the implication is that about six major "checkpoints" are in order, even if there are more iterations than that. For example, a two-year project might have 10 iterations, but only six of these will require the highest level of management scrutiny upon their completion.

There is nothing wrong with each sub-team's having some finer granularity tasks, if that helps. It is up to each team leader to organize his rope to make sure his party arrives in synch with the others.

Monitoring and Recordkeeping

Most experienced team leaders I know keep some records in real time. For climbers, a small pocket notebook and stubby pencil usually come out at rest points, and some notes are written down. When I examine these notes after the climb, I find that although I did not capture a lot of information, it is always very much to the point. Typical notations are about arrival times, discrepancies from planned arrival times, and unusual conditions. Sometimes there are informal notes on how the individuals and teams are performing. When you're planning a climb, notes like these about similar mountains can prove useful for adjusting initial estimates. For software projects, similar notations can be useful for gaining insight into actual project performance.

Handling Risk

Project plans also need to address contingencies. In climbing, the two variables that represent *forces majeures* are surprises in the selected route and the weather.

If the route chosen beforehand turns out to be too risky, an alternative route needs to be selected. This usually occurs because the ice or rock is not in the same condition it was in the last time this route was explored. A good plan uses natural stopping points in the climb to assess options and choose among alternative routes. The software development analogy is to assess technical direction continuously and then, based on the results achieved with each iteration, change the route slightly for the next iteration. Note that the goal, the mountain's peak, is a constant. However, changing conditions may affect our judgment as to the best way to get there. It is rare that there is only one path, and the superior mountaineer distinguishes himself by finding the right path in the face of new data.

The weather is a different thing entirely. When the weather turns on you, the whole nature of the enterprise changes radically. Now it is not an issue of getting to the top, but one of survival. Even if the party decides that further immediate progress is impossible and that the correct strategy is to "hunker down" until the storm blows over, everyone may still perish if food runs out before the weather abates. Because you have absolutely no control over the weather, you must view it with the utmost caution; the strength of your team can become irrelevant. More people die of ego on mountains than any other cause; failure to turn back at the right time can be fatal.

The programming analogy is when you find yourself dependent on things you can't control directly. This includes new, untested technology, scheduled miracles, required violation of known laws of physics, and internal and external suppliers and subcontractors. Ignoring changes of weather in these areas can lead to death, either instantly or in a painful and protracted fashion.

Decisiveness

I have never met a good climber who was indecisive. I have known climbers who confused recklessness with decisiveness. There is a difference. (I might also add that I have known old climbers, and I have known bold climbers. I have not known any old, bold climbers.)

The main thing I learned when climbing was that you don't have the time to agonize over decisions. That doesn't mean you can afford to shoot from the hip. You often have to consider alternatives that are difficult, situations in which one wrong branch can mean the difference between success and failure or, in the extreme, between life and death. Sometimes the choice is not obvious.

However, what you cannot afford to do is to become paralyzed and continue to defer the decision—also known as the "paralysis by analysis" syndrome. You must take some time, consider the options, gather data, and then decide. Once you decide, you go forward and don't second-guess yourself.

This may mean walking a fine line in terms of team dynamics. It is critical to build consensus around important decisions. However, consensus building itself can lead to paralysis. At some point, it is the leader's responsibility to make the decision if there is an impasse. If the team has been correctly assembled, they will then execute, understanding that this "best" decision is better than no decision at all.

I once was perched on a rock trying to decide which of two ugly paths to follow. My climbing partner humored me for a little while and then said, "Well, you can make a decision or you can sit here and freeze to death." It's the same thing in software development.

Common Goal and Focus

On a good climb, everyone agrees on the purpose. Usually, that means getting to the top. Anything that doesn't contribute to the goal is ruthlessly avoided: no side trips, no one going off to pick flowers, no one stopping for a half hour to take pictures, and so on. The team can agree beforehand that some of these activities are part of the climb and thus sanctioned; however, it is very important that there not be confusion as to the principal objective and how it is to be attained.

The software development analog is staying focused on the objective, which is usually to build a software system. Interesting software side trips can sabotage the whole effort, especially if one sub-team ends up in a crevasse. On a related subject, don't worry about style points. Mountaineers don't award any. Getting to the top "ugly" beats an aesthetic retreat anytime. This is not a personal opinion; this is the way most of the world keeps score.

Taking the Long View

In talking about climbing a mountain, it is common practice to make the mistake of focusing on getting to the top, as though that were the only goal. Getting to the summit and then getting the whole team back down the mountain in one piece is the real objective. (In a similar vein, the objective of the space program in the sixties was not to put a man on the moon; it was to put a man on the moon and bring him back alive.)

The software analogy for this mistake, to stretch the point a little, is to focus all the effort on the development necessary to ship the initial version of the product. This allows you to "plant the flag," as it were. (Sometimes we proclaim victory even earlier—on shipping a first beta copy, for example.) I contend that the moral equivalent of climbing the mountain and getting back down safely is shipping a software product that you can support and maintain. It means putting together a product whose software is robust, whose documentation is complete and understandable, and whose support burden doesn't kill the rest of the organization. So when the team plans a software project, it must plan to do the entire job, not just plant the flag at the summit.

Competition Can Cause Irrational Behavior

Our two sons, David and Marc, were both very young children when we were in Switzerland. Later on, they got to share some of my enthusiasm for climbing. Dave pointed out to me that the "purity" of mountaineering stems in part from the romantic notion of an isolated team striving against the elements to achieve a noble goal. He also remarked that this ideal is often violated in the real world by competition between teams. There may be two or more groups striving for the same peak, all desiring to "plant the flag at the summit" first. (Some areas of scientific research suffer from a similar gap between the romantic ideal and the real world.) In software development, of course, the competitive pressures are even more intense, as the product under development is a competitive weapon that the rest of the organization wants in its arsenal immediately. The effects of this pressure can be catastrophic; often, *en route* changes to plans in response to the competition cause the team to take risks that are too high, leading to failure or worse.

Common Causes of Failure

Having pointed out the similarities between a mountaineering expedition and a software development project, I assert that software projects fail for some of the same reasons climbing expeditions fail. Many of these issues will come up over and over again in later chapters. Let's take the mountaineering "failure modes" and find their software development analogs:

- Trying to get to the summit too quickly.

  Analog: Unrealistic schedule from the start.

- Trying to get to the summit with clearly inadequate resources.

  Analog: Not enough good people or tools.

- Climbing with a team that is too big; the logistical and communications burdens overwhelm the team.

  Analog: Too many mediocre developers in relation to superior developers.

- Taking too long; teams that stay on the mountain too long lose their verve, energy, and desire—fatigue takes its toll. Also, they may simply run out of resources.

  Analog: Software projects that stretch out forever, taking so long that the requirements get changed, sometimes multiple times.

- Sticking to the wrong route in the face of new information.

  Analog: Ignoring data from early iterations; failure to adjust the plan during the course of the project.

- Getting wiped out by circumstances beyond the climbers' control.

  Analog: Supplier or subcontractor failure; failure of a key component that was really an R&D activity, not product-ready.

- Not having a reasonable plan that everyone understands, believes can succeed, and is totally committed to.

  Comment: Usually the result of a top-down, hierarchically mandated plan.

- Failing to execute, within tolerances, according to the plan.

  Comment: Sometimes results from the accumulation of many small slips, rather than any one spectacular failure.

- Losing gumption when the going gets tough; not understanding that adversity is part of the endeavor.

    Comment: Just as bad at the office as on the mountain.

- Not having any reserve for emergencies.

    Comment: Usually the experience of the senior players can provide some of this reserve; they'll know what to do when the unexpected happens.

Ingredients for Success

In a similar fashion, I should be able to deduce the hallmarks of successful teams by looking at other aspects of the metaphor. Here are a few:

- Successful teams are good planners, but they're not obsessive about it.

    Comment: A small amount of good planning beats a lot of detail every time.

- Ability to move fast with small teams; get on and off the mountain before Mother Nature changes her mind and decides not to let you climb this one this day.

    Analog: Get it done before the requirements change too much.

- Talent for assessing incoming data in real time and making appropriate changes to the plan at appropriate times.

    Analog: Use iterative development, integrate and test early and often, and use the information to adjust your plan.

- Good balance between top-notch individual contributors and good team players and leaders; the key here is usually very wide communications bandwidth.

    Comment: Need to have balance and shared mindset.

- Monitor against plan at the appropriate granularity.

    Comment: Need a sense of when you are getting in trouble, and what to do about it.

- Leaders display maturity and good judgment.

    Comment: Knowing when to amplify and when to dampen is important.

- Stamina: Understand that overall extended performance is much more important than burst-mode performance. It is no surprise that most climbing leaders come into their own in their forties, not earlier.

    Analog: It would be interesting to see the statistics on software leads.

- Toughness: Ability to bear down when things go badly.

  Analog: Important when tracking down really hard bugs, for example.

- Focus: Team stays centered on a clearly defined objective.

  Comment: All members know what, why, when, and how.

- Creativity: Willingness to experiment and to experience genuine joy in what they are doing.

  Comment: Just like the rest of life.

The Human Factor

Well, in some respects this comes down to saying that people are everything. For software projects, as in almost everything else worth doing, I'd like to paraphrase the novelist Irving Stone: "Give me men (and women) to match my mountains." The human factor is so important that I devote an entire section to it later.

Recap

Many software managers I talked to about this mountain-climbing metaphor pointed out that I missed an important point: *scaling*. No pun intended there; what they mean is that the general principles remain regardless of the size of the mountain or the size of the project. Things change in the details, of course: a weekend ascent of a 4,000-meter peak by a team of 10 is different from an assault on Everest. On the other hand, violation of the general principles will cause either expedition to fail. While very large software projects need somewhat different organization, one wonders if they would not be more successful if they were modeled on the small-team approach, only with more teams. The interesting issue in both cases is the tradeoff between increased communications overhead with more teams, versus the intrinsic failure modes that seem to set in when teams grow too large. In any event, this mountaineering metaphor did stimulate a lot of really interesting discussion on the true nature of a software development project.

I am still a member of the Swiss Alpine Club, but most of my climbing feats these days involve extricating myself from especially deep sand traps on various golf courses around the world.

The next chapter deals with some other ideas on general management that I have accumulated throughout the years.

CHAPTER 4

Managing

There has probably been more nonsense written about management than just about any other subject. If everyone knows so much about this activity, why is it that the folks down in the trenches universally disdain it?

This subject has puzzled me for decades. I remember as a young worker falling into the trap of believing that my bosses were idiots. A little later on I realized that this was just a variant of Mark Twain's feelings about his dad when he was 15 or so. I began to see that the job was not as easy as I first thought it was. And, in some sense, I was a little lucky; I didn't get to manage people for the first time until I was somewhat older than the average brand-new manager. So maybe I was able to make fewer blunders early in my management career.

Nonetheless, I am sure that I made at least my share along the way, and some of them were doozies, believe me. Looking back on it now, with the luxury of hindsight, I take comfort in a few things. First, every time I screwed up I felt pain—most of it self-inflicted. That pain was useful, because it caused imprinting, sort of like touching the hot stove as a child. I like to think that I didn't repeat too many of my big mistakes, but instead found variety in my errors. More seriously, I began to study what the really good managers did. Finding good role models is hard, but when you do find one, the crucial thing is to carefully analyze what makes him or her great. I would spend time with these folks, who were sometimes (but not always) willing mentors, trying to extract every secret I could from them. My theory was that life was too short to make all the mistakes myself; rather, it was more efficient to try to learn from the mistakes of others.

Managing Teams

I try to distill some hard-earned experience in leading and managing groups into a few basic instructions for success. The blend of leadership and management strategies I describe are effective for both product- and service-related efforts. If you've ever been in a leadership position, you may find that I am articulating much of what you've already discovered through experience—and by applying common sense.

1. Focus on building a strong team that can solve hard problems and add genuine value for the customer.

The key words here are *focus, team, hard problems,* and *the customer.* You need to have a focus; otherwise, your energy will not be well-directed.

And, as it is your team that will ultimately produce the results you need, your main focus should be on building and supporting that team.

The best definition of "team" I've found is that of Katzenbach and Smith:[1]

A team is a small number of people with complementary skills who are committed to a common purpose, performance goals, and approach for which they hold themselves mutually accountable.

Your first challenge is to find the right combination of people with the right combination of skills and personal qualities. Then, to maintain a sharp edge, the team you assemble needs a performance challenge—to tackle and solve hard problems. There is no point in forming a superb team and then letting it loose on a trivial problem.

These problems also need to be customer-focused. Avoid tasking your team with self-serving internal research and development work. If you keep the customer in your sights, there is a much better chance that you will be aiming at a real target. More fundamentally, you need to produce something that adds real value to the customer's situation. Sometimes this involves understanding what customers really *need,* as opposed to what they think they *want.*

[1] Jon R. Katzenbach and Douglas K. Smith, *The Wisdom of Teams* (New York: Harper Business, 1993).

2. Leaders inspire; managers enable. To be both a good leader and a good manager, you need to communicate the vision and understand the details.

There is a difference between leadership and management. In an ideal world, we'd all embody the best attributes of great leaders and effective managers, and avoid the stereotypical failings of each.

Leaders are often charismatic, but they do not have to be. A leader who displays quiet determination and steadfast endurance can be as inspirational as one who breathes fire. What the best leaders do is transmit a sense of mission—a vision—to the rest of the team that inspires and sustains; they lead by example. This encourages teams to accomplish great deeds.

Managers, like leaders, also need to understand the big picture (vision) that drives each project. But they also need to grasp the details that will allow the team to fulfill that vision. Managers need to be enablers: planners, negotiators, pulse-takers, and removers of obstacles. You cannot do this kind of work effectively without understanding the details. And, the more technically challenging the problem domain, the more important this understanding becomes.

Managers and leaders need to know one another's business but remember that they have distinct specialties. A leader's primary job is to communicate the vision. The manager's primary job is to understand the details and enable the team to work effectively and move forward.

Rarely do outstanding leadership and managerial qualities reside in one person. If you are charged with setting up a team, finding one person to fill both roles may be too hard. Instead, understand whether your primary candidate is mainly a leader or a manager, and then find a complementary person for him or her to work with. And analyzing your own strengths and weaknesses will pay dividends when you select a partner to help you lead or manage your next project.

3. Anticipate obstacles, and eliminate them while they're small.

Nothing fancy here. Most problems seem small when they're either far off in the future or way back in the past—but in their own "time neighborhood," they loom large. This is partly a trick of perspective, but there are other, more insidious reasons, too.

The simple fact is that small problems, left unattended, grow over time. This is certainly true for employee discontent; left unaddressed, it festers and becomes worse. Better to brush plaque from your teeth every day than to let it build up and destroy them.

Some items, such as capital equipment acquisition, are naturally "long lead." If you address them far enough in advance, you can handle such needs administratively. You can budget for capital equipment, order it, plan for it, install it, and so on. Ordinarily, it's not a problem. But what if you don't do the required homework well in advance? You'll have to beg, borrow, or steal when lack of equipment becomes a crisis. The small obstacle will become a big one.

Typically, two types of management animals wind up in this situation: ostriches (problem avoiders) and sloths (procrastinators). The ostriches never lift their heads out of the sand to look for present and future obstacles, so they are perpetually being unpleasantly surprised. The sloths know about the problems but put off doing anything about them. The problems, of course, take no offense; they'll stick around whether or not anyone pays attention to them.

To lead well and manage effectively, you must aggressively seek out potential obstacles and attack them. There's no excuse for getting blindsided: good management is the art of intelligent anticipation.

4. Take the time to listen to others carefully, but don't worry too much about what other people think.

Not listening is a cardinal sin. If you think you're too busy to listen, then you have your priorities wrong. You don't have to listen to absolutely everyone, and you don't have to listen to everyone equally, but listening is a must.

Scientists know that they ignore data at their peril. You may want to discount certain data after gathering it. But get the data. And get it first-hand whenever possible. Raw, unfiltered data is always valuable—even redundant data, because it allows for cross-checking.

Remember, however, that you don't have to be a slave to your data givers. Sometimes you'll come up with ideas that others find strange or unpopular, and they'll let you know it. Listen to them, weigh what they're telling you—both the words and the music—and then choose your course. Don't let what others think dissuade you when you know what needs to be done. You are not being paid to be popular; you are being paid to get a job done. If you worry too much about the opinions of others, then you will succumb to the weathervane effect—you will change direction every time the wind does.

This counsel may be controversial, because we live in a time and a culture that favors consensus. But consensus-based decisions can be wrong or, in some cases, represent bad compromises that a team makes when driven by severe time constraints. If your team can't achieve a strong consensus and paralysis sets in, it becomes imperative for you, the leader, to make a decision and go forward. In such cases, whatever decision you make will inevitably leave some, or even all, of the participants unhappy, at least for a time. What you must make clear to everyone is that making *no decision* is the worst course; a decision, after all, will inevitably have to be made, and in the meantime, valuable time is being lost. You'll achieve the best outcome in these situations if you make sure that all the players feel they've "had their day in court"—that you've heard them out. They don't have to agree with the decision, but they do have to accept it. This is fundamental to team success.

5. Focus on facts.

For many reasons, we frequently violate this guideline, almost always with disastrous consequences. Deal with reality. Always relate to what *is,* not to what you would have liked or what could have been or what might be in the future. Stay in the present, and deal with the facts.

Separate facts from opinions. Also separate facts from their consequences or implications; often people report these concurrently or confuse them.

When engaged in discussions, evaluations, critiques, and other issues that involve performance, stay focused on the facts as opposed to the personalities of the people involved. Evaluate data based on its factual content, not on the source. Gather facts first and reserve judgment until later.

I have found that writing things down helps me focus on facts. Sometimes this involves making lists, writing things in a standard format, or just creating notes for future reference. When I do this, it becomes very clear when I can legitimately use verbs like "is" and "are" rather than verbs like "appears to be" and "seems to."

6. Provide stability by being an attenuator, not an amplifier.

This is an important attribute.

Most of our information channels are "noisy." Every organization has a rumor mill that is constantly churning out misinformation. As managers and leaders, we need to avoid amplifying the noise so that we don't mask the signal. Rarely is a new situation as good or as bad as it looks at first. Take in the data, absorb it, and then decide on appropriate action. A measured response is almost always best. As crises spike within your organization, remember that "this, too, shall pass," and be the one who sets an example for the rest of the team. To lead effectively, you must keep your head while those around you are losing theirs. Your job is to dampen the spikes and surges and restore regularity to the daily flow of energy.

Occasionally, you may be forced into acting quickly, or an "unmeasured" response may even be desirable. For example, if someone lures away a key employee with a "Godfather offer,"[2] then you need to react quickly if you hope to turn the situation around. Or if your team makes a major breakthrough, you'll want to react with unbridled enthusiasm, no holds barred. You'll recognize these exceptional situations when they crop up.

7. Never attribute to malice what can be explained by incompetence.

If someone says or does something that may affect you or your team in an adverse way, be very careful not to jump to the wrong conclusion; paranoia can get you into a lot of

---

[2] A "Godfather" offer is one that cannot be refused. It comes from the film of the same name.

trouble. If the act seems wrongheaded, first assume that it was a mistake. Try to imagine the erroneous set of assumptions that might have led the person to this action. Put yourself in his or her shoes.

Only after eliminating all possible "error scenarios" should you even entertain the notion that impure motives were at work. Why? Consider the consequences. If you assume malice and you are wrong, then you will almost certainly make an enemy—and enemies have a nasty habit of accumulating. It's silly to make them unnecessarily.

If you incorrectly assume incompetence, on the other hand, then, yes, you may get burned. But you will be burned only once. When you give the perpetrator a chance to reconsider his "mistake," then he's sure to expose his true colors. In the long run, you'll have earned the trust of other team members by treating your enemy with respect.

I also believe that incompetence is far more widespread than evil. This may be a naïve view, but I believe statistics are on my side when I take this approach.

8. Cultivate a sense of humor as a counterweight to intensity: take the job seriously and yourself lightly.

I have sometimes been called an intense person. This quality is both a blessing and a curse.

Intensity is the flame to brilliancy's spark. It allows you to focus, and it can help transmit a sense of purpose to the rest of the team. The refusal to give up, even in the face of adversity, is important.

But there is a dark side to intensity. It violates the Greek ideal of "everything in moderation": There's no such thing as "moderately intense." If you're a person who doesn't let go easily, then you need to be careful; don't let large, ongoing doses of your intensity poison your team.

Having a sense of humor helps. Even in times of crisis, you may need to step back enough to recognize the absurdity of it all. Laugh. Make fun of yourself. Recognize your mistakes and be proud of them, even though it hurts. My theory is that you have already paid for the mistake, and getting a laugh out of it at least brings you a little return on your investment.

I'm not talking about gallows humor here, which is scarcely better than no humor at all. I mean a real, robust appreciation for the follies that inevitably go along with working in an organization, trying to create something out of nothing, and being human.

Teams will forgive a lot of transgressions on the part of their managers, but incompetence, sloth, lack of reward for performance, and humorlessness are not among them.

9. Have a life outside of work, and read 25 books a year.

Go back and read number 8 again. Work is a part of our lives. Sometimes we get so caught up in what we are doing that "life" seems to be an adjunct to our work. This is an out-of-balance situation, and you cannot be a good manager if you are chronically out of balance.

You cannot lead effectively—or even survive—if you don't have something else to think about besides your job. For me, it has been family, physics, golf, and a few other miscellaneous interests. Go out to the movies, see plays, play poker, dance, howl at the moon. Whatever works for you. But remember, alcohol is a depressant.

Hot baths and long walks have also helped me. I've found that you have to do some kind of exercise to stay in shape, even if the only muscle you use during the day is your brain. That's why world champion chess players do rigorous physical training.

If the stress gets really bad, then talk to people outside your project and your company. They can help you gain perspective. Inside the company, your chief architect and your boss should be your main confidants.

Regular reading is another activity that's crucial for effectiveness and survival. As we grow older, we tend to recycle what has worked in the past instead of learning and trying new approaches. We gain more and more knowledge through experience, and less and less through formal channels. In addition to periodicals, you should set a goal of 25 books a year, which comes out to a book every two weeks. They don't all have to be new, and they don't all have to be technical. If travel is a part of your job, reading is an excellent way to use the time you might otherwise waste waiting around in airports or on the plane.

10. Trust your instincts: if it doesn't feel right, then it probably isn't.

It's easy to get overly analytical. Sometimes we run the numbers until we're blue in the face without bothering to examine the underlying assumptions that went into collecting those numbers. Then, we come to a conclusion that doesn't feel right.

What's maddening about these situations is that we're unable to articulate the reasons for our discomfort. Nevertheless, fearing that this perverse situation will paralyze us, we forge ahead with the analysis and then take action, even though it doesn't feel right.

In the vast majority of these cases, I have regretted the decision. Here's my advice: If it really doesn't feel right, then trust your instincts. You didn't accumulate your "gut wisdom" overnight; you are feeling the sum total of all your past experiences when this happens. At the very least, force yourself to try to understand what is causing the discomfort and then address it.

In my case, most of these bad decisions have revolved around hiring. Never hire someone with whom you don't feel comfortable, which is not to say that you should never take a risk. If the risk level is high enough to make you uncomfortable, however, go with your gut, and don't make the offer. Hiring mistakes are among the most expensive you can make.

I've always believed that it's better to make a bad decision than to make no decision at all. When your important decisions and your tummy disagree, however, be careful!

Summing Up

If the 10 ideas I've presented seem like a bit of a grab bag, that's because they are. Management and leadership are still arts, not sciences; disciplines that attach the word "science" to themselves—such as computer science, management science, and social science—are suspect.[3] We learn what works empirically: by trying things, observing success and failure over a large number of attempts, and then trying to discern patterns. These 10 ideas have worked for me over an extended period of time, and all I can do is pass them on for your consideration and use. Your results may vary, because it is all in the application.

Recap

It has been observed that Moses did not come down from the mountain with The Ten Guidelines. Any time I see (or create) a list with 10 items, I become nervous. Even Woodrow Wilson received some ridicule for his "Fourteen Points": his critics pointed out that God had been able to fit all His wisdom into only 10.

On the other hand, calling this list "Joe's 10 Tips" seems to undervalue it just a tad. These are ideas that have proven useful to me time and time again. They are synthesized from watching some extremely good managers ply their trade during a 40-year time span. And when I see a manager grossly violating one of them, I can be pretty sure that there will be adverse consequences.

Now people will look over the list and remark, "What does this have to do with managing a *software development* project?" Well, two things. First of all, a software development project is a project; you can't get away from the fundamentals of good management just because you are managing software development. Second, I have noticed throughout the years that software developers are perhaps a touch more cynical about their managers than engineers in other domains. This is fairly easy to understand; they work in a rapidly changing field, and it is easy for them to dismiss their managers if they (the managers) are even a half-step behind technically. The only way to compensate for that perceived deficiency is to demonstrate extreme management prowess. For, if your developers think you are an old fart from the technical perspective *and* a screw-up as a manager, it is unlikely that you will be able to effectively lead them.

---

[3] This observation was originally communicated to me by Wayne Meretsky, a former developer at Rational.

PART 2

SOFTWARE DIFFERENCES

We now turn to those parts of our discipline that require that we go beyond just good general management.

In Chapter 5, "The Most Important Thing," I discuss the most important differentiator in software development project success: the iterative development concept. It turns out that the single biggest factor in the timely delivery of a quality software product is this: Has the team effectively practiced iterative development?

Chapter 6, "Modeling," talks about one of the few new tools that have helped raise the level of abstraction and better communicate what software is all about. The downside of this trend has been a tendency to undervalue coding, which is what programmers spend most of their time doing.

So, in Chapter 7, "Coding," I talk very briefly about programming languages and how developers and managers can adapt to the *"language du jour"* that seems to appear with great regularity every 10 years or so.

Finally, I note in Chapter 8, "Getting It Out the Door," that one must first ship a product to have it be successful—those products you work on forever are rarely profitable. But it turns out that getting the product out the door is not as simple as it first appears. I provide some help for those who have not yet mastered this "annoying" yet essential part of our discipline.

CHAPTER 5

The Most Important Thing

I get to make two introductions in this chapter. The first is the concept of iterative development, and the second is the character Roscoe Leroy.

Iterative Development

As a profession, we've learned a lot in trying to understand why software development projects succeed or fail. By far, the most important concept to come out of the last 20 years is iterative development. Aside from the obvious prescription that you can't develop great systems with mediocre people, the most important methodological consideration is how you go about building the software. What I have observed time and time again is that those teams that practice iterative development succeed more often, whereas those that employ other methods have a greater tendency to fail. Of the best practices advocated by Rational Software, I find iterative development to be the most compelling.

Why is this?

The iterative development approach breaks away from the overly rigid waterfall approach that had come to dominate large projects in the eighties. It is an approach that is grounded in risk mitigation, incremental construction, and progress measured by actual working code as opposed to documents. If you need more background on the details of iterative development, see Royce[1] or Kroll and Kruchten.[2]

In this chapter, I describe some of the technical reasons why iterative development has proven superior time and again. But more important, I discuss the business reasons why you should use it. This should help bridge the gap between the software development manager and his manager, in the following sense. Iterative development is something that is new and unique to software development. Many general managers feel more comfortable with the waterfall approach, which is closer to classical project management as they know it. So this chapter can be used in two different ways:

- A software development manager can have his manager read it, so that the two of them can have a common understanding of how the project will be managed.

- The general manager can have his software development manager read it if the software development manager is not going to employ iterative development. The question, of course, is—why not?

In both cases, the chapter can be used as a springboard for discussion as to how the project will be managed, monitored, and reported. It is a discussion that is well worth having before the project is launched, because it will help establish the rules of engagement between the software development manager and his manager. Along with the budget and team-selection discussions, this one is mandatory.

Roscoe Leroy

The first thing to know about Roscoe is this: Don't make fun of his name. "It shows my parents had a sense of humor. Besides," he always adds, "it could have been worse. They could have named me Leroy Leroy."

Roscoe is an old war buddy of my dad's. According to Roscoe, they both served under Patton, although my guess is that my dad served directly under Roscoe, and Roscoe served somewhat remotely under Patton. Roscoe is one of those old salty dogs who have an opinion on just about everything. The annoying thing is that he is right so much of the time. Of course, when he is wrong, the results are not pretty, because he is willing to back his convictions to the hilt. I have seen Roscoe push all his chips to the center of the table,

[1] Royce, Walker, *Software Project Management: A Unified Framework* (Reading, Massachusetts: Addison-Wesley, 1998).

[2] Kroll, Per and Philippe Kruchten, *The Rational Unified Process Made Easy: A Practitioner's Guide to the RUP* (Boston, Massachusetts: Addison-Wesley, 2003).

confident that his poker hand was the best. The results were spectacular, but not always in the way Roscoe would have liked.

His wisdom is simple and easy to understand. It comes in the form of very prescriptive advice: As long as you don't probe for deep theory, you'll be fine. Going with Roscoe is a leap of faith, one that benefits us all when the chips are down. With his "been there, done that" swagger, he boasts of having finished the eighth grade, but I have it on good authority that he graduated from an excellent high school some time in the thirties. My dad explained this discrepancy to me simply by saying that Roscoe felt it unnecessary to flaunt his education.

At various times, Roscoe has served in the military, fought oil well fires with Boots and Coots, and been a mining engineer. Those experiences made him a pragmatic kind of guy, but they also taught him how to perform under pressure. He does manage to get all the dirt out from under his fingernails if you invite him to dinner, but you can't expect much use of the salad fork.

Roscoe doesn't do math, really; he does arithmetic. Answers tend to come out of his mouth in whole numbers. When asked about this, his reply is along the lines of, "Well, it always comes down to how many sticks of dynamite you need to make the hole, and how many men you need to clean it up. I don't cut my dynamite in half, and I don't hire fractional people." When he puts it like that, you know you are done with fancy mathematics.

Roscoe has good background, solid values, and a world of experience. And he is a great general manager. From our point of view, his only defect is that he knows very little about software engineering.

We turn that "defect" into a feature. A few years back, when the mine closed, Roscoe decided to go into software engineering. I took on the job of educating him but, of course, he spent a fair amount of time educating me.

Going Over the Waterfall

One day Roscoe and I were walking across his backyard to toss a round of horseshoes. I had told him that even though I hadn't played in years, I bet I could beat him. "OK, now we'll see who's going to beat whom, Sonny," Roscoe said. "And before I teach you the right way to throw a horseshoe, I'm going to demonstrate to you why waterfall development is doomed to failure."

I had to smile. Six months ago, I was the one who wanted to talk about software development. Now it was Roscoe who kept bringing it up. Always on the prowl for new ways to look at things, I was eager to see what he had to show me.

When I picked up my pair of horseshoes, I suddenly realized that the big, omega-shaped things were heavier than I'd remembered. "C'mon, get ready," Roscoe ordered. "There's the stake. See if you can hit a ringer on your first toss."

Naturally, I felt a little pressure after my bragging. I swung the horseshoe a bit, back and forth, getting a feel for it, then took one big swing. Of course, I didn't hit the stake. I didn't come anywhere near it, in fact. My horseshoe just bounced away and landed about 15 feet from its target.

"No fair!" I exclaimed. "You need to let me have a few practice throws."

If you are unfamiliar with horseshoes, it is normal to take several practice tosses before you get competitive. It's like anything else, really. You need to get used to your equipment, which in my case was an arm that hadn't seen a lot of exercise lately. "Well," responded Roscoe, "that might or might not help, because you missed for three reasons. First, as you point out, the target wasn't where your arm thought it was, due to some miscalibration.[3] Second, you will always have some imperfection in your execution; none of us is perfectly steady—the horseshoe doesn't always go where we aim it. And third, between the time you let go and the time the horseshoe hit the ground, the stake moved!"

"Bull bleep," I responded. "Nobody moved the stake."

"True enough, but after you let that horseshoe fly, there was an instantaneous gust from a 40mph crosswind that you hadn't taken into account. The effect was the same as if someone had moved the stake in the opposite direction," Roscoe replied. "Plus, any angular deviation is multiplied by the distance the horseshoe has to travel, so it is no wonder you failed."

"Well, at least in project management, I don't have to score a ringer every time," I said.

"Fair enough," responded Roscoe. "That's where the expression 'Close only counts in horseshoes and hand grenades' comes from. 'Close enough' is often just fine in project management. What really hurts is missing the target by a wide margin, especially after your 'horseshoe' has been in the air a long time. Yet, this happens all the time with the waterfall approach, because you only get one toss. And typically, just as in horseshoes, there are three critical problems at work:

- The target isn't where you perceive it to be.

- You make human mistakes in your execution.

- The target moves, to boot."

It made sense. Taking one shot at anything seemed silly. But I thought I would tease Roscoe a little by taking a completely contrarian position.

---

[3] It turns out that there were two very good reasons for my "miscalibration": Roscoe's horseshoes were a little heavier than the normal set, and his distance between stakes, end-to-end, was a little longer than the standard setup. Both of these were small effects, around 10 percent, and hard to discern immediately, but they led to the target "not being where I thought it was." This is why warm-up tosses are so important: Your mind-body computer makes adjustments automatically after some practice throws.

The Other Extreme

"Well, I can see your point. Suppose we just forget about all this planning stuff, and just constantly reevaluate where we are and where we need to go," I smiled sweetly.

"Stop trying to bait me, Sonny," replied Roscoe. "We know that anarchy doesn't work either—just produces lots of senseless reaction to local events. I think you physicists call it 'Brownian Motion.' Lots of activity, little progress.

"The real issue is this: You have to do any project in a series of steps. The crucial things you need to understand are the best *length* for each step, and how many steps are required." I could see that he was on the verge of a big exposé, and I wanted to pursue it, so I said, "OK, Roscoe, what you're getting at interests me a lot more than horseshoes, and besides, my wrist is sore. Let's take a break."

Roscoe charitably let me off the hook, horseshoe-wise.

"Yes, let's go get a cup of coffee, and I'll introduce you to the concept of 'short vectors'," said Roscoe. "I'll draw you some pictures while we talk."

So we tramped back up to Roscoe's house, grabbed ourselves some coffee (he keeps his coffeemaker going all day), and adjourned to the back porch.

Roscoe's First Picture

No sooner had we settled into a pair of creaky old rockers when Roscoe took a stubby pencil out of his pocket and drew a picture on a paper napkin. This picture is reproduced as Figure 5.1.

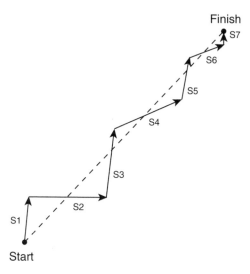

Figure 5.1   Roscoe's first drawing—short vectors.

"Now, we know from elementary geometry that, in a perfect world, the shortest distance between the start of the project and the finish (the 'target') is the straight dotted line I just drew. Waterfall guys are under the illusion that they can follow that path, but we have just demonstrated the three reasons why they can't. Really good project managers follow a path like the other one I drew, that goes from S1 to S2 to S3, and so on—that involves a series of small steps before you converge on a result. I call each of these steps a *vector*, which comes from air traffic control lingo. You software guys would call each step an *iteration*."

"Looks like a sailboat tacking into the wind," I remarked.

"Sure enough, but let's just stick to the geometry for a minute. I want to contrast this path with the path a project manager might follow if he were trying to do everything in just a couple or three iterations." Roscoe took another sip of coffee and grabbed another napkin.

Roscoe's Second Picture

"Here's the path that manager would take," he said, as he drew Figure 5.2.

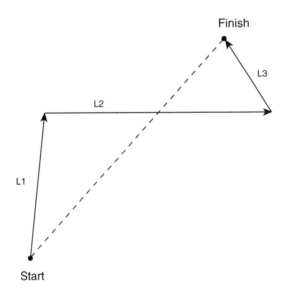

Figure 5.2   Roscoe's second drawing—long vectors.

"Note that in this case, as in the first one, we have made the simplifying assumption that the target doesn't move, although we know it always does," he added.

I noticed immediately that L1 was in the same wrong direction as S1 in the previous diagram, and I pointed that out to Roscoe. "Sure, they both get off to the same bad start because of errors in aim and execution. But notice that Mr. Long Vector, as I like to call him, stays on the deviant path much longer."

It was also true that, at the first correction point, both Mr. Short Vector and Mr. Long Vector made the same wrong "guess" for their second direction; L2 and S2 are basically in the same direction. But once again, Mr. Long Vector persisted too long before making a correction.

"Now, let's measure all three paths," Roscoe said. "The dotted line comes out to 10 inches. Let's see...hmm...L1-L2-L3 comes out to about 15 inches. And S1-S2-S3-S4-S5-S6-S7 comes out, let's see, to around 12 inches. So Mr. Short Vector is 20 percent longer than optimum, and Mr. Long Vector is 50 percent longer than optimum."

Wait a Minute!

I smelled a rat. "Hold on there, Roscoe," I exclaimed. "I can draw Mr. Long Vector's path so that the total length is the same as, or less than, Mr. Short Vector's."

"True enough," replied Roscoe. "There is nothing, geometrically speaking, that says Mr. Short Vector will always take a shorter total path. If Mr. Long Vector is very lucky, he can come out better. But that is not what we observe in practice. Statistically, averaged over many Mr. Long Vector projects and Mr. Short Vector projects, we find that Mr. Short Vector projects come out better. The reason for this is that short vectors allow you to do some other things that you can't usually accomplish with long vectors. I'll talk about those in a minute. Although you are right that there is no geometrical 'proof' of this, it is an empirical fact, and the geometrical analogy still has a lot to recommend it."

Just as I was beginning to accept this line of reasoning, Roscoe drove his point home: "Besides, neither of these drawings takes into account the third factor: that you are constantly aiming at a moving target. Because, unlike the horseshoe stake, targets always move in the real world. That means Mr. Long Vector faces much more risk than Mr. Short Vector, because Mr. Short Vector gets to take aim more often. As the target moves, he gets to readjust and therefore spends less time moving in the wrong direction."

Keeping the Vectors Short

"So," said Roscoe, "let's continue with our analysis. In our geometrical analogy, if time and resources are proportional to path length, we can see that Mr. Short Vector only needs 20 percent more than the minimum required for success, while Mr. Long Vector needs 50 percent more than the minimum. So Mr. Short Vector has much more margin for error.

"Another way to look at this is to measure scrap and rework. Out of the 12 units that Mr. Short Vector expends, 10 are required to get the result, and 2 are wasted, so his scrap and rework represents about 16 percent of the total effort. Mr. Long Vector wastes 5 out of 15 units expended, so his scrap and rework represents 33 percent of the total. Using scrap and rework as a metric, Mr. Long Vector is twice as bad as Mr. Short Vector." Roscoe was quite convincing.

"OK, Roscoe," I conceded. "It seems that short vectors are a good all-around principle in project management. But why is the concept even more important in software development projects?"

"I'll be glad to tell you, Sonny," said Roscoe triumphantly. "Why don't you get us some more coffee first?" Then he lit up one of his favorite stogies.[4]

The Application to Software Development

When I returned with our refills, Roscoe took a long puff on the stogie and started in again. "It seems to me," he began, "that software development projects tend to have, in general, the following characteristics:

- Resources are very tight; there always seems to be little margin for error.

- The 'target' is hard to get in focus at the outset; just as in horseshoes, we have to get used to our swing and calibrate as we go. Another way to state this is that requirements are usually poorly understood at the beginning.

- Execution errors are unavoidable, especially at the beginning.

- The target *always* moves during the course of the project.

- Staying on a bad path too long is typically catastrophic; it means throwing out work you thought you'd 'accomplished' and starting over again.

When you take these characteristics into account, an iterative development approach with short vectors starts looking pretty darned important."

The argument was persuasive. It was clear that errors, particularly in early iterations, could have a really big impact unless they were detected and corrected. When I mentioned this to Roscoe, he nodded emphatically.

---

[4] The Surgeon General wants me to remind you that smoking is bad for your health. Roscoe may live to be a hundred, but if you smoke, you shouldn't count on it. And, by the way, "stogie" has an interesting etymology. It comes from a town in Pennsylvania named Conestoga, where they made an inexpensive, slender, cylindrical cigar that was popular in the 1840s. It is also likely that drivers of Conestoga wagons (also manufactured in Conestoga!) smoked stogies. Roscoe's grandfather probably drove a Conestoga wagon, also known as a prairie schooner.

Applied Learning and Short-Vector Direction

"You are not as dumb as you look," he rejoined. "You need to work with short vectors so that the whole team learns as it goes and makes course corrections as a consequence. When you get to calibrate your machinery as you learn, you make smaller 'aiming' errors. You get to execute better on each succeeding iteration, given what you have learned, so you deviate less and less from your intended path. And each time you combine what you've learned with the discovery that the target has moved, you are better able to anticipate future movements. You might even get smart enough to 'lead the target' a bit.

"So a short vector approach means a shorter total path for two reasons. One, you spend less time on bad paths early on (short vector principle). And, two, your later vectors are closer to optimum (learning principle). Although there might be lucky exceptions, statistically these are the two features responsible for shorter total path length when averaged over many projects."

"Was there a systematic technique for getting maximum learning out of the early iterations?" I wondered aloud.

Risk Targeting

"Yes, it's called *risk targeting,*" replied Roscoe. "Risk targeting is about understanding where the threats are on our project. For example, suppose we are using some new technology that has never been used in production before. That has the potential to take us on a vector in a very wrong direction, because if the technology is inappropriate, we might have to spend a long time working with it, only to abandon it and replace it with another. So let's look at how this might play out in an early iteration."

Roscoe began. "Having identified 'using this new technology' as a risk, we need to rank order it with all the other perceived risks on the project. Suppose we identify it as the number one risk on the list. What do we do then?"

"As a software guy, I think I can answer that," I offered. "The first step is to remove or reduce the risk of this new technology on the next iteration. But, according to your short-vector principle, we want to limit the scope of each iteration. So we need to design a part of the system that will 'wring out' this new technology as quickly and thoroughly as possible. We want to make a decision, and we want to be clear and quick about it. Designing the iteration is a little like designing a scientific experiment: What do we want to determine? How will we determine it? And how can we do it with a minimum of interfering effects?"

"Couldn't have said it better myself," Roscoe chimed in. "So how would you answer the folks who say, 'Arggh, that's not iterative development; that's just prototyping!'"?

"Sure, it sounds a bit like prototyping," I continued, "but there is an important distinction: We need to test the technology in the context of how it will eventually work in the full product, so we need to consider scalability and performance, too. 'Toy' experiments at this stage are dangerous, because they can lull us into a false sense of security and make us complacent. A well-designed iteration leads us to build a piece of the system that either validates or invalidates the technology. At the end of the iteration, we need to be able to assess our working software and answer the simple question, 'Do we continue down this path, or not?' If 'yes,' then what we built in that iteration *remains a part of the product,* unlike a prototype, which gets thrown away.

"And," I summed up, "the bias has to be 'What experiment will show that the new technology is inappropriate?' rather than 'What experiment will make us feel better about the new technology?' Sometimes in our desire to go down a certain path—in this case, using the new technology—we design iterations or experiments to make us feel more comfortable. This might have the unfortunate consequence of making us feel much more uncomfortable later on, when we discover that we have been engaging in wishful thinking."

"Yeah," said Roscoe. "A good recipe is to be 'tough' early to avoid big trouble later.[5] Using risk targeting gives us a focus for each iteration. We might target more than one risk per iteration, but we should always be addressing the risks in priority order. Remember, the earlier we start working on the hard problems, the more time we have left to solve them," he continued. "This leads me to a huge pitfall I've seen over and over again on software development projects."

I could hardly wait.

Have You Heard This One Before?

"Sometimes I hear software development project managers say 'We'll tackle that risk later; that'll give us much more time to think about it while we're doing all the easy stuff.' Whenever I hear that, my blood pressure goes through the roof!" exclaimed Roscoe.

"Ah, Roscoe, I know where that wrong thinking comes from," I said. "It's what we tell American students about how to take tests in a time-constrained setting. Over and over again, we admonish them to do the easy stuff first, to 'get money in the bank' and reserve the remaining time at the end to work on the harder stuff. The logic is to get as much credit as you can for what you know, and 'don't leave money on the table' because you run out of time."

Roscoe reflected for a moment. "Well, that might be a legitimate strategy for certain environments. The problem is, software projects are different. You don't get partial credit

---

[5] John Walker reminds us of the importance of killing off really bad ideas early. Figure out a way to "falsify" an approach, and then see if you can. Sometimes a literature search can be revealing. As F.H. Westheimer so cogently put it, "A month in the laboratory can often save an hour in the library."

for an unfinished project the way you get partial credit for an incomplete test. In project settings, you *must* solve the hard problems. So the situation is not only not analogous; it is diametrically opposite."

I agreed. "So what you're saying, Roscoe, is that the idea that a team will work on the 'hard' or 'high-risk' problems in the background is an exercise in wishful thinking, because:

- While the team is working on 'the easy stuff,' they will *not* be thinking about the deferred risks. Teams have difficulty focusing on too many things at once, and once they start working on the easy stuff they will forget about the risky stuff they deferred. 'Out of sight, out of mind.'

- Parkinson's Law says that the 'easy stuff' will expand to fill out the schedule. This will squeeze out the harder, more risky stuff. I have seen this happen over and over again. After taking 20 to 30 percent longer than expected on the soft issues, sometimes due to excessive perfectionism, the team finds itself behind schedule. Then it gets hit with the really hard problem. Which, of course, was there all the time; it didn't go away because they ignored it.

- The net result is that the team winds up having *less* time to work on the hard problem rather than more time.

- And here's the ultimate disaster: Sometimes, to solve the hard problem, you have to throw away the work you did on 'the easy stuff' and do it all over again."

I concluded with, "So once again, the moral of the story is: Prioritize your risks, and attack the biggest ones first. If there is not enough time left over to do 'the easy stuff,' then you were certainly going to fail anyway."

"Now you're striking oil, Sonny," said Roscoe, and added one more cogent observation to supplement mine: "If I were behind schedule, I would feel much more comfortable going to my boss and asking for more time *if I could demonstrate that my team was executing on a plan that had already squeezed out most of the risks*. On the other hand, if I had to admit that not only were we behind schedule but also that there were still high-risk items on the table, I'd be in a very weak negotiating position. I probably wouldn't get my extension, and the project might be cancelled. And maybe it should be."

More on Applied Learning

It was all coming together for me: short vectors, risk targeting, and hard problems first. One thing really hit me between the eyes: In iterative development, we are forced not only to learn as we go, but also to *use* what we have learned.

I pointed out to Roscoe that we can't plan the next iteration unless we take stock of what we learned in the previous one. There is no "autopilot" in iterative development; we can't be asleep at the switch. In some sense, iterative development not only encourages applied learning: it demands and requires it.

"Contrast this with organizations that don't develop iteratively," said Roscoe. "How often have you heard people say, 'Well, that's a mistake I won't make on my *next* project,' or 'We'll have to remember that for *next* time'? This happens because their project plan is so rigid that they cannot incorporate lessons learned right away. They have a 'plan of record' that either can't be changed or is very difficult to change. This is tragic for two reasons: One, the team becomes resigned to 'going down with the ship' because they think it's 'too late' to change the plan; and two, because the lesson will likely be forgotten by the time the next project rolls around, and the same mistakes will probably get repeated."

The vein on Roscoe's temple was starting to bulge, so I knew we were approaching a crescendo. "This is 'planning' run amuck," he exclaimed. "It amounts to confusing the map with the territory. Or using a tool as an excuse for failure. If the current plan is going to lead to disaster, then CHANGE THE PLAN!!!" He slumped back in his chair.

I had to agree. Iterative development mandates that you immediately apply the lessons you've learned on this project to all successive iterations of the *same project*. As any educator can tell you, learning is most efficient and effective when you apply lessons learned as soon as possible. This is a very crucial difference between iterative and waterfall development. Iterative development insists that you "strike while the iron is hot," even if it involves pain; if you apply the right technique while the pain is still fresh, then everyone involved will remember the lesson better and longer.

Business Implications

Roscoe had one more point he wanted to make. Once again, he reached for the napkin holder and pulled out a fresh "canvas" for his final sketch.

"No doubt you have seen curves like this that contrast waterfall development with iterative development," he said, as he sketched Figure 5.3.

"The basic message here is that waterfall development remains high risk for much longer, because until there is meaningful system integration, we don't really know where we stand. With iterative development, which employs risk targeting and meaningful integration-and-build activity from the first iteration, risk is squeezed out early. In both pictures, point 'D' represents the decision point at which we might decide to cancel the project. That is, if the risk curve does not begin to plummet at that point in time, we might decide that we can't go on; without a diminution in project risk, maybe we cannot and should not continue to invest."

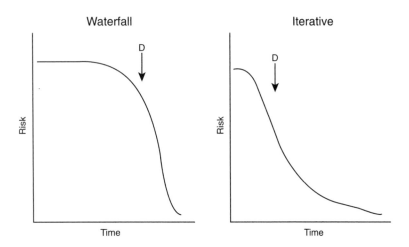

Figure 5.3   Roscoe's third drawing—waterfall versus iterative.

"Sure, Roscoe," I said, "I've seen Dave Bernstein[6] draw those curves for years. No news there. Clearly, it is better to make this decision early rather than late. So waterfall is the inferior approach."

"Yeah," countered Roscoe, "but there is a second, less well-understood reason that makes iterative development even more compelling. And I'm going to show it to you right now."

The Staffing Effect

Roscoe grabbed his pencil. "Let's superimpose a staffing profile on the previous curves. Waterfall projects staff up early, whereas iterative projects defer staffing, relatively speaking. Small, elite teams that can go fast are best for doing most of the work in the early phases, in other words, for the Inception and Elaboration iterations.[7] Then, you add significant numbers of people as you move into iterations for the later phases, Construction and Transition. The difference looks something like this..." as he drew some new curves to produce Figure 5.4.

---

[6] Dave Bernstein managed product development for more than 20 years at Rational Software. Anyone who can stay in the saddle that long must be doing something right.

[7] Standard practice is to divide the project into four phases: Inception, Elaboration, Construction, and Transition. Each phase has one or more iterations. We'll return to this in Chapter 12.

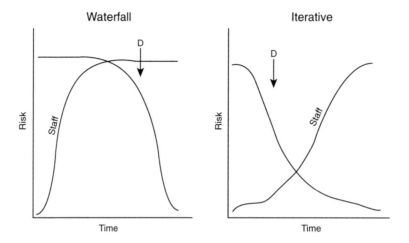

Figure 5.4 Roscoe's third drawing, amended—waterfall versus iterative, with staffing.

"Now, let's consider a project that gets canceled at point D on each curve. The resources that will be consumed to that point are indicated by the shaded areas on the curves—the area under the staffing curve from the start to point D, when cancellation occurs." His shaded additions are shown in Figure 5.5.

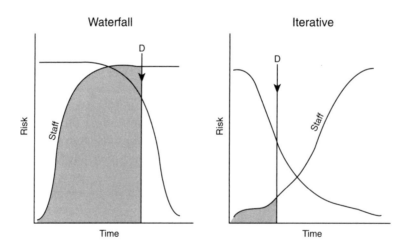

Figure 5.5 Roscoe's third drawing, further amended—waterfall versus iterative, with staffing shaded.

"Compare the shaded areas. The iterative scenario is superior for two reasons: You decide to abort earlier, and you have much less invested because you started small and planned to staff up later."

Roscoe was right, but there is one small detail I should mention here. Although iterative development uses far fewer people early in the project than waterfall, in general those people are more experienced and therefore more costly. So the shaded areas reflect manpower loading, but not necessarily actual staffing costs. This is often a second-order effect, however, simply because of the huge differences in number of people employed.

Roscoe continued. "The implication here is that you can launch more iterative development projects, because you can cut them off early with relatively small losses. This benefit is undercut somewhat because of the limited number of really good people within most organizations who can be deployed on early iteration work. These people are always in short supply."

Roscoe was coming in for his landing. "Remember, too, that waterfall is a disaster, because as staffing costs grow—the shaded area—it becomes organizationally and politically harder and harder to cancel the project. When you cancel an iterative development project early, you have a relatively small number of people to redeploy. When you cancel a large waterfall project late in the cycle, it dislocates a large number of people."

I saw his point. In the end, if you have to cancel a project for any reason, it just makes good business sense to cancel it early, before you have too much in the way of sunk costs. And the staffing approach for iterative development keeps these costs to a minimum in the early phases.

Just Plain Horse (shoe) Sense

Often, arguments for iterative development focus on the "technology" involved in software development. We point to issues like R&D content, the imprecision of requirements, architectural risk, performance risk, integration risk, and so on, to justify developing iteratively.

What Roscoe showed me was that iterative development makes good sense from a general project management perspective. And in particular, certain characteristics peculiar to software development amplify the benefits of short vectors, risk targeting, and applied learning. So what makes good sense in general makes even better sense when the project involves software development. Furthermore, intelligent staffing during early iterations ensures that, even if you cancel it, a software development project does not need to incur significant financial losses.

As Roscoe put it, stubbing out his stogie and swinging his feet up onto the porch railing, "If it makes sense from the technology point of view and it makes sense from the business point of view, it makes sense to me."

Recap

There is a somewhat widespread misconception that criticizing the waterfall method is akin to beating a dead horse, or one that never really lived. Contrary to popular belief, waterfall is alive and well, so to speak, and continuing to undermine projects today. The software development world is moving away from it much more slowly than we would like to believe.

In his project management book, Walker Royce points out that his father, Win Royce, intended for waterfall to be used much more iteratively than it came to be used. So clearly there is confusion even on this point.

Rather than focus on what's bad about waterfall, I think it's much more constructive to focus on what's right about iterative:

- Focus on architecture

- Learn early, and then produce more later

- Progressively and incrementally grow the system with each iteration

- Measure progress by working code, not documents

- Integrate, build, and test on each iteration

- Progressively reduce risk by attacking hard problems first

- Adjust the plan by carefully reviewing the results of the previous iteration

If you remain unconvinced about iterative development, the only thing I suggest is to find a manager who has done it both ways and have a chat with him. The rest of this book assumes you accept the iterative way of doing software development, and lots of other concepts I will discuss tie into it. For instance, I'll talk about "high trust" work environments, which are essential to the effective use of iterative development. Another related concept is a stable, underlying "software architecture," which allows iterative development technique to keep a complex project on course. The best way to express and communicate this architecture is through the use of a model. So I'll attack the subject of modeling in the next chapter.

CHAPTER 6

Modeling

People have been drawing pictures since the time of the cave paintings at Lascaux, and probably even before that. Man is a *visual* animal, so even after the advent of language we continued to record history and communicate with each other through graphics.[1] It is hardly a matter of dispute that our eye-brain computer is a powerful tool that integrates an incredible amount of information extremely quickly and enables other forms of cognition to take place. Even our daily language reflects this; when we finally "get" something, we often say out loud, "I see it!"

Software developers allowed this visual capability to go unexploited for many years. Even though many people around them tried to describe (and get them to describe) the software they were building with rudimentary sketches, the response usually was, "Let's look at the code." That might have been OK if two software developers of approximately the same skill level were talking to each other; in fact, this notion led to the practice of *code reviews*, which is not a bad idea at all. But once you get away from the lowest level of detail, code is probably the worst vehicle one could imagine for describing software.

This is because it operates at the wrong level of abstraction. Simply put, it is too fine-grained. As soon as you need to describe how various parts of the code work within a subsystem, or how various subsystems interact amongst each other, you are at sea. Managers

---

[1] Just to be clear, I would classify the wolf as primarily an *olfactory* animal.

listen, draw their sketches of what they think they are hearing, show them to the developers, and usually get the response, "Yeah. Whatever."

Now I have to be careful here. In my advocacy for graphics, I need to also describe their limitations. For, as much as graphics can transmit valuable information, they can also convey lots of misinformation. I am not talking about technically detailed but inaccurate diagrams; those are quickly exposed. The truly dangerous graphics are the "management level" pictures that one so often finds in PowerPoint presentations. These pictures purport to tell us something, but in fact they are usually extremely vague and fuzzy. They are better than clip art, but not much. They can mean all things to all people. Because these pictures can be quite content-free, most software developers disdain their very presence. And, as most developers don't think it is part of their job to accurately communicate through graphics what they are building, we come to an impasse.

Our pictures are often content-free because everyone draws them differently. Different people use different symbols for classes, objects, subroutines, functions, databases—you name it. When there is no common notation, everyone struggles; it is as though you are all speaking the same language, but there are too many "dialects," and the dialects lead to miscommunication. Because graphic representation is generally pretty arbitrary, no one can be "right." But that doesn't stop people from defending "their" notation, sometimes with an almost religious fervor. The diversity of styles actually retarded the adoption of a graphics notation. So that was a problem.

This, of course, masked an even deeper problem. Because there was no common graphical notation, we could not even begin to attribute semantics to the pictures. What do I mean by *semantics*? Semantics, in some sense, is what adds true content. But first of all let's get a better understanding of the problem of notation.

How to Explain the UML

The one true test of your understanding of any concept comes when you must explain it to someone unskilled in the art. For those of us who deal daily in technology, the most maddening variant of this challenge is to transmit your understanding to *civilians*, that is, other intelligent people who have little or no background in technology. The reason this is so difficult is that you cannot fall back on technical jargon—the shorthand that permits high-bandwidth communication with peers, while at the same time presenting a barrier to those unfamiliar with the lingo.

In fact, I have found that software people have difficulty explaining the nuances of their craft to other engineering professionals. On a trip to China, I needed to explain the UML (Unified Modeling Language) and its significance to technical managers who were not software professionals themselves. I had not anticipated that this would be a problem, but when I first mentioned "UML," I got nothing but blank stares. Before I could advance, I needed to get them grounded in the UML. But how?

What follows is the 10-minute presentation I improvised and subsequently polished. When we're done, there's a neat irony that wraps up the tale.

What Is the UML, and Why Is It Important?

Let us begin with a simple example. If I write on the whiteboard:

$$1 + 1 =$$

anywhere in the world, people understand what I am trying to say. In fact, at this point, someone in the audience always volunteers "2!" When that happens, I complete the equation:

$$1 + 1 = 2$$

and explain that not only are we understood around the world, but also we usually get the right answer, too.

This is a good example of a *universal notation*—that is, the number system. People all over the world use it to communicate with each other. An English speaker can write it down, and a person speaking Mandarin in China can understand it.

Although this example seems trivial at first sight, it really does reveal an amazing fact: Numbers are universal, and certain symbols such as + and = have the same meaning all over the world.

The other really nice thing about this example is that anyone who has a *first-grade* education can understand and appreciate it. It has the unfortunate disadvantage of appearing to be more trivial than it really is.

A Second, Less Trivial Example

At this point, I acknowledge that perhaps this first example is a little too simple. So I then draw a triangle on the whiteboard that looks like Figure 6.1.

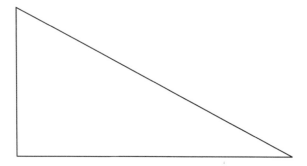

Figure 6.1   Triangle.

I then point out that the triangle takes on additional meaning when I complete the diagram with the addition shown in Figure 6.2.

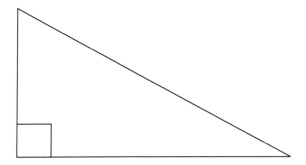

Figure 6.2   Right triangle.

Now this triangle is unambiguously a *right triangle*, because the little square doohickey is a worldwide convention meaning "right angle." Furthermore, I can now label the sides of the triangle A, B, and C, as in Figure 6.3.

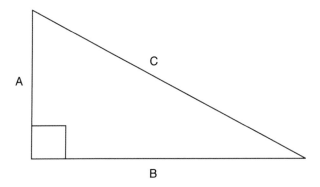

Figure 6.3   Labeled right triangle.

And, immediately, I can write down that

$$A^2 + B^2 = C^2.$$

Now this has a few very endearing properties. First, it is once again an example of a universal notation. Right angles, right triangles, and the symbols representing them are the same all over the world; someone from ancient Egypt could in principle reason about right triangles with a modern Peruvian by drawing such diagrams. What's more, once the diagram for the right triangle has been written down, the relationship of A, B, and C is defined. A, B, and C can no longer have completely arbitrary values; once any two of them are specified, the third is determined as well. The diagram implies the Pythagorean Theorem. One could even go so far as to say that the diagram has some "semantics," that there is a well understood relationship between the picture and the values implied by the letters.

What is truly amazing about this example is that anyone with a *high school* education can understand it. If the person has seen any geometry at all, they have seen triangles and right triangles, and if they remember anything at all from their geometry, it is good old Pythagoras.

So now I have a diagram with semantics, and I have moved up a level of abstraction at the "accessibility cost" of moving from the first grade to the high school freshman level of mathematics. Also, at this point, people are definitely intrigued as to where I am going with all this. So I try to bait the hook with a very tasty worm.

The Third Example

So far, these examples demonstrate the utility of a universal notation. The problem is, they are both from the world of mathematics; although math has concrete manifestations, it is intrinsically abstract. Are there any examples *not* from mathematics?

I then draw Figure 6.4 on the whiteboard.

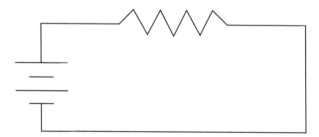

Figure 6.4   First electric circuit.

What is stunning about this picture is that as soon as I complete the drawing and say the words, "Here I have a simple circuit with a battery and a resistor," heads begin to bob. Of course, this is probably the simplest electrical circuit you could draw, but no matter. Just as the audience will applaud for itself when it recognizes the opening notes of Beethoven's Fifth Symphony, it will feel good about recognizing something technical.

Without giving them too much time to think about it, I quickly add the symbols for a volt-meter and an ammeter, as shown in Figure 6.5.

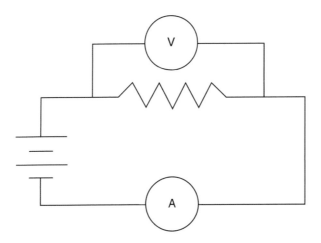

Figure 6.5   Second electric circuit.

And, in a final bold stroke, I note that if the battery is 6 volts and the resistor 6 ohms, then 1 ampere of current flows in the circuit, as shown in Figure 6.6.[2]

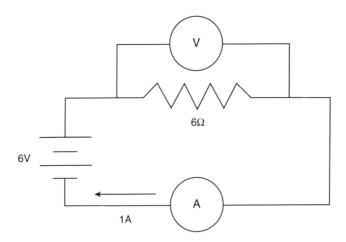

Figure 6.6   Third electric circuit.

---

[2] It is important for the effect to use the symbol for ohms, not the word "ohm."

Now, people know what a 6 volt battery is; they can buy one in the store. And most people will have a recollection, however vague, that resistors are measured, or come, in units of ohms. So when you finally draw the "1 A" on the diagram, indicating that 1 ampere of current flows in the circuit (note that I even indicate the direction of flow!), people are totally convinced they know what you are talking about, even if they never could remember Ohm's Law.

This is a very good time to mention that a Swedish student and an Australian hobbyist can communicate about this circuit without knowing each other's language. Once again, an international standard notation has come to the rescue. Only this time it is not purely mathematical; the objects in the diagram have real physical instantiations. Moreover, semantics is in play: Not only is Ohm's Law implied, but also implied is the direction of current flow that comes from our notions of the positive and negative terminals of the battery, represented by the long and short horizontal lines. I typically spend a few moments on the richness of the information communicated by this simple diagram, and remark how hard it would be to do any electrical engineering at all if we didn't have this notation that is the same all over the world.

Incidentally, I have moved the accessibility threshold up to anyone having had one year of introductory physics.

And Now for the Relevance to Software...

Now is the time to summarize that we have seen how progress is made in all fields by having a common notation that can be used to express concepts, and how diagrams begin to take on precision and meaning once we attach semantics to the pictures. The most useful of these notations are understood the world over.

But before 1996, there was no common notation for software. Before the UML became an international standard, two software engineers, *even if they spoke the same language*, had no way to talk about their software. There were no conventions that were universally accepted around the world for describing software. No wonder progress was slow!

With the advent of the UML, however, software engineers have a common graphic vocabulary for talking about software. They can draw progressively complex diagrams to represent their software, just the way electrical engineers can draw progressively complex diagrams to represent their circuits. Things like nested diagrams become possible, so different levels of abstraction can now be expressed.

Rational Software's contribution in this area was huge. Formulating the UML and bringing the world's most influential companies—IBM, Microsoft, HP, Oracle, and others—to agree on it was a major step. Getting an international standards body—the Object Management Group—to ratify it as a standard was the formal process that irreversibly cast the die. Everyone agreed to end the Tower of Babel approach and also agreed about how to talk about software.

The significance of the UML is now established, and we can move on.

Raising the Level of Abstraction

Of course, the UML itself is an example of "technical jargon." It is now the way software professionals talk to each other about software. As each example of a notation becomes deeper and denser, it can become an esoteric and subtle way of expressing ideas and designs that are very rich and complex. Yet, at the outset, this (and any) notation, at its highest level of abstraction, is useful for communicating between professionals and "civilians." That is because its fundamental elements can still be used to transmit fundamental ideas. A truly great notation "nests" and has many levels of abstraction; the highest levels facilitate communication between people who are "farthest apart" in terms of background and context, whereas the lowest levels (with the most technical detail) aid communication between people who are "closest together" in terms of their understanding of the domain—the technical specialists.

What has been interesting about our journey is that I have used analogy to explain a technical notation. I have avoided the "self reference" trap—in other words, I have explained the UML without describing the UML itself. I have explained the jargon without using the jargon. Although this seems like a subterfuge at first ("Hey, wait a minute; I never even got to see a UML diagram!"), it is, in fact, a requirement that you be able to explain it without using it.

Otherwise, those "civilians" are going to balk the first time you draw one. With this introductory context, however, I believe that the first UML diagram you do draw will be much better received. They will hark back to "1+1," Pythagoras, and Ohm's Law, and know that you are doing the same thing for software constructs.

Recap

Indeed, the UML has become the *lingua franca* for describing software. It is a good example of what happens when instead of trying to maintain a proprietary standard, one instead opens up to giving away intellectual property with the aim of creating momentum behind an industry standard. What happened was that several companies could now focus on building tools to support the UML. Each one did not have to create its own standard, and competition could take place at the tool level instead of the notation level. This in turn had the benefit that diagrams produced by different tools could all be understood, because they used the same underlying notation and semantics. In most areas of human activity, we call this progress.

Right. But developers still have to write code. Maybe less of it, if they reuse standard modules that their UML diagrams might suggest. But, still, cutting code is primordial. It is never going to go away.

Nor, I'm afraid to say, is the turmoil engendered by advances in programming languages. Our languages are getting better and more sophisticated, but they are a form of planned obsolescence. Developers have to learn a new language every 10 years or so, and this is a very disruptive process. Those that don't make the leap to the "next great thing" become consigned to maintaining legacy code in one of the older languages. This is the software developer's version of Purgatory.

As managers, we have a slightly different problem. Our code-cutting days are behind us, but languages march on. How can we familiarize ourselves with the latest language? That is the subject of the next chapter.

CHAPTER 7

Coding

Sooner or later, it all comes down to "the code." As much as we would like to eliminate this pesky step, you just can't build software without writing code. Even if you think you are going to put together an application using preassembled parts, you still have to write the code to glue it all together, to pass results from one module to another.

This is both a blessing and a curse. Great code allows us to have robust systems—the kind that don't break—as well as high-performance systems—those that respond quickly to our demands on them. Writing great code allows us to field superior products that give us a competitive edge in the marketplace. But what about all that positively awful code that is foisted onto the general public? Anyone who thinks that "it's just code" should consider the difference between the writing for *USA Today* and *The Economist*. Both are written in approximately the same language, but the differences in level, quality, and style are obvious. To say that "it's just English" misses the point entirely.

Or, as we say in the trade, "You can write garbage in any language." This poses a problem for the software development manager. Most managers did write code at one point in their careers, and they were probably pretty good at it; that's why they were promoted in many cases. But it's likely that they used some language other than the one their team is using on the current project. This causes what you might call a *first-level disconnect*: Although the software development manager understands general programming problems and issues, he may not be crystal clear on why the current language *du jour* is offering new and ever more interesting challenges.

This problem pales in comparison to the problem the software development manager has with *his* manager who, in many cases, has never written a line of code. Explaining to him that the project is being held up by a coding bug is like telling him that his car has to go into the shop because its frammis is broken. In fact, it's worse, because the car mechanic can probably tell him how long it is going to take to fix or replace the frammis; we, unfortunately, can offer no such prognostic. When your software frammis is broken, it could be a long time.

I must admit that I don't have a solution to this second problem, other than to suggest you explain the truth of the situation as clearly as you can. On the other hand, I do have some advice relative to the first problem of the software development manager and a "new" language. My solution is simple: The software development manager should attempt to gain familiarity with the new language by trying it out.

How Managers Can Learn a New Programming Language

Every few years, a new programming language arrives on the scene that promises to be the answer to a maiden's prayer and superior to all languages that have gone before it. The first reaction, for those of us who have been around the barn a few times, is, "What, again?" We're jaded enough to believe that all these languages are more alike than they are different, and we are quick to dispense with the hype surrounding each new introduction.

On the other hand, hope springs eternal; maybe this time there is more gold than dross. Maybe someone has invented a better "do" loop. The point is that simply dismissing the new candidate out of hand is not an option for those of us seeking competitive strength wherever we can find it. So we grit our teeth and once more leap into the breach.

But how can you discover the true value of a new language without sinking too much valuable time into learning it? Reading books on new programming languages is rarely an uplifting experience. Frankly, most of them are awful. Every now and then you can find a gem that not only kick-starts a new generation of programmers but also stands the test of time; for example, *K&R*[1] has been the classic manual on C programming since the language first became popular. It introduces C and supplies everything you need in a reference manual—packaged in a short, readable, and (once) inexpensive paperback. (Today that slim paperback costs $42.) But as I said, this kind of brief, well-organized, and highly informative book is a rarity.

So, after mucking around in a few of the early books available on a new language, most professionals start to learn a new programming language by writing their first pro-

---

[1] Kernighan, Brian W. and Dennis M. Ritchie, *The C Programming Language*, *Second Edition* (Upper Saddle River, New Jersey: Prentice Hall, 1988).

gram. This enables more learning than simply reading the somewhat contrived and artificial examples that most books set forth to introduce you to the language. To learn anything, it is usually efficacious to try to solve a problem.

The Problem, Better Defined

Once you decide to write a program, you must then get calibrated. Ever since *K&R*, it has been almost a cliché to write your first program to do nothing more than print or display the message **Hello, world**. While this does teach you how to print out a string and use the compiler and linker/loader, it doesn't do much else. You don't get enough return on your investment to consider this even a first effort.

I believe that the first program shouldn't be so trivial. Nothing ventured, nothing gained. On the other hand, you don't want to make this into a huge effort. You want a project that is just hard enough to cause you to learn how to implement things in the idiom of the new language, yet you don't want to get confused by having to do new domain learning. What this means is that you need a *standard problem*, so to speak, so that each time you have to re-implement its solution in a new programming language under evaluation, you have a *calibration*. In other words, you don't want to have to invent new science or devise new algorithms. Theoretically, the exercise should get easier each time you do a new implementation in a new language, because the problem space is already familiar to you, and you can spend more of your time judging how well the new language articulates the solution. If the new language takes you four times as long as usual to solve the standard problem, then you might begin to ask questions about the new language and/or its learning curve characteristics.[2]

What Should the Standard Problem Contain?

Glad you asked. Here are a few of the things I like to discover in any new language:

- **How to print out a string.** This is useful in terms of prompting the user for input, for example. As mentioned in the previous section, this is as far as you get with the **Hello, world** problem.

- **How to accept input from the user.** You can start with simple strings, working your way up to formatted numbers. You can do an awful lot by just reading character strings, so that's a good place to start.

---

[2] There is, of course, the possibility that we are losing prowess with the passage of time. Only the true pessimists among us would admit this possibility.

- **Simple algorithmic stuff.** You should manipulate some data. You don't need to try anything fancy here, maybe just some simple assignment, arithmetic operations, and so on. This will expose whether you need to call in math libraries or not, and so on. It's not necessary to test your ship's rigging under storm conditions at sea, but you do have to get the boat out of the slip.

- **How to store data persistently.** This is a big step up, because it asks that you write out a result and store it somewhere that survives the execution of the program. Ideally, you would like your sample problem to both read and write to the permanent store. Generally speaking, this exposes the language's interface to some sort of file system. Note that the file need be nothing more elaborate than a text file.

- **How to implement a "typical" data structure such as a linked list.** Because these beasts come up over and over again in programming chores, it is good to have one in your sample problem so you can see how this trick works in the new language. Note that this option is just an extension of "Simple algorithmic stuff" discussed earlier.

- **How to do simple error handling.** What do you do when user input or a data file is not what you expect—when it's blank, corrupt, or just plain silly?

- **How to evaluate the abstraction and encapsulation capabilities.** Will it be easy or hard to react to a change in requirements or problem definition?

I offer one big *caveat* here. What you are exploring are "programming in the small" features of the language. While these are important, they do not test the other very important "programming in the large" features—things like the capability to have public and private interfaces, interactions with other programmatic infrastructures, and, of course, graphics. In particular, much of the power of recent additions to our language arsenal comes from the richness of class libraries and the like; you won't have a chance to appreciate these until and unless you invest a lot more time exploring. Nonetheless, those things can be more easily investigated once the programming-in-the-small issues are better understood.

The Animal Game

Here is the program I have been re-coding as my own standard problem since the 1960s.[3] It is called "The Animal Game."

The program is an interactive dialog between a user and the program. The user is prompted to "Think of an animal." The program then begins by asking, "Is your ani-

---

[3] I must admit to being proud of having delivered production-quality software within five different decades, starting with the sixties. In the early days, I wrote much of it myself; later on, my colleagues did everything they could to prevent me from writing code. During that span of time, I have had to deal with many different languages.

mal a beagle?"[4] If the user was thinking of a beagle, he answers, "Yes"; the program congratulates itself on its perspicacity, thanks the user for playing, and the game is over.

If, on the other hand, the user is not thinking of a beagle, he answers, "No." Downcast, the program responds, "Sorry, I did not guess your animal. Tell me your animal and give me a question that has the answer 'Yes' for your animal, and 'No' for a beagle."

For example, if the person is thinking of a trout, he would enter "trout," followed by the question, "Is it a fish?" The answer is yes for a trout, and no for a beagle.

Having stumped the program and entered his animal and his question, the user is thanked, and the program again terminates.

However, the next time the user plays, something different happens. After being prompted to "Think of an animal," the first question asked is, "Is it a fish?" If the user answers "Yes," then the program asks, "Is it a trout?" But if the user answers "No" to "Is it a fish?" then the program asks, "Is it a beagle?" If the user was thinking either of a beagle or a trout, then the program wins by guessing right. On the other hand, if the person was thinking of some other animal, then once again the program admits defeat and asks for the new animal and a question that will distinguish the new animal from either a beagle or a trout, as appropriate.

So, in the beginning, the program is exceedingly "dumb." But by storing up the new animals and the new questions, it gets "smarter" as it plays. It won't always guess your animal by the shortest possible route, but after a while it can fake intelligence and "guess" your animal almost every time. That's because as its database gets bigger, it appears to "track down your animal" more and more surely.[5]

Does the Animal Game Fit the Criteria?

You betcha. Here they are again:

- **Output strings:** The program needs to give the user instructions and to respond to his responses to your questions.

- **Input:** The program needs to take strings from the user and do something with them. The dialog nature of the problem requires some (but not much) parsing of the input.

---

[4] Homage to Snoopy and his creator, Charles Schulz.

[5] There is a flaw here. A user can insert a bad question or otherwise get things bollixed up—like reversing the roles of "yes" and "no." Don't laugh; I have seen it done. I have even seen a player forget the animal he was supposed to be thinking of in mid-game. Once this happens, the database is contaminated for future use. Historically, I have had more success with third-graders than with adults; apparently, the simplicity of the game is perfect for eight-year-olds and daunting for their parents.

- **Simple algorithm:** The program is going to branch to different questions depending on the answers. Thus, depending on the "Yes" and "No" responses, it will traverse a data structure.

- **Interaction with a permanent store:** The program needs to keep the current animal and question database file somewhere, and read it in on program invocation. This data will be used to exhaust the question set. If the program does not guess the animal, it will have to update the file with the new animal and the new question. Then it will have to store these for the next user session.

- **Prototypical data structure:** Once again, the program will traverse some sort of linked list to achieve the result. When the user adds a new animal and a new question, the program will have to add those links and update some of the old links to point to the new information.

- **Error handling:** The program needs to be able to deal with blank input from the user when actual values are required, and it has to cope with the data file's being corrupted. This area has lots of latitude, depending on how user-friendly you want the program to be. For example, what do you do if the user quits halfway through?

- **Abstraction and encapsulation:** You can easily generalize the problem to be a vegetable game, a mineral game, or a famous-person game. These variations should depend only on loading a different data file; the language should let you do all of them with the same program.

Note that I have kept this very simple. For example, you shouldn't allow several people to play the game simultaneously; this would vastly complicate the problem. But even for serial interactions by different users, it makes for a nice programming problem.

Does It Pass the "So What?" Test?

Throughout the years, I have implemented "The Animal Game" in the following languages:[6]

FORTRAN

BASIC

APL

---

[6] The list reveals my programming roots: I come from the scientific side of the house, not the business side. Although I did have to manage a group of COBOL programmers once, I was so busy at the time that learning their lingo was way down on the priority list. And, to tell the absolute truth, I still suffered from "language snobbery" at that point in my career.

Pascal

FORTH[7]

C

Ada

C++

I would have done Java, but[8]...

In general, it takes me a few hours to recall how to make the linked list work and get something on the air. To allow someone else to play the game unsupervised (which means doing some error handling) usually takes me a few days of programming. I could probably go faster if I could ever find legacy code for any of the previous implementations, but I never can. The exercise gets repeated with a periodicity of every four to five years, which is just long enough to lose the last example.

But, you say, why should you need legacy code? Don't you have a design spec, a pseudo-code document, or a UML diagram lying around that would enable you to do the implementation without referring to the last piece of code you wrote?

The answer is twofold: Yes, I do develop the diagrams and pseudo-code, but I get to do it over again each time because I can never find that, either. Second, seeing how you did something in the last language is a useful crutch when trying to do the same thing in the new language. If I had my druthers, I'd be able to locate both my last diagrams and pseudo-code version *and* my last language implementation. Together, they would give me a quicker start. If only I kept better records. Oh well. Although this would be a grievous infraction for a software development organization, it is a somewhat lesser sin for what is, after all, a small, personal, programming effort.

By far the most bizarre implementations I've done were in APL and FORTH. Practitioners of those languages will probably understand why, and it is futile to try to explain this to non-practitioners. Absent from the list of likely suspects are LISP, Smalltalk, PL/I, and COBOL. There is nothing to prevent you from trying these; I just never have.

Incidentally, one of the other things you learn each time you do this exercise is the nature of the development environment and the available tools. I learned, for example, that the early C++ debuggers were not that wonderful; on the other hand, the utility of

---

[7] FORTH is the exception to the rule that programming languages are all caps only if they are acronyms. Charles Moore, the inventor of FORTH, wanted it to be a fourth-generation language, but the computer he was working on only allowed five-letter identifiers and capital letters, or so goes the folklore. The individual letters of FORTH do not stand for anything themselves.

[8] I really am getting too old for this. And to be perfectly even-handed about it, I will decline the opportunity in C# as well.

the Rational Environment was apparent, and my Ada implementation was done in record time. When I did it in FORTH, I learned how to reboot my machine every time there was a runtime error.

It's Your Game

The best way to get one's feet wet with a new programming language is to program a standard problem that you are already familiar with. This allows you to explore the language and learn "How do I do this?" on a known set of useful questions. My standard problem is one that I have used for many years, one that I believe forces you to confront a minimal but useful set of basic issues.

Recap

The biggest problem with this approach is that it does tend to focus on the "programming in the small" issues. Each new language that comes along has more expressive power, and often that power is not shown off by using small examples. For instance, it is hard to see how this example would help you understand the inheritance feature of C++, although I am sure you could find a way.

What I have observed over and over again is that the majority of developers use the subset of the latest language that allows them to get the job done. Only a very few effectively use the "power features" that are often touted in the books and in the hype surrounding the new language. It also concerns me that these languages are more sophisticated to the point that when power users employ the most advanced features, the code becomes very obscure to the average programmer. This is especially dangerous when one considers that the maintenance of the code will be done in almost all cases by a programmer who is less competent than the person who wrote the original code. This is not a slam on modern programming languages; it is an advisory to managers to be sure that the code they produce will be maintainable over the long haul.

We now pass to the last chapter in our section on software differences. This involves that little-known art called "Getting the Product Out the Door." It is what we get paid for, and, I am sorry to say, in too many cases we are not very good at it.

CHAPTER 8

Getting It Out the Door

I have on occasion claimed that I can build the perfect product. Just don't ask me to ever ship it.

As soon as you require that I ship a product on a given date, I can guarantee you that the product will be imperfect. It will disappoint someone along some dimension. It will lack some feature, exhibit some annoying minor bug, or will lack some piece of documentation. No doubt there will be rough edges in its user interface. If only we had more time…

This is not a phenomenon unique to software products. A shipped product is always a compromise between the product we would ideally like to ship—the one that approaches perfection—and the one we really need to ship because we must begin generating revenue. And sometimes, believe it or not, the product we ship *is* good enough, even though it represents a compromise. The test is whether or not it serves the greatest good for the greatest number.

Consider an *update release* of an existing product, one that will add some new features and fix many annoying defects resulting from the previous compromised release. You can work on this update as long as you like; the longer you take, the more features you can add and the more bugs you can fix. But here's another way to look at it: The longer you wait to ship that update release, the longer your existing customers will have to live with the bugs in the version they are currently using. So the tradeoff becomes this: Is it better to ship 50 bug fixes today, or 55 in another two weeks? If you have thousands of customers who are suffering with Bug #29 on the list every day, I think I can make a pretty good argument for shipping *yesterday*.

Once you realize that shipping the product is not only part of your job but in fact the critical step—Bob Bond[1] would call it "running it through the tape"—you need to consider exactly what is required to go from some assemblage of working bits to a package that you can put on the loading dock or, alternatively, some set of files that you can stage on your download server. You need to consider testing, installation, documentation, preparing the support organization, and many, many other details. Like the death from a thousand cuts, getting this all right can be extremely painful the first hundred or so times you do it. It is one of those exercises that require method and persistence, and extremely meticulous follow-up.

The purpose of this chapter is not to bludgeon you to death with the obvious. What I focus on in this chapter is a small subset of the problem: How do we "close out" development of the software so that we can ship the product? When we are on "final approach" to shipping the product, what changes? The answer is this: If you have been doing it right, the change is imperceptible. If you have neglected thinking about this problem all along, then you will suffer large, severe, and disruptive change at the end, and your ability to ship will be endangered.

If You Build It, They Will Come[2]

In the world of software products, there are successes and failures, determined by the free market system. We must, of course, add to the list of failures those projects whose products never see the light of day—the ones that are worked on for various lengths of time but never ship. As obvious as it sounds, you cannot be successful unless you meet the precursor of shipping your product.

As you cannot ship what you cannot build, actually putting together the pieces becomes critical. Intrinsic in this is the concept of a *repeatable* build process. You will build the product over and over again, until one of your *candidate releases* passes muster and you let it out the door. I now confront the issues involved in creating such a repeatable build process for your product.

---

[1] Bob Bond ran sales and marketing at Rational for many years. He was a very positive mentor for me.

[2] In fact, the line from the movie "Field of Dreams" was, "If you build it, he will come," the "he" being either Shoeless Joe Jackson or the principal character's father. The line has been so frequently misquoted that most people use this one. Of course, at the end of the movie "they" come, as illustrated by the stream of headlights across the Midwestern plain.

In the Beginning, There Was the Sandbox

Products come out of projects, and projects tend to begin in haphazard ways. Organizations with well-defined processes have developers building their components in local work areas, sometimes called *sandboxes*. They provide for mechanisms whereby the sub-products of these sandboxes can be assembled, sometimes in *ad hoc* ways, so that each development team can test its progress in the context of the whole product. Configuration management systems allow for appropriate partitioning such that each developer (or team of developers) has the autonomy and isolation to work on his piece without stepping on the other guy's toes, while at the same time providing for a loose integration context.

This works fine in the early, chaotic days when everything is changing very rapidly, and before architectures are well-defined and interfaces are nailed down. However, before too long even modest projects outgrow this framework. At that point, one of two things happens: Either the organization makes *the build* a priority and adds some structure, or it doesn't. In general, those that do establish a regular "heartbeat" for the project—a periodic, regular, and dependable build cycle—improve their chances for success. Those that don't establish this rhythm find that entropy begins to take over, and that building the product becomes more difficult over time.[3]

Many organizations vastly underestimate the effort it takes to put a good build process in place. Because of this, projects in their latter stages often have a "new" problem to deal with: In addition to having buggy software, incomplete parts, and so on, they also struggle with something that they have taken for granted—the simple assembly of their product. This is a trap for the unwary. In order to not fall into the trap, you need to understand more about the process of assembling a product.

Why Should the Product Build Be Hard, Anyway?

First of all, the product you are going to ship has more pieces to it than the prototypes you have been putting together for internal consumption. Here's a classic example: Developers and testers rarely look at the help system, because they know the product well enough to play with it and test it. Once you are going to have outsiders try to use it, you need a well-elaborated and working help system for people to use. Further, you need instructions for installing the software in different computing environments, as well as various other adjuncts that you can live without when you are only consuming your software

---

[3] *Entropy* is the tendency that all systems have to move from an orderly state to a disordered state when left alone. It is a fundamental physical law. One might say that all attempts at progress, by any civilization, fly in the face of entropy. Another way to say this is that to bring order out of chaos takes work, and that once you stop working, entropy will cause the system to spontaneously move to a more disordered state. I will talk some more about this in Chapter 18, "Bad Analogies."

internally. So the first problem that comes up is one that might be dismissed as *packaging*. You need more pieces to ship a product than to use it internally; and further, you need to document all the little details that the internal team has always known or taken for granted.[4] Making the product ready for outside consumers is sometimes called *sanding off the rough edges*. Some of these "rough edges" can be very sharp, and because you don't catch them all the first time, your first consumers may cut their fingers on them.

Let's assume, however, that this is just a logistical exercise and that with enough planning you can avoid the "packaging" trap. In some sense, it can be put in the "annoying detail" category: If you ignore it, it will bite you; but if you are aware of it and plan for it, then it is relatively easy to overcome. So, forewarned is forearmed: Treat packaging as a purely technical problem and you will be fine.

In fact, there are three much more fundamental obstacles to success that come up over and over again. They are distinct and interrelated, and all three must be worked on to achieve a successful build process.

Obstacle 1: Organizational Politics

Many software development managers lose sight of the simple fact that controlling the build process is first and foremost a political problem. To put it simply, he who controls the build has an enormous amount of power. After all, the build cycle itself defines the rhythm of the entire development and test organization. Think of the build cycle as the software equivalent of a factory assembly line. The person who gets to define the characteristics of the line and its speed determines, to a very real extent, the output of the factory. Line workers are very aware of their subservience to the line. The cardinal sin in the factory is to slow down, or—Heaven forbid!—shut down the line. The software equivalent is submitting a set of changes that *breaks the build*.[5]

Now the build process is something that everyone must participate in, but only one group can control. By its very nature it is not a democratic enterprise; it requires a certain amount of hierarchical and structural apparatus to work at all. Everyone agrees on this, more or less. The sticky wicket is determining who gets the responsibility and authority to make it work. That group will, from that day forward, wield a lot of power and clout.

Because human beings are, in general, reluctant to give up this sort of power, the build process becomes a political football. Myriad discussions ensue as to who will have

---

[4] The standard vehicle for this is called the *release note*. The release note documents the limitations of this version of the software, known bugs, and so on. It is an attempt to characterize the state of the deliverable, as it is better to tell your consumers things you know about rather than have them discover them on their own. Sometimes the release note is called the *readme file*.

[5] There are legitimate reasons for shutting down the line, and sometimes the person on the factory floor is the most appropriate person to do this. On the other hand, shutting down the line by mistake is definitely not a good idea.

the right to do what to whom in the interest of the build process. All of the negative political tendencies of your organization will be exposed during these discussions.

The purists among you will cry out that political tendencies should be discouraged or even condemned, pointing out that the job is hard enough from a technical point of view and should not be "polluted" by politics. In most organizations, however, *wishing* politics away will not necessarily make them *go* away. Politics is a fact of life that must be dealt with.[6] However, you must get through this phase, as unpleasant as it first appears. Else, you will be incapable of dealing with the next two hurdles.

Here are some specific suggestions:

- Try to get the group to agree that someone has to be in charge, because a loose confederation approach is doomed to failure.

- Try to reach a reasonable compromise between the autonomy of the constituent teams and the centralized authority that will be required.

- Always make sure that the management team understands the importance of the issue and has the very best people assigned to the build.

- Later in this chapter, we will talk about having a *czar of the build*. Make sure it is a person who is technically competent, firm, fair, and respected by everyone. Install him or her early in the process and have this person guide you through the political shoals.

- Enlist management's support in crushing "bad politics," should it rear its ugly head.

Obstacle 2: The Process

Having hacked through all the political jungles that accompany conceding power to the build group, the participants must now agree on the process they will use. Just as form follows function, the process will often be shaped to mirror the political compromises that were made to get to this juncture. There is plenty of interaction between the first and second obstacles. In fact, often the process obstacle presents itself early on, in Phase 1, because it is being used as a surrogate by those who don't want to openly admit that there are unresolved political issues. In some organizations, we see these two obstacles mashed together into one giant hairball, which in turn gives "process" a bad name. You cannot use "process" to solve what are intrinsically political problems, much in the same way that you cannot "solve" technical problems through political compromise.

---

[6] My perspective is that there are "good politics," akin to the notion of "fighting fair," and that a healthy political process can and should work toward making good decisions. Then there are "bad politics," which make organizational objectives subservient to personal agendas and self-aggrandizement; this sort of politics needs to be stamped out wherever it is found. The problem, of course, is the gray zone in between. I treat this subject in more detail in Chapter 13, "Politics."

The basic tension at this point revolves around the people who want a strict, rigorous process—sometimes called *lots of rules and no mercy*[7]—versus the people who want a looser set of policies. Acknowledging that there is no single, simple, right answer is usually the best place to start here. Your process will have to be tuned to your organization, because all organizations have their peculiarities.[8]

That does not mean that you need to invent new process. I used the word "tune" advisedly in the previous paragraph because I am firmly convinced that the best way to deal with this issue is to start with a base process that has been demonstrated to work before. Rational Software's Unified Change Management (UCM), for example, has a rich legacy of successful application. We know it works across a broad spectrum of domains, applications, and organizations. Why start over? Do you really think you are going to do better?

There are a few traps you don't want to fall into at this point. One is the *religious wars* pitfall. In every organization there are process gurus who believe that they, and only they, have the magic formula. And sure enough, every time there are others who resist, quite certain of their own convictions.[9] Regardless of who is right or wrong, these crusades are totally unproductive, often revolving around obscure details of little importance. The strong manager needs to identify the religious process fanatics and stifle them early. Sometimes the only answer is to tell them to put a cork in it. Remember always that process is not an end in and of itself; it is a means to an end—shipping the product![10]

Another trap is to think that any process, no matter how good, can substitute for thought or judgment. For every ironclad rule, there is bound to be an exception. You will have to watch what is going on and make midcourse corrections, no matter what your

---

[7] I believe the world is indebted to James E. Archer for this characterization. Jim is one of the most effective development managers I know, having been the godfather for Rational's programming environments products from the very beginning. He and I had many interesting discussions on the right amount of process.

[8] Some people argue at this point that you should endeavor to get your process "right" and then tune your organization to fit the process. While this is a laudable objective and *theoretically* the right approach, I have rarely found it to be successful in practice. You cannot allow a regressive organization the prerogative of rejecting reasonable process; on the other hand, it is difficult to implement any process that is too far out in front of the organization that must carry it off.

[9] To illustrate how far out of control this can become, the wars are often characterized as struggles between the "process Nazis" and the "anarchists." With such value-laden labels, it is difficult to have discussions that will get to the right place.

[10] In a like manner, the anarchists will be hard put to demonstrate that they can ship product without any process. As is the case in almost all these debates, neither extreme position is defensible.

process is. As called out previously, you will need to modify and tune your process in real time as you discover what works for you and what doesn't.

Lastly, get on with it. Perfect is the enemy of good.[11] You will develop your process iteratively, just the way you develop the software. Get to Iteration 1 quickly. Learn. Change. Improve. Repeat until done.

Obstacle 3: Tools

Just as the first obstacle (politics) and the second obstacle (process) are intimately related, so are the second and the third. The third, of course, is the toolset that you will use to implement the process. Needless to say, choosing the tools first is getting it bass-ackwards, but surprisingly enough, that's the way many organizations go about it. They then wind up with the tool determining the process, which can be loads of fun when the process thus derived is inconsistent with the political philosophy of the organization.

Obviously, you need tools that will automate and enforce the process you have chosen to use. If you have a process that admits mistakes, you will be "backing out" changes from time to time. Does the tool support that easily? Are developers going to be checking in their work to a common baseline from multiple remote sites? If so, then your tool had better support that model. Do you want to build your entire product from top to bottom every night? If so, then I hope your tool has the performance and turnaround characteristics that will permit that. Do you want to automate your regression testing as part of the build? Once again, tool support is crucial.

Even organizations that have done a good job with the first two problems sometimes flounder with the third. And sometimes it is not the tools' fault either. Once again, using our factory analogy, you need someone to monitor the line and to do quality control for the product coming off the line. Without constant vigilance, it is easy to automate a process that produces a low-quality result. Every successful build process requires a foreman or the equivalent thereof; sometimes he or she is called the *czar* (or *czarina*) *of the build* or, more simply, the *buildmeister*.[12] The buildmeister monitors the health of the line and makes sure that a steady stream of good-quality product is produced.

---

[11] I first heard this from Mikhail Drabkin of Riga, Latvia, and assumed it was Russian folk wisdom. He may have in fact been (mis?)quoting Soviet Admiral Sergei Georgievich Gorshkov, although that citation turns out to be only an approximation: Gorshkov's ended with "Good enough." Dr. Stephen Franklin of U.C. Irvine points out that very similar sentiments have been attributed to both Clausewitz and Voltaire. Clausewitz is much more verbose, and there seems to be evidence that Voltaire "borrowed" from an Italian proverb. Though these pithy sayings sometimes have a provenance that is difficult to pin down, one can deny neither their truth nor their wisdom.

[12] Here's a cautionary, funny, and politically incorrect tale: I once made a big deal about having a czar of the build, and then appointed a fellow who was, shall we say, altitudinally challenged. He unfortunately became known as the czardine of the build. Ouch!

One last semi-technical note: Beware of the old saying "We can always write a script that can do that." The problem is that these scripts always start out small and simple and then grow in ways that are random and unsupervised. Scripts, unlike programs, are rarely designed; they just grow. They become compendia of special cases and are inadequate to respond to the ever-increasing demands of the organization; they are brittle. They are a maintenance nightmare, especially if the original author moves on. And they are very, very difficult to debug. Just as the road to Hell is paved with good intentions, the road to "build Hell" is paved with the out-of-control products of general-purpose scripting languages.[13]

What About Iterative Development?

Iterative development sidesteps one of the great dangers of the waterfall approach: leaving system integration to the last minute. One of the reasons so many waterfall projects fail is that, very late in the game, developers are trying to assemble their product for the very first time. In addition to finding many bugs, mostly in the interfaces, they grapple with the normal logistical and organizational problems of putting together a build chain for the first time. Often, things that pass for bugs are nothing more than the artifacts of broken builds. But the organization is in such chaos at this point—running out of time, nothing working, people frazzled—that it is hard to separate the sugar from the salt. It is also a very bad time to be trying to solve political and process problems.

By contrast, iterative development requires that you construct your build chain to accomplish the deliverable for Iteration 1—a working program. So you begin to debug this process early in the project, not at the end. By the time you get to Iteration 3 or 4, the build process is actually starting to work pretty well. For the last iteration, the one that will deliver the final bits, the build should be working like a finely lubricated Swiss watch.

As with pretty much everything else in software development, there are a small number of ways to get this right and almost an infinite number of ways to get it wrong. If you view the build as a detail that will "just happen," then the odds are against you. Make sure you attack the build process as a conscious effort that is critical to your success, and devote the time, energy, and resources to it that it demands. To do any less is sheer folly.

---

[13] Some scripting languages have been favorably likened to duct tape; would you want to begin the final assembly of your jet aircraft by having some guy yell out, "Time to get out the duct tape!"?

Recap

I've frequently been called in late in the software development cycle when projects are in trouble. Often, it is difficult at first to judge the depth of the yogurt. Usually the developers are focusing on how much they are "behind," as measured in things that are coded but just don't work, and things that are not coded at all but should be.

While this is one important aspect, I always begin to also look at the health of the build process. If the build process is non-existent or badly broken, it needs attention *immediately*. The reason for this should be obvious; at this stage of the proceedings, the lack of a reliable, repeatable build process will impede all further progress. You can't test what you can't build, and repeated testing is a necessity at this point; else, how can the developers know what they've fixed and what remains problematic?

Sadly, in many organizations the build process is something that is relegated to the B Team. This is a huge mistake. You must have A-list players in this part of the organization. As soon as people understand how much you as the senior manager appreciate the contribution of this team, you will have no problems getting volunteers.

The other thing that proves very slippery is answering the question, "How do we know when we are done?" Getting agreement well in advance on some clear criteria is incredibly useful; such agreement reduces the odds that the bar will move radically up or down as the ship date looms. One of the major objectives when moving into the Transition Phase of iterative development is to define reasonable criteria for shipment. Without a clear "exit plan," the project risks a series of never-ending last-minute slips.

Thus ends Part 2 on the basics. In Part 3, I will look at software development from a project management perspective.

PART 3

THE PROJECT-
MANAGEMENT VIEW

The third section of this book looks at software development from a project-management perspective. The view is that in the zeroth-order approximation, managing a software development project is just like managing any other project.

In Chapter 9, "Trade-Offs," I look at that age-old problem of how to get "those eight great tomatoes in that little-bitty can." Or, why is it we always seem to be trying to do too much in the time we have allotted to us?

I turn in Chapter 10, "Estimating," to some rudimentary notions about how to estimate software development projects; our old friend Roscoe Leroy reappears.

In Chapter 11, "Scheduling," Roscoe continues with his theory of how to schedule software development projects, injecting some predictive science into the domain.

Finally, we note in Chapter 12, "Rhythm," that all successful projects and the teams that execute them have a certain rhythm to their activity. This rhythm is disarmingly the same when observed over many, many projects, so I look for some underlying causes.

In all these chapters, I of course try to compare and contrast software development with "other" projects, so that you can understand the differences as well as the similarities.

CHAPTER 9

Trade-Offs

The biggest problem every project manager faces is explaining to his team members how they are going to get all that work done with the ridiculous deadline they have facing them. The same developers who were wildly optimistic ("No problem!") during the exploratory phases of the project suddenly become glum, even sullen, when management says, "Go ahead." The problem, of course, is that management always wants more. Yesterday.

As well they should. For if management doesn't set the bar high, they know they will get even less. The problem is that most software development managers take the following point of view: "Yeah, it's a stretch, but it's a good team. With a little bit of luck, we should be able to pull it off. And, so long as we come close, we'll be OK." The developers, on the other hand, know better. They know that lots of things will go wrong; people will quit, suppliers of critical components will fold their tents in the middle of the night and disappear, and so on. The emerging system will inevitably be too slow compared to the prototype. Things will just bog down.

Management, on the other hand, has a "contract view" of the situation. They have opened the corporate vault and funded this project. Elevendy-seven weeks later, to the minute, they expect a software product to be on the loading dock. When the product is late, all hell will break loose, because many other wheels have been set in motion that critically depend on this one deliverable.

How do we get this level of disconnect, and how does it happen over and over again? I have watched this scenario play out for the last 40 years or so. It is as though we never learn. The simple fact is this: We try to do too much in too little time. All our other problems stem from that fundamental error.

The software development manager is the person who always gets caught in the middle. He is the one who gambled on the "slightly optimistic" estimate and schedule which, having no margin for error, was doomed from the start. He is squeezed between his developers, who feel as though they have been signed up for yet another death march, and his management, who can't understand why these things are always late. Sometimes, in an effort to save the bacon, he agrees to ship a product roughly on time, with the usual consequences: the product is buggy, the customers are unhappy, and the support organization is badly overloaded answering the phones.

There are only two fundamentals every software development manager needs to keep in the forefront of his brain at all times. The first is *scope management*. If you cannot control the scope of what is being developed, you are destined to fail; "feature creep" will kill you every time. The second is the *primacy of time*. Of all the things that affect the outcome, time is the one that governs all else. After that, everything else is a question of trade-offs.

The Project Pyramid

I've long been fascinated by the now famous "scope, resources, time—pick any two" paradigm, which states that trying to maximize scope while simultaneously minimizing resources and time will impose too many constraints and inevitably lead to project failure. Max Wideman talks about "the *iron triangle*" on his excellent website on project management wisdom, www.maxwideman.com.[1]

Max makes the important point that we need to add a critical fourth dimension—quality—to the paradigm. As he wrote to me,

> Interestingly, quality ultimately transcends all else, whether in terms of performance, productivity, or final product. But a remarkable number of people in

---

[1] The relevant links are http://www.maxwideman.com/musings/irontriangle.htm and http://www.maxwideman.com/musings/triangles.htm. In this chapter, I use the term *resources* to mean all costs, including burdened people costs.

the project management industry don't seem to have latched onto that. Who cares if last year's project was late and over budget? That's all lost in last year's financial statements. But the quality [of the product] is enduring.

It is hard to argue with that point of view. Most of us software developers can recall some time when, in our zeal to make our commitments and ship on time, we let stuff get out the door that caused us heavy regrets later on.

So Max extends the iron triangle to a star, as shown in Figure 9.1.

Figure 9.1   Max Wideman's extension of the "iron triangle"—resources, scope, and time—introduces "quality" as a fourth element.

As an alternative to this star, Max's correspondent Derrick Davis suggests using a tetrahedron to illustrate these relationships. This allows you to maintain the original triangle but create a third dimension to depict the quality aspect. The nice thing about the tetrahedron is its intrinsic symmetry; the four attributes populate the vertices, and any three can be used as the base. Max has illustrated this in a thoughtful way, tying the vertex pairs together with another descriptor (see Figure 9.2).

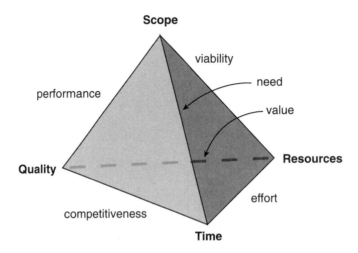

Figure 9.2   The tetrahedron model allows any three attributes to serve as a base, placing the fourth attribute into the third dimension.

Five, Not Four

Although I agree with Max's insistence on quality as a critical fourth factor, I believe that his model still leaves something to be desired. When thinking about a project prior to beginning work on it, management is typically interested in the "shape" of the project—an interest that maps nicely to the four parameters illustrated in Figures 9.1 and 9.2. That is, we can state *how much* we intend to do (scope); we can describe *how well* we are going to do it (quality); we can predict *how long* we will take to complete the project (time); and we can estimate *how much it will cost* (resources). But then are we done with our project description?

I don't think so. Management is always interested in a fifth variable: *risk*. That is, given the previous four parameters we've identified and the plan that goes with them, management wants to know whether the project represents a high, medium, or low risk to the business. We know from vast experience that projects have different risk profiles, and good managers try to balance their project portfolios by planning a spectrum of projects with different risk levels. The more risky ones have a greater probability of failure, but they might have bigger payoffs, too. Just as it is judicious for individuals to have diversified financial investment portfolios, it is smart for a company to diversify its portfolio by having many projects with different risk/reward profiles. Statistically, such an enterprise is bound to prosper.

Now, how can I use geometry to visualize this new, important, and—I believe—final, parameter?

Enter the Pyramid

I propose a model that represents the first four variables as the four sides of the base of a pyramid. We'll assign *extensive properties* to the sides so that the lengths are meaningful. Note that this is different from the Davis tetrahedron model, in which the attributes occupy the vertices.

For simplicity, let's assume that all sides of the base are of equal length, so that the base forms a square. This is reminiscent of Max's star, except that I have moved the attributes from the corners to the edges. Of course, these lengths can be independently adjusted, so the base is actually an arbitrary quadrilateral. Conceptually, however, I lose nothing by assuming for now that the base is a square.

Now let's redefine the length of each side of the base. I will also adjust the terminology slightly to reflect more accurately what the sides represent. Bear with me, and you will see why:

- **Scope.** More "things to do" represents a larger scope, so the length of this side increases as the scope increases.

- **Quality.** Higher quality standards mean a tougher job, so the length of this side increases as our quality metrics increase—in other words, as we "raise the bar" on quality.

- **Speed.** This is our way of capturing the time element; we increase the length of this side as the speed increases. Conversely, the slower you go—the more time you have—the shorter this side becomes. Completing five function points per month is harder than completing two function points per month; think of this side as work accomplished per unit time.

- **Frugality.** (Max suggested this term instead of my original *parsimony.*) When we consume fewer resources, we are being more frugal. So higher frugality corresponds to a longer length for this side. If we use up more resources, then this side gets shorter.

Notice that if I use these definitions for scope, quality, speed, and frugality, the project becomes easier if the sides are shorter. That is, the project is easier if we do less, lower our quality standards, proceed more slowly (take more time), and can afford to be less frugal (have more resources). Thus all four variables "move in the same direction."

Note also that with these definitions you increase your profitability as you increase the area of the base. This is because the value of the product goes up as you make it bigger, better, and get it sooner, while at the same time are the most frugal in producing it. Maximizing value while minimizing cost optimizes for profitability. It's perfectly logical that attempting to make our profit larger also makes the project harder and more risky.

The Altitude Variable

Now let's build a pyramid on this base, keeping in mind that no matter what lengths the sides are for a given project, the volume of the pyramid will be proportional to the area of the base times the altitude. The altitude abstractly represents the *probability of project success,* which is the inverse of its risk. That is, a high-risk project will have a low probability of success and a low altitude. A low-risk project will have a high probability of success and a correspondingly higher altitude.

Now all I have to do is link it all together (see Figure 9.3).

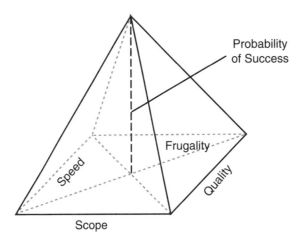

Figure 9.3   The project pyramid. A high-risk project will have a low probability of success and a low altitude. A low-risk project will have a high probability of success and a higher altitude.

The Pyramid's Volume Is Constant

We can now posit that the volume contained in the pyramid is a constant for a given team. That is, reality dictates that only so much "stuff" will fit into the project pyramid, based on that team's capabilities. This makes sense, because the pyramid's volume is proportional to

$$\{\text{difficulty}\} \times \{\text{probability of success}\}$$

As one goes up, the other must go down. This is another way of saying that there is a "conservation law" at work here: The product of the base area—which represents the project difficulty due to the specification of the four parameters—times the altitude (representing the probability of success) is proportional to a "conserved" volume.

What determines the pyramid's volume? Two things. First, the capabilities of the project team, as I have already mentioned. And second, the degree to which the project team members are grappling with unfamiliar problems. A highly capable team implies a larger volume:

more capacity = more "stuff" = more volume

and lots of new problems and unknowns implies a smaller volume:

more unknowns = higher risk = less volume

So, given a constant volume corresponding to the project team and initial set of unknowns, what do you have to do if you want to make the altitude higher—that is, if you want to increase the probability of success? By the logic of elementary solid geometry, you must make the base smaller. You do this by reducing the lengths of one or more sides of the base, thereby making the project easier.

Remember: Volume is proportional to base times altitude, regardless of the base's shape.[2]

A Statistical Interlude

At this point, I can attempt to figure out the right "scale" for the altitude. I can measure the edges along the base in familiar units:

- **Scope:** Function points or features.

- **Quality:** Inverse of number of defects allowed.

- **Speed:** Function points or features/month.

- **Frugality:** "Inverse" dollars or person-months.

But what about that pesky probability of success—our altitude?

We know that "longer is better," that a higher altitude corresponds to a higher probability of success. But there is a slight problem with using probability—a percentage-based measurement—as the scale. For example, if I have a pyramid with an altitude corresponding to a 60 percent probability of success, I cannot, under the constant volume assumption, improve that percentage by cutting the area of the base in half in order to double the altitude. That would give us an absurd answer of "120 percent probability of success," and I know that probabilities must be between zero and 100 percent.

To resolve this conundrum, I must investigate how the outcomes of software development projects are distributed. Can I assume that these project outcomes are distributed

---

[2] The formula for the volume of a pyramid is $V = (1/3) \times$ (area of base) $\times$ (altitude).

according to the standard normal distribution—the well-known "bell curve"? The diagram in Figure 9.4 is worth a thousand words.

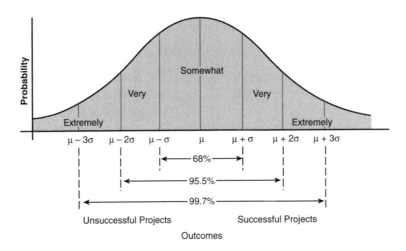

Figure 9.4 How software development project outcomes relate to the standard probability bell curve.

If you happen to be rusty on what a probability distribution function is, recall that the x-axis represents the outcome, and the y-axis represents the number of events with that outcome which, properly normalized, is the probability of that outcome. If you start from the left edge and sweep out the area under the curve, you measure the cumulative probability of attaining that outcome. In Figure 9.4, the percentages beneath the x-axis show us how much area is contained between the x-axis coordinates that are spanned.

Note that the distribution is "normalized" here, with the midpoint called μ, and the "width" of the distribution characterized by the standard deviation sigma (σ). The distribution extends to both plus and minus infinity, but note that the "tails" of the distribution past the plus and minus 3 sigma limits are quite small; the two tails share less than 0.3 percent of the entire area under the curve. The graph tells us that 68 percent of the projects will be either somewhat successful or somewhat unsuccessful, that only about 27.5 percent (95.5 percent minus 68 percent) will be either very successful or very unsuccessful, and that only 4.2 percent (99.7 percent minus 95.5 percent) will be either extremely successful or extremely unsuccessful. To get the relevant percentages for each of these, you can just divide by two, as there is symmetry around the middle. For example, you can predict that around 34 percent—approximately a third—of all projects will be somewhat successful.

In many applications you assume that μ is zero, so the outcomes range from minus infinity to plus infinity. But the standard normal distribution is also used to model things that are only positive, such as the heights of people. In that case, μ is shifted to represent the mean value of the distribution. What is the situation for project outcomes?

You can think of the x-axis as the net payoff or reward. Although I am sure many software development projects have had zero or negative payoff, it is hard to conceive of a project having a very large *negative* payoff.[3] This is because all projects will be cancelled by management long before they even start to approach minus infinity! So the symmetrical standard normal distribution centered on zero with tails to infinity in both directions seems to be the wrong model. What about the "shifted standard normal?" Here again, there are lots of reasons to suspect that the distribution is skewed, with a very long (if not infinite) positive tail and a shorter, finite tail in the negative direction. For example, the total net payoff on a project such as MS-DOS is very, very large. On the other hand, it is hard to imagine a project not being cancelled long before its net payoff was the symmetrical negative number! What we'd prefer is a distribution that has a finite limit on negative outcomes.

Right Idea, Wrong Distribution

For this purpose, my dear friend and colleague, Pascal Leroy[4], suggested the skewed lognormal distribution[5], which more accurately reflects many phenomena in nature.

Unlike the standard normal distribution, the lognormal distribution is asymmetrical and lacks a left tail that stretches to infinity. Figure 9.5 shows what it looks like.

We still use a sigma to represent the standard deviation, but we interpret it differently for the lognormal distribution, as explained next. Note that μ is now coincident with 1 sigma. Half the area under the curve is to the left of 1 sigma and half is to the right; if we believe the universe of projects has this distribution, then we want our project to fall to

---

[3] Part of this has to do with the *finite horizon* of a project. If we ship a defective product, the company will suffer huge support costs post-deployment. But these costs are rarely charged back to the project. This is rather unfortunate, because it shifts the burden away from the place that originated the problem. True project cost would include some measure of the post-deployment support cost.

[4] No relation to Roscoe! Pascal is a real person living in France, who has often improved the quality of my writing through insightful criticism.

[5] The lognormal is actually a "family" of distributions, of which we have chosen just one. For more information on the ubiquity of the lognormal distribution, see *LogNormal Distributions Across the Sciences: Keys and Clues*, Eckhard Limpert, Werner A. Stahl, and Markus Abbt, *BioScience* May 2001, Vol. 51, No. 5, page 341.

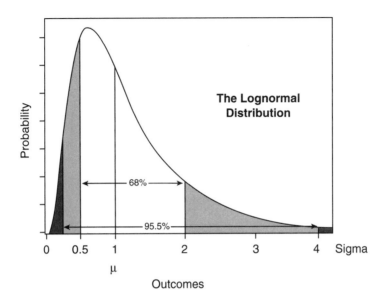

Figure 9.5 The lognormal distribution for depicting positive outcomes only.

the right of the 1 sigma line, which means its reward will be above the average.[6] This is the equivalent of saying that we are willing to invest μ (or 1 sigma) to do the project; any outcome (payoff, reward) less than that represents a loss (red ink), and anything above that is a win. To put it another way, we have "shifted" the lognormal distribution such that μ ($\sigma = 1$) corresponds to breakeven or zero net payoff.

Unlike the standard normal distribution, the lognormal distribution clumps unsuccessful projects between zero and 1 sigma, and successful projects range from 1 sigma to infinity with a long, slowly diminishing tail. This tells us that we have a small number of projects with very large payoffs to the right, but our losses are limited on the left. This seems to be a better model of reality.

The meaning of sigma is different in this distribution. As you move away from the midpoint, which is labeled here as 1 sigma, you accrue area a little differently. Each confidence interval corresponds to a distance out to $((1/2)^n \times sigma)$ on the left, and out to $(2^n \times sigma)$ on the right. This means that 68 percent of the area lies between 0.5 sigma and 2 sigma, and 95.5 percent of the area lies between 0.25 sigma and 4 sigma. This is how the multiplicative nature of the lognormal distribution manifests itself.

---

[6] Actually, the math is a little more complicated than that. For the standard normal distribution, the mean and the median are identical because of the symmetry of the distribution. For the lognormal distribution, they are not. So taking the 1 sigma point here is a little off, but the effect is small. We will ignore it in all that follows, as the effect is on the order of a few percent, and our overall model is not that precise anyway.

Mathematically, the distribution results from phenomena that statistically obey the *multiplicative central limit theorem*. This theorem demonstrates how the lognormal distribution arises from many small multiplicative random effects. In our case, one could argue that all variance in the outcomes of software development projects is due to many small but multiplicative random effects. By way of contrast, the standard normal distribution results from the *additive* contribution of many small random effects.

Implications for Real Projects

What are the implications of this distribution for real projects? Because the peak of the curve lies at approximately 0.6 sigma, we see that the most likely outcome (as measured by the curve's height) is an unsuccessful project! In fact, if the peak were exactly at 0.5 sigma, your probability of success would be only around 16 percent:

$$50\% - {}^{1}\!/2(68\%) = 50\% - 34\% = 16\%$$

Because the peak is not at 0.5 sigma but closer to 0.6 sigma or 0.7 sigma, the probability of success is a little higher—around 20 percent.

Now this is starting to become very interesting, because the Standish CHAOS report[7], of which I have always been somewhat skeptical, implies about a 20 percent success rate.[8] I will have more to say about this report later on. But it is interesting to note that the lognormal distribution predicts the Standish metric as the most *likely* outcome, which may mean that most development projects have a built-in difficulty factor that causes the lognormal distribution to obtain.

What Does It Take to Get to a Coin Flip?

What project manager wants to start with a less-than-even chance of success? At the very least, we would like to get the chances up to 50/50 for our projects. So, using our pyramid model, what do we have to do to the base to increase the altitude?

---

[7] See, for example, http://www.costxpert.com/resource_center/sdtimes.html.

[8] One quotation from the report is: "…the software success rate is 24 percent overall, with numbers even lower for large projects, especially those in the government sector." In another place, we find the notion that "…only 16 percent said they consistently meet scheduled due dates." So I have two numbers: 16 percent using one definition and 24 percent using another. Because I am biased somewhat towards large projects, I derate the 24 percent to 20 percent anyway, which leads to the assertion. Note that we probably can't distinguish 20 percent from 25 percent given all the different criteria people use for defining "success." At any rate, success rates in this range are nothing to crow about, either way.

Using units of sigma for our pyramid's altitude, I begin with a plan that gives us a starting point at the most probable outcome: at the distribution peak of 0.66 sigma. To get to a 50 percent probability of success, I need to accumulate half the area under the curve, which I know is at the 1 sigma point. So I need to go from 0.66 sigma to 1.0 sigma, which is an increase of 50 percent. That says I have to increase the altitude of the pyramid by a factor of 1.5, which means decreasing the area of the base by 1.5, or multiplying it by two-thirds.

In turn, this implies that I must multiply the lengths of sides of the square base by the square root of two-thirds, which is about 0.82. Therefore, to go from a naïve plan with only a 20 percent chance of success to a plan with a 50 percent chance of success, you must *simultaneously*

- Reduce scope by about 18 percent.

- Reduce quality standards by about 18 percent.

- Extend the schedule by about 18 percent (in other words, reduce speed by 18 percent).

- Apply about 18 percent more resources (in other words, reduce frugality by 18 percent) relative to what you had planned in the original scenario.

You could, of course, change each of these parameters by a somewhat different amount, as long as you reduced the area of the base by a third.

Let's call this new plan—the one that gets us to a 50/50 footing—"Plan B." I'll refer to the original, most likely, and somewhat naïve plan as "Plan A."

More Confidence

Can I do better? Suppose I wanted to go out to the 2 sigma point. This would then lead to a probability of success of around 84 percent:

$$50\% + 1/2(68\%) = 50\% + 34\% = 84\%$$

This would bring up our odds to five-to-one, which any project manager would gladly accept. In fact, this would be standing Standish on its head: five successful projects for every unsuccessful one.

What would it take to get us there?

Well, I can do the math both ways, either starting from our original Plan A or from the 50/50 Plan B. For consistency's sake, let's begin with Plan A. The math is pretty much the same. I now have to go from 0.66 sigma to 2 sigma, increasing our altitude by a factor of 3. That means I must multiply the area of the base by a third, which in turn means that I must multiply each side by the square root of 0.333. And in our previous list of things we'd need to change simultaneously to achieve better results, we'd have to replace 18 percent with 42 percent.

Let's now summarize, using rough numbers so that we don't assign spurious precision to the model.[9] Plan A has a probability of success of only around 20 percent. As we have seen, if we simultaneously reduce the difficulty of all four of the base parameters (scope, quality, speed, and frugality) by about 20 percent, we get Plan B, which has a 50 percent probability of success. To achieve an 85 percent success rate, we'd need to reduce the difficulty on the base parameters by around 40 percent relative to Plan A. Table 9.1 summarizes these relationships.

Table 9.1 Results of Using the Pyramid Model and Lognormal Distribution

Plan	Description	Location on Lognormal Curve	Probability of Success	Values for Base Parameters
A	Naïve and most likely starting point	0.67 sigma	20 percent	Per Plan
B	More realistic	1 sigma	50 percent	Reduced by 20 percent relative to A
C	High efficiency	2 sigma	85 percent	Reduced by 40 percent relative to A

Clearly we've gone way out on a thin limb here, but the numbers in Table 9.1 represent the pyramid model's predictions, based on the lognormal distribution for project outcomes and a constant volume assumption.

Important Caveats

At this point, it is important to step back for a moment and consider the limitations of this model. I have made many implicit assumptions along the way, and now I must make them explicit.

- Let's begin with what I mean by "success." Remember, I said I would define success as an outcome greater than 1 sigma in the lognormal distribution, which would mean that about half of our projects would be successful.

    But the Standish report says that four out of five projects fail. Does this mean they are so constrained and therefore so difficult that this is the result? Perhaps.

---

[9] Remember also the detail we ignored earlier about the mean and median not being identical for the lognormal distribution. Here is where we can bury some of that approximation.

Many software development projects are doomed the instant the ink dries on the project plan. But I think there is more going on than that.

I have always had a problem with the Standish report, because I think it overstates the case, and in so doing it trivializes the real problem. If we were to take all original project plans and then apply our four base metrics to assess the projects at their conclusion, Standish would probably be right. And the lognormal distribution seems to support this scenario. But do we really have four failures for every success?

Here is what I think really happens: Along the way, as a project progresses, management realizes that the original goals were too aggressive, or the developers were too optimistic, or that they really didn't understand the problem. But now the project has incurred costs, so that scrapping it would seem wasteful and impractical. So instead the project is redefined, and the goals are reset. This may involve scaling back the feature set, deferring some things to a subsequent release. Sometimes, especially if the team discovers problems near the end of the development lifecycle, it will sacrifice quality and ship the product with too many defects. And even then, the team is likely to exceed its schedule and budget. But does this mean that the project is a failure? Not necessarily.

I maintain that lots of these projects fall into the "moderately successful" bucket, and some into the "only somewhat unsuccessful" bucket. So, as in everything else in the world, we revise expectations (usually downward) as we go, so that when we are done we can declare victory. This is important both politically and psychologically. It avoids what the psychologists call *cognitive dissonance*. No one likes to fail, and you can always salvage something. So we tend to gently revise history and "spin" actual results. In reality, the Standish metrics apply only if you use the original project plan as a measuring stick. But no one actually does. In this context, having about half the projects judged "successful" is the result.

- The parameters scope, quality, speed, and frugality are not all independent of each other. For example, as the project slips and takes more time, it also incurs increased cost because of the increased resources consumed, so both speed and frugality tend to suffer in parallel. You could try to offset one with the other—for example by spending more money to hire more people and go faster. But, as Brooks so clearly pointed out almost 30 years ago[10], adding people to a software project usually has the effect of slowing it down! If you wanted to make this kind of trade-off, counter-intuitively you would do better to spend less money per unit time by having fewer people and going more slowly. You might not even lose that much time, because, as Brooks pointed out, smaller teams tend to be more efficient.

- The different parameters do not have perfectly equal impact. Time, or the inverse of speed, appears to play a more critical role than the other three, although this

[10] See Brooks, Frederick P. *The Mythical Man-Month: Essays on Software Engineering, Second Edition* (Boston: Addison-Wesley, 1995).

is always open to debate. Typically, managers resist reducing scope and quality, and they are always in a big hurry. From their point of view, the only parameter they can play with is resources. So often they opt to throw money at the problem. This usually fails, because they don't take the time to apply the money intelligently and instead spend it in ineffective ways. This is exactly Brooks' point. In the end, he said, more projects fail for lack of time than for all other reasons combined. He was right then, and I believe he is still right.

- In general, you cannot trade off the four parameters, one against another—at least not in large doses. That is, you cannot make up for a major lacuna in any of them by massively increasing one or more of the others. Projects seem to observe a law of natural balance; if you try to construct a base in which any one side is way out of proportion in relation to the others, you will fail. That is why I opted to assume our base was a square, with all sides (parameters) conceptually on a somewhat equal footing. I acknowledge that you can adjust the sides up and down in the interest of achieving equivalent area but caution against the notion that you can do this indiscriminately. Again, you can't increase one parameter arbitrarily to solve problems in one or more of the other parameters. Max Wideman likes to think of the base as a "rubber sheet." You can pull on one corner and adjust the lengths, but eventually the sheet will tear. Geometrically, of course, one side cannot be longer than the sum of the other three sides, because then the quadrilateral would not "close."

- To some extent, I have ignored the most important factor in any software development project: the talent of the people involved. Over and over again, I have seen that it is not the sheer number of people on a team that matters but rather their skills, experience, aptitude, and character. Managing team dynamics and matching skills to specific project tasks are topics beyond the scope of this chapter. However, the pyramid's volume to some degree corresponds to the team's capabilities.

- We should all be careful not to specify product quality based solely on the absence of defects. Quality needs to be defined more generally as "fitness for use." A defect-free product that doesn't persuasively address an important problem is by and large irrelevant and cannot be classified as "high quality."

- What about iterative development? Unfortunately, this treatment looks at the project as a "one shot," which goes against everything we believe in with respect to iterative development. But perhaps the unusually high failure rate documented by Standish is caused by a *lack* of iterative development. That is, by starting with an unrealistic plan and rigidly adhering to it throughout the project, despite new data indicating we should do otherwise, we bring about our own failures.

    However, if we are smart enough to use an iterative approach, then we can suggest a workable model. We start out with a pyramid of a certain volume and altitude during inception, based on our best knowledge of the team and the unknowns at that point. As we move into the next phase, our pyramid can change both its volume and shape. The volume might shift as we augment or diminish the team's capability, or as we learn things that help us mitigate risks. This is a natural consequence of iterative development. In addition, the shape of the pyramid may change, as we adjust one or more sides of the base by reducing scope, adding resources, taking more time, or relaxing the quality standard a bit—or by making changes in the opposite direction. This should happen at each of the phase boundaries; our goal should be to increase the altitude each and every time. As the project moves through the four phases of iterative development, we should see our pyramid not only increase volume but also grow progressively taller as we reduce risks, by whatever means necessary. If this does not happen through an increase in volume, we must accomplish it by decreasing the base area.

- The issue of whether projects follow the lognormal probability distribution is debatable. I agree with Pascal that it makes more sense than a standard normal distribution. Here's why.

  The normal distribution occurs when you add together many small effects that influence the final result. Often we say colloquially: "Some things will go better than we planned, and some things worse, and in the end it averages out." Implicit here is the notion of symmetry, that is, the idea that it is equally likely that an effect will be greater than or less than its average. These two assumptions—addition and symmetry—make the normal distribution symmetrical around its central value, and give it tails out to infinity in both directions—a reflection of the low probability of having all the effects go in one direction or the other. So long as we add "symmetrical" things to produce a result, the normal distribution is a very solid concept; in fact, something called the *Central Limit Theorem* virtually guarantees it, even if the constituent effects themselves are not normally distributed.

  The normal distribution, or "bell curve," has become part of our collective mindset. It dominates every probability and statistics course taught today; it is intuitive and has lots of easy-to-calculate characteristics. But in life, results don't always come about from the cumulative addition of their constituent causes. So we need to be careful about applying the standard normal distribution everywhere without examining the underlying causes. Despite its amazingly wide applicability, it is a mistake to just assume "standard normal" applies universally.

  The lognormal distribution occurs when you multiply together many small effects that influence the final result. Note that there is a crucial difference between adding lots of small things and multiplying lots of small things. Obtaining a large result by multiplication requires that some of the factors be "large," while only one factor needs to be close to zero for the result to be close to zero. Hence there is a lack of symmetry, and the distribution is skewed to the low end. It strikes me that many composite events in life may be better simulated by a lognormal distribution: to get a large positive result, lots of things have to go right; to get a small result—

a negative outcome, so to speak— one needs to have only one thing go very wrong. And even one "zero" will make the result zero, independent of all the other factors combined. In the case of project management, my experience tells me that nature will tend to distribute outcomes lognormally rather than normally.

- Finally, the conservation law expressed as a constant-volume pyramid is just a model. It provides a convenient visualization of the phenomenon, but it is a guess—and the simplest geometric model I could come up with. To determine whether it reflects reality, we'd need to examine empirical data.

Although it is long, this list of caveats does not negate the value of the model; I think its predictions are valid and consistent with my previous experience. Indeed, many mid-course corrections that teams make during a development project to improve their probability of success turn out to be mere Band-Aids and don't come close to addressing the real issues. As a profession, we have demonstrated over and over again that to improve your chances of success substantially, you need to do more than relax a single constraint by 10 percent, and this model underscores that point. Therein lies its greatest value; I believe it represents a fundamental truth.

It's All About Risk

Risk is perhaps the most important parameter to consider in funding and planning a project. That is why the simple model I have defined in this chapter correlates four traditional project parameters—scope, quality, speed, frugality—and then adds risk as a fifth variable. If you were planning to paddle a canoe down a river, you'd want to know whether the rapids were class three or class five. The latter would be a lot riskier, so you might decide to spend a little more money on your boat. The same is true for software development investments: It is worthwhile to assess the risks before deciding what resources to allocate to a project. But remember, resources are only one side of the square base; you must consider them in concert with scope, time, and quality. It is the combination of these four parameters, along with the quality of the team, which ultimately determines the risk profile.

The simple pyramid model also shows how much you *must* trade off to improve your probability of success. Although it is speculative, the model helps us to soberly decide whether we are willing to invest the resources required to raise our probability of success above the minimum threshold acceptable for our business, given the scope, quality, and time constraints that we specify.[11]

---

[11] Max Wideman has incorporated some of the material of this chapter in his recent book, *A Management Framework for Project, Program and Portfolio Integration* (Victoria: Trafford Publishing, 2004) with my blessing. His Chapter 8 begins with the project pyramid idea and further extends it. As I began my study with "his" tetrahedron, this is only fitting and proper.

Recap

As you might well imagine, I take a fair amount of flak for my mathematical models. There are several reasons for this.

First of all, there is an interesting cultural effect. Although our civilization has untold millions of dollars in the total sunk cost of assembling our mathematical toolbox over the millennia, the average manager uses about 29 cents' worth of it. I have always found this puzzling. It's not like we don't teach any math at school. The reasons I usually hear have to do with "bad data," or "no data," but I think that is just an excuse.

Why do I like mathematical models? My response is simple. We all have rough ideas, even instincts, about how things work in the real world. What we don't have is a good grasp on how much, how severe, the effects are. So, when a project gets in trouble, and the manager uses good instincts—reduce scope instead of adding people, for example—we are moving in the right direction. But to do even better, he or she should have an idea of *by how much* the scope needs to be reduced to make a difference. Absent this information, the manager is apt to cut too little. He then incurs the wrath of management for leaving something on the cutting-room floor and, at the same time, still being late because he didn't cut enough. This is the worst of both worlds.

The models I propose are all simple in concept. They usually don't involve any math more complicated than the notions of areas and volumes, and the idea that if things need to be conserved, something must go down when something else goes up. In this chapter I invoked some ideas about statistics, but I was careful to explain them as I went along. The lognormal distribution is somewhat obscure, but that does not undermine its validity. It is the correct distribution to use.

It is, of course, very difficult to compare the results of these models with experimental data. But I don't think that should keep you from inventing models. If you don't like mine, create some of your own. See how much your results differ from mine. What I have discovered over and over again is that when you finally get three or more competing models side by side, their predictions are remarkably similar. That is, if the models are at all faithful to reality in some regard, they will all get similar results, independent of their details.

What the model on trade-offs teaches us is that improving the probability of success is not easy. We have to modify parameters a lot to materially affect the outcome. In turn, this means that our estimating and scheduling activities need to be effective. I turn to these topics in more detail in the next two chapters. As you might expect, Roscoe Leroy has something to say about this. It will be interesting to compare some of his math models to mine.

CHAPTER 10

Estimating

One of the mysteries of software development is why even the best programmers are so bad at estimating the time it will take them to get done. Either their estimates are wildly optimistic or, at the other extreme, overly conservative. When you get an estimate of "a couple of weeks" for some major subsystem to be created from scratch *and, the same morning*, the same estimate for what you think should be a two-line fix, you know that something ain't right. It's even worse if the two estimates come from the same programmer, although that would be a pretty rare occurrence!

I have to admit that I have not discovered any great secrets to good estimating. What I have discovered is that younger, more inexperienced developers tend to be too optimistic. A good antidote is to review their estimates with more senior people, including the architect for the project. In some cases, the developer may be thinking of a particularly "clever" implementation that will get the job done very quickly. On the other hand, if his approach is at odds with the overall architecture of the project, it will all be for naught. So, very aggressive estimates need to be put under the microscope and thoroughly discussed. The usual outcome is a better understanding of the problems and a better, albeit longer, estimate.

What about the other fellow? The overly conservative estimates come from doing a detailed "bottoms up" study of the problem, and they suffer from including safety factors at every step. All these safety factors accumulate; it is almost as though you are planning for everything to go wrong at every step, which rarely happens, Murphy notwithstanding. These estimates also suffer from the *compartmentalization effect*. Good developers work on problems in bunches, especially if they are fixing bugs. Often, for example, several problems can be isolated to one part of the code that needs overhaul; by getting into that section and cleaning it up, developers can address several problems in one pass. If you did an estimate on a bug-by-bug basis, you would likely wind up with something at least two to three times as long as the job will really take.

It turns out that some developers do "sandbag." That is, they purposely give long estimates, either because they have been burned in the past, or because they really don't want to work on that particular problem. The good manager needs to be very patient and work on establishing an environment of trust surrounding estimates. No one should be severely punished for honestly missing an honest estimate. On the other hand, irresponsible estimating—giving a number without sufficient thought—and sandbagging should be actively discouraged.

What If We Used Common Sense?

We sometimes tend to get a little wrapped up in the jargon of our trade: process frameworks, multiple inheritance, polymorphism, and the like. What would happen if we had to explain this stuff to "civilians"? In particular, how would our methods of estimating look to them? Roscoe Leroy gives us his slant on estimating.[1]

Chocolate Versus Vanilla

Roscoe showed up at my house awhile back with a copy of *USA Today* under his arm. "Looks like even McPaper is starting to understand," he said, knowing I would be unable to resist taking the bait. When I asked him what he was talking about, he showed me one of the little squibs in the corner of the page: 52 percent of the population prefers vanilla ice cream, 48 percent chocolate. From my perspective, that registered pretty high on the "So what?" meter.

---

[1] If you haven't read Chapter 5, "The Most Important Thing," you don't know who Roscoe is. You might want to read its introduction now so as to better understand where Roscoe is coming from.

Then Roscoe offered the following. "Notice what it says below the little bar graph: Accuracy is plus or minus 3 percent.[2] Now that is significant. For years, they published these factoids without any indication of the error bars. We must be getting less stupid about polls, if they think they have to tell us the likely error."

I had to admit I had never thought about it that way. I also was intrigued by why Roscoe thought it was interesting.

Roscoe Explains

"Of course," he said, "3 percent error is important, because the total spread in the preference is only 4 percent. So we can't be really sure. But I'll tell you one thing: I bet I know how many people they asked."

Certain that Roscoe had never taken a probability and statistics "seminar" that didn't involve poker chips, I was about to learn otherwise.

"Here's my guess," he continued. "They talked to about 1,000 people. The error on 1,000 answers is roughly the square root of 1,000, which is 31.4. Thirty one over 1,000 is 3.1 percent, which of course is roughly 3 percent."

"Wait a minute, Roscoe," I jumped in. "The square root of 1,000 is 31.6, not 31.4."

"There you go, letting your education get in the way again. Any fool can remember that the square root of 10 is pi, which is 3.14. For 1,000, move the decimal point one place in the answer—31.4, done deal."

Well, my math was more accurate, but seeing as how we were going to round off anyway, the difference did seem academic. And it did seem like a fairly reasonable calculation.

Roscoe Goes Deeper

"I'll tell you another thing," Roscoe continued. "You'll never see that kind of squib with an error bar of, say, 1 percent."

---

[2] Sometimes the term *precision* is used instead, but precision and accuracy are not the same. *Precision* indicates the degree to which the measurement is reproducible. If you have a high precision measurement method and measure many times, most of the measurements will fall within narrow margins. On the other hand, *accuracy* is a measure of how close the measurement is to reality. Precision talks about measurements on the sample; accuracy reflects how close your measurement of the sample is to defining the properties of, in this case, the underlying population.

Roscoe may appear to be sloppy in his use of these terms, but he is not; we shouldn't be either. Shooting for high precision is silly in the face of low accuracy, because high precision costs money, and we should never pay lots of money for an inaccurate result. Just always remember that high precision does not necessarily imply high accuracy.

I thought about that for a couple of seconds, but Roscoe wasn't patient enough to wait for my thoughts on the subject.

"Doesn't take an Einstein to figure out why, either. If you use the same logic, you'll see that they have to talk to *10,000 people* to get the error down to 100, or 1 percent. That's 10 times as expensive as talking to 1,000 people. So to push the error down from 3 percent to 1 percent, it costs you an incremental factor of 9."

"Ten," I thought to myself. Then I realized you could reuse the first thousand in the second sample. Never misses a trick, that Roscoe.

Roscoe's Calendar

By now I had developed a belief that Roscoe had learned about square roots. This was confirmed when I talked with him about projects and schedules. His assumption about the number of weeks in various periods was, well, curious. Table 10.1 encapsulates my discovery.

Table 10.1   Roscoe's Calendar

Duration	Roscoe's Duration
Two years	100 weeks
One year	49 weeks
Nine months	36 weeks
Six months	25 weeks
Four months	16 weeks
Two months	9 weeks
One month	4 weeks

When I asked him about three-month projects, Roscoe replied, "Don't like to do those."

It was clear from these numbers that some Leroy square root arithmetic was in the offing. You don't set out a pattern like that without some underlying motivation. Another thing that was interesting was Roscoe's unwillingness to talk about time intervals of less than a week. "We ain't day laborers, son," he'd say. "I pay my engineers by the week. So that's the smallest interval I ever use when estimating."

Seemed about as reasonable as his argument about fractional people.

Roscoe Computes

"Actually," said Roscoe, "I can compute square roots lickity-split. And without a square root button on the old calculator."

"Fifty-three!" I shouted out, challenging him on the spot.

"No sweat," he said, talking and punching numbers simultaneously. "Fifty-three is close to 49, so we'll start with a guess of seven. Seven into 53 goes 7.57 times. Now we know that because 7 is too low, 7.57 must be too high, so let's take the average. In my head, that's 7.28. Then, 7.28 into 53 goes, well, gosh, would you believe it, 7.28 times. So I guess the answer must be 7.28."

For the guy to have extracted the square root to two decimal places with two divisions was impressive. But Roscoe had a different point of view.

"Too tiring," he said. "Prefer to work with round numbers. Sticks of dynamite and whole people…"

Roscoe Gets into Software

Just when I thought the world was safe, Roscoe 'fessed up. "They closed the mine, son," he said. "Looks like I need to find a new job. Think I could manage one of those software projects?"

Thank heavens the "dot-com" frenzy has abated, I thought. How the hell would I ever explain *that* to him? On the other hand, he would certainly bring a fresh point of view to our business. We might actually learn something in the process.

"Sure, Roscoe," I replied. "Go off and learn about iterative development. That's the best place to start. Read up on that, talk to some people, and then come back to see me." I figured that would keep him busy for a while.

"I'll get back to you," he said, being careful not to let the screen door slam as he left.

Roscoe Reports In

About a month later, Roscoe showed up as usual, with no notice and a chip on his shoulder. I figured he had had enough time to understand the essentials, and I was interested in what he had to say.

"Well, there sure seems to be enough written about this stuff," Roscoe opined as he pulled up a three-legged stool. "In fact, it's amazing to me that you could know so much about something so screwed up."

I allowed that our success rate in software projects was not quite up there in the spectacular category. Roscoe was unimpressed.

"Seems like folks think this stuff is really hard. Shoot! Digging for coal is hard. This is just software, after all."

I said, well, maybe we should use the word "difficult," not "hard," but Roscoe was not to be convinced.

"Hate to remind you, but the Egyptians built the pyramids. Of course, they did have that fella Euclid, who was nobody's fool.[3] But, even today, the Amish can put up a barn in one day, for crying out loud."

"But," he continued, "there are some signs of hope."

Guess We Did Something Right

"It strikes me that the iterative development boys are on the right track. Although it's just a fancy name for what every cowboy carpenter does—cut and try.[4] Those boys know that they can't measure or cut that accurately, so they rough it out first, and then fix it until they're done. Of course you guys would call it 'successive refinement on subsequent iterations.'"

I detected a small note of sarcasm in Roscoe's summary. But he was not to be deterred.

"Of course, the cowboy carpenter has to be more careful than you guys. He knows that he can always take a little more off, but adding material back is hard. Learned that from his barber. So he always has to make his first cut the right way. Some big city comptrollers use that algorithm, too."

Now Roscoe always pronounces the "p" in comptroller so that you know that he knows the right word. But "algorithm" came out of his mouth sort of like "I'll-go-rhythm." Oh shoot, I thought. We are in big trouble. Roscoe has learned a new word.

"Roscoe, where did you pick up that word 'algorithm'?" I asked.

"Well, son, I've been talking to some software architects…" he trailed off.

"Huh," I replied, "who told you to do that?"

"First of all, you did. You said talk with people. Hey, I may look stupid, but I know what I don't know. There's a big difference between reading a set of blueprints and producing one. So I went and palavered a bit with those good old boys."

"Fair enough," I said. "What did you learn?"

---

[3] This is a good example of Roscoe not letting his education get in the way: Euclid came after the pyramids, by a lot. He lived around 300 B.C., and the pyramids were built circa 2500 B.C. Makes the pyramids seem even more impressive, doesn't it?

[4] What Leroy is referring to here is the kind of carpentry ranchers and farmers do—building rough structures like barns and fences. The other end of the spectrum would be fine craftsmanship, as exhibited by a professional woodworker or cabinetmaker. I think most software professionals view themselves more at the craftsman end of the spectrum, so Roscoe is probably a little out of line here with his analogy. But there is a middle ground. We do not start most software projects with a detailed drawing of the cabinet precise to the millimeter.

Roscoe Sums It Up

"Well, it makes sense to me. Basically, when you start a project you don't know spit, so the initial phases are important. After all, you don't want to build a $50 fence to keep in a $10 horse, so understanding what it is you're trying to do just makes sense to me. Likewise, I like the idea of keeping the payroll down until you have a pretty good idea of what all those people are going to do. Otherwise, you're just paying them to chew tobacco until someone figures out what they should be doing."

I was starting to be impressed with Roscoe's appreciation of the situation.

"Then I got into the scheduling and estimating end of things. Some pretty smart fellas there. In particular, that guy Barry Boehm and that guy Walker Royce seem to have a handle on some of it. Although their Coconut model is a little high falutin' for me."

I cringed, but didn't have the heart to correct him. COCOMO and coconut do sound a little alike, after all. And there were lots of other interpretations you had to make in parsing Roscoe-speak, so this would not be too much of an additional stretch.

"Then I got around to reading some Kruchten and Booch, and even stumbled onto your name. Right here," he said, pointing to a page in a dog-eared copy of Grady's book, *Object Solutions*.[5]

Sure enough, he had me dead to rights. There I was, in black and white, in a footnote on page 136.

Roscoe Picks a Bone

"Well, it says here that you and that Kruchten fella have observed that the duration of an iteration in weeks seems to be equal to the square root of the size of the code to be developed, as measured in thousands of lines of code."

It was hard to argue with him. It was a direct quote. I figured I was in for it now.

"Hmm. I even talked with my architect friend, and he said there's a term for 'a thousand lines of code.' Claims it's called a *KSLOC*, for 'kilo source lines of code.' Whoosh!"

Roscoe was clearly warming to the task.

"Buncha B.S., I'd say. Like trying to estimate how big a project the pyramids are going to be, and using the 'brick' as your unit of measure. Only that would be ridiculous, so you invent the 'kilobrick.' Dumbest thing I ever heard of."

The man was gaining momentum, and I was not going to lie down in front of that locomotive just yet.

"But the real problem, as I discovered in talking with my architect friend, is that nobody knows how to count SLOCs or KSLOCs. Do you count every line, including

---

[5] Booch, Grady. *Object Solutions: Managing the Object-Oriented Project* (Boston: Addison-Wesley, 1995).

comments? Do you count both your headers and your implementation source files, where there is obviously lots of repeated stuff? And how do you deal with those huge libraries that you're gonna use, but not write from scratch? Basically, you have a number that you can get from 'Dial-a-Prayer.'"

I made a note to talk to the architect about telling Roscoe about headers and such. I knew he didn't make that up on his own. But the man had a point: We had concocted a formula that was based on a number that was, to put it charitably, subject to some interpretation. The prediction would be no better than the definition we used for SLOCs.

Guess We Did Something Right, Part Two

Just when I thought Roscoe was going to write me off completely, though, he came up with a compliment, sort of.

"You did get something right, Joe. The square root is the key. The whole idea is that you don't want to have too many iterations, because each beginning and end of an iteration has overhead, which as we all know is just plain unproductive. On the other hand, you don't want to have too few iterations, because then you lose all the benefits of iterative development. It's like Goldilocks and the porridge—it needs to be just right.

"Now, I think you were right to peg the iteration length to the square root of the size of the project. And picking the week as the unit of measure was surely the right thing to do, as it is the fundamental unit of labor measurement. All you did wrong was get tangled up with that KSLOC idea. I've got a much simpler way to do it."

I listened. Carefully.

"The main problem is that you start from the wrong place. You need to use that Coconut or some other technique to negotiate the total time you are going to be allowed to have to complete the project. Management always wants it sooner, and you'll always wind up discussing a date, not the number of lines of code. You might get to barter the date against the size of the team, or against the feature set, for instance, but in the end what you will have that is fixed is the length of time.

"Once that's settled, it's easy. The duration of an iteration should just be the square root of the total duration of the project. Let me show you this little table I made up." With that he whipped out Table 10.2.

I was not surprised to see Roscoe's calendar make a guest appearance. Nor was his fondness for square roots absent from the proceedings.

Damn! Wouldn't you know it, when I went back and checked against my database of projects, Roscoe's estimates weren't that far off. As he would say, "Plus or minus one stick of dynamite."

And no SLOCs. I was impressed.

Table 10.2   Roscoe's Iteration Estimating Guideline

Duration	Roscoe's Duration	Iteration Length	Number of Iterations
Two years	100 weeks	10 weeks	10
One year	49 weeks	7 weeks	7
Nine months	36 weeks	6 weeks	6
Six months	25 weeks	5 weeks	5
Four months	16 weeks	4 weeks	4
Two months	9 weeks	3 weeks	3
One month	4 weeks	2 weeks	2

Roscoe Admitted to Software Project Manager Fraternity

Based on this little exercise in figuring out how long an iteration should be, I deemed Roscoe competent enough to take on his first iterative development project. But I had a warning for him.

"Roscoe, listen up," I said. "You are going to find out that 'calling the shot' in software projects is incredibly slippery. If you come up with any ideas there, I'd be really glad to hear from you."

"Sure 'nuff," he said. "See you next month."

Recap

Of course, what I am trying to do with old Roscoe is to inject some common sense into our software engineering management discussions. The best way to do that is to try to clear away as much of the jargon as we can. You might find that helpful in your discussions with others as well.

Of course, I'm not really done with estimating. The "rubber meets the road" part of estimating is coming up with a schedule.

In the following chapter, Roscoe opines on software development schedules.

CHAPTER 11

Scheduling

This is, of course, where the trouble really starts, because the average software development manager thinks of his schedule as a *working document*, and his general manager tends to view it as a *contract*. This "subtle" difference has accounted for lots of grief throughout the years.

This has led to the infamous "two-schedule" game, whereby there is an "internal schedule," purposely held tight—so the developers don't use up all the time they think they have—and an "external schedule" for the rest of the company, which has the safety margin added on to the internal schedule. Frankly, I've never been a big fan of this ruse. It is hard to keep the two schedules from becoming known, and once that happens, neither schedule has much credibility, no matter how hard you try to explain that one is the "development schedule" and the other is the "business schedule." My recommendation is to have one schedule, and have that schedule have as much integrity as possible.

In the end, a general manager has a difficult time trying to reason with a software development manager about his schedule. In a similar vein, it is often hard for the software development manager to intelligently discuss one component's or one subsystem's schedule with the technical lead for that piece. The reason is that there is very little to grab on to. Sure, you can start discussing whether this or that could be done faster, but ultimately it is a matter of judgment, and it is rare that any one piece is very badly estimated. In point of fact, the weakness in all scheduling activity comes from two principal causes that crop up over and over again in software development projects. First, there are interdependencies that are unknown or unclear at the beginning of the project. What tends to happen is that one part starts slipping, and other pieces start slipping in the background because their developers are waiting on the heretofore-unknown critical component. Only after the secondary components show slippage, too, is the dependency discovered.

A really good antidote to this form of schedule slippage is *iterative development*. In the early iterations, putting together the big pieces to get the first example of a working system will flush out these "hidden" dependencies. Once it becomes clear, various strategies can be employed: forced decoupling, more attention/resources put on the critical piece, and so on. Another way to mitigate this problem is to ask each team to iron out its subsystem interfaces well in advance of implementing the internals. That way, other groups can continue to make progress based on the published interfaces. So long as the interfaces remain stable, or mostly stable, the internals can change quite a bit without causing too much pain.

The second and more insidious reason that software development schedules slip so badly is that they do so gradually and progressively. Fred Brooks pointed out many years ago that projects get to be a year late one day at a time. If you miss your first milestone by a week or two, it is most likely that you will *never* make that time up and will slip all succeeding milestones by that much or more. It is the proverbial death by a thousand cuts, and even with the most assiduous management, it is difficult to avoid. On the other hand, if, as a software development manager, you do take your eye off the ball, well, look out!

Roscoe Poses the Problem: How Late Are You Gonna Be?

We've previously made the acquaintance of Roscoe Leroy,[1] a crusty old retired mining engineer. It was a dismal, rainy day when he pulled up in front of the house, running from his pickup to the front door, his slicker flapping in the wind. "Here comes the sun," I thought to myself.

As you may recall, Roscoe is an old war buddy of my dad and has a wealth of real-world experience from the school of hard knocks and cruel treatment. The reason I listen to Roscoe is that he brings a fresh perspective to anything he looks at, and his thinking is not overly encumbered by conventional wisdom, accepted doctrine, or theoretical considerations. My sources tell me that he has saved more than one engineering manager's bacon in the course of his "career."[2]

---

[1] See Chapter 5, "The Most Important Thing," and 10, "Estimating," for more background in case you are reading the book out of order and this is your first contact with Roscoe.

[2] If you asked Roscoe, he would scoff at the notion of a "career." "Just trying to get the job done, son," is what he would usually say when asked about any of his accomplishments or failures.

"So," I led off, "how's the new career in managing software development going?"

"Well, what we have here is a failure to communicate,"[3] Roscoe started off. The road boss's reflecting sunglasses from *Cool Hand Luke* flashed before my eyes when he started that way. I hoped this would end better than in the movie.

"In the first place," he said, "software projects are always late. And I mean *always*. That just doesn't seem right. After all, most estimates of pretty much everything else have an error that is stated as 'plus or minus such-and-such.' In software, you people seem to have lost the 'minus.' The estimator might just as well say 'This is the best we think we can do.'"

I admitted that his observation seemed to be mostly correct. Roscoe excoriated me for the "mostly." He defied me to show him *one* project that had been completed early. I squirmed. I did remember a milestone being early once, but a whole project…

"So, it would seem to me that the problem in calling the shot is to figure out just how late you are going to be," he said, smiling.

Joe Makes a Slight Comeback

Having had a bit of crow somewhat inelegantly jammed down my throat, I figured I'd use my years of being late on software projects to good advantage. I'd show that recycled roustabout he didn't know everything.

"Actually, Roscoe," I said calmly, "there isn't just *one* estimate. There's an initial estimate at the beginning of the project. Then, when you get partway in, you make another one. In fact, you make estimates of your time-to-completion all the way along. So what you really need to tell people, at any point in time, is how late you are going to be *based on the latest estimate*. Because, after all, the latest estimate includes everything you know up to that point."

"You got a point, Sonny," retorted Roscoe. "And I'll tell you another thing. Them estimates had better be getting more accurate as you move along. For two reasons: One, you are learning more and getting smarter as you go, and two, there is less left to do. At the start, you have lots of uncertainty and lots to do. On the other hand, you do have more time to recover from your mistakes. Let me think about this a little bit more."

I counted that round as a draw. Roscoe finished his coffee—black, no sugar—and somewhat aggressively stamped out his stogie. I could tell I had given him something more to think about. It was also clear that he was having a tough time figuring out why estimates for software projects were so much more slippery than those for other projects he had managed in previous lifetimes.

---

[3] Famous quotation, often repeated, from the movie *Cool Hand Luke*, starring Paul Newman.

Roscoe Returns

It wasn't long before Roscoe was back for another sit-down. I was about to have my well-ordered universe stood on its head again.

Roscoe was much calmer this time around. "As I pointed out the last time, mostly we are going to be late. The question is, how much? Well, I think I've got a handle on it.

"As usual, the solution involves the square root, and the unit of measure is…ta da, the week. I believe that a well-managed project can be late by a number of weeks equal to the square root of the predicted number of weeks left. So when you tell me you have, for example, 16 weeks to go, I am going to assume that you will take somewhere between 16 and 20 weeks to finish."

This was getting a little deep. The square root again? How could this be? Did Roscoe not have any other tricks in his bag?

"Actually, there're five distinct cases," he went on. "I've worked it all out."

This time, Roscoe had come loaded for bear.[4] The more he got going, the harder I listened.

"First of all, there's the well-managed project, headed by a guy who really knows what he is doing. He will be somewhere between his estimate and one square root late.

"Now, every now and then one of these gentlemen is going to do a really good job of estimating and an even better job of straw-bossing.[5] The 'powers that be'[6] are going to smile on him, and so on, and he will be early. Maybe even up to one square root early. It could happen." I remembered my embarrassment at not being able to come up with examples the last time we talked.

"Those are the good cases," he added.

Roscoe's Rogue's Gallery

"Of course, there is the other 75 percent of the known universe. They make up the three other cases.

"First of all, there are the guys who finish more than one square root early. These varmints we call *sandbaggers*, and they are dangerous because they cost you money—not by being late, but by overestimating everything. The only way to be more than one square root early is to fudge the estimate. Actually, the guy you should fire here is the boss who bought that estimate. On second thought, fire them both."

---

[4] This quaint Americanism means he had brought the heavy artillery, fully loaded for the task at hand.

[5] For our overseas friends, a *straw boss* is the fellow who manages the workers on a day-to-day basis. Sometimes he is called the "butt kicker."

[6] My guess is that Roscoe is referring to divine intervention here.

I was starting to get the idea that Mr. Leroy might revolutionize the way we thought about the problem.

"Next, we have the guys who finish between one and two square roots late. There is hope for them. They are probably just starting out, and need to hone their estimating and execution skills. They are costing us money, but with some work, we might be able to get them into the 'one square root band.' If they have some gumption, we might be able to coach them to the right place.

"And last, there are the guys who are off by more than two square roots' worth. These fellows are either out of control or have no idea how to estimate in the first place. When you have to decide whether they are just rotten estimators or actually can't manage their way out of a wet paper bag, it doesn't matter what the answer is. The only solution is to just run them off, because the train wrecks they produce will put you out of business."

Roscoe's Graph

Roscoe then proudly whipped out the graph shown in Figure 11.1 to display his theory. He was so proud he could use his new toy, Microsoft Excel, that he almost burst. "The good

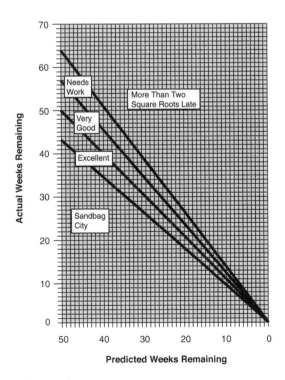

Figure 11.1   Calling the shot.

guys I've marked 'Very Good' and 'Excellent.' Between one and two square roots late I've marked 'Needs Work.' The other two pathological cases are clearly marked as well.

"There you have it. The border between 'Very Good' and 'Excellent' is 'On Time.' All you need, on one sheet of paper."

And Roscoe leaned back and rested his case—sort of.

One Last Objection

"Well, Roscoe," I replied, "as usual you have put your finger on something that makes sense. And I am impressed that you are willing to *quantify* how late you think you are going to be. But there is a flaw in your theory."

Roscoe perked up immediately. He loves a challenge.

"The problem is, how do I know which one of these zones my project manager falls into? If I know he is an ace, then I'm fine. But what if I've never worked with the guy before?"

"Sheesh," replied Roscoe, "that ain't nothin' more than a calibration problem. Here's how I do it.

"First of all, every time I ask someone to do something, I ask for an estimate. And then— *pay attention now*—I write it down."

At this point, I made the mistake of making a wisecrack about his stubby pencil.

"Listen up, Mr. Smarty Pants. The shortest pencil is longer than the longest memory. And don't forget that when Tiger Woods is out there competing for all those millions, he uses that same short pencil to keep his score."

Chastised, I decided to shut my trap and open my ears.

"So then for software I would try to get them to commit on a variety of subprojects and tasks of various durations. As a matter of course, you should get an estimate at the start of every iteration in an iterative development project. And I write down every estimate. And then I check later on how they did.

"What I get is a bunch of points on my graph of predicted versus actual. Some guys are consistently in one zone. Wonderful. They're calibrated.

"Some guys are gonna be all over the map. If I were you, I'd try to sit down with them and understand that. But sooner or later they have to become predictable, or you'll have to move them down the road. And even you know what to do with the guys in the sandbagger and 'more than two square roots late' categories. Just make sure the door doesn't hit them in the behind on the way out!

"The tool is really pretty useful for the guys who fall in the 'Needs Work' zone. We can show them what they need to do to start helping us make money instead of helping us lose it. It gives them a decent target to shoot at. They need to work at being consistently no more than one square root late, regardless of their estimate.

"See, Joe," he sat back and smiled, "I don't much care, so long as it's predictable. I can always live with one square root late if I know that will be the extent of the damage. I can plan around that."

Beat the tar out of anything I'd ever thought of.

Roscoe's Parting Shot

"By the way," Roscoe finished, "I hope you noticed what happens in my model when we get near the end of the project." I hadn't, but it did strike me as an interesting limiting case.

"When you get to a prediction of one week left, the square root of 1 is still 1. So you are at the limit of the method's precision. Inside of one week, you will always have a week to go because, if you are honest with yourself, you will find things to do as fast as you scratch them off your list. So, even theoretically, projects can go on forever, a week at a time.

"That's why we call it 'getting down to the short strokes.'[7] In the last week, the kinds of decisions you have to make are different, and estimating how much you have to go is beside the point. I can get you to the last week, but finishing is your job."

I sure hope Roscoe continues in his new career. We have so much to learn.

Recap

There were two things that resonated with people whenever we talked about software schedules. The first was the notion of *predictability*. Over and over again, managers have lamented to me, "It's the unpredictability I can't live with." As Roscoe points out, it is having results come in wildly at variance with the plan that throws everything off. If people were systematically late, we could deal with that.

This led to the second resonance, the idea of *calibration*. In order to achieve some measure of predictability, you really do need to calibrate, almost at the individual developer level, what the historical record says about the quality of the estimate. If you can know who is systematically optimistic and who is systematically way off, well, that's information.

My guess is that all good managers do this qualitatively. What Roscoe introduces here is the idea that we should gather data as we go, calibrating *and recalibrating* our

---

[7] One of Roscoe's rare golf references. In order to finish a hole in golf, one needs to putt the ball into the cup. These are usually "short strokes." So, getting down to the short strokes means doing the last remaining work to finish the job.

people's estimates *all the time*. By better understanding how much credence to attach to their estimates, we can perhaps achieve greater predictability in our schedules.

It is interesting how compact this chapter is. I attribute that to Roscoe's ideas' being short and sweet. He proves once again that you don't have to be long-winded to have a good idea.

In the next chapter, I examine a curious phenomenon. All successful projects seem to have an internal rhythm that governs their progress. Where does this come from? I propose a model that perhaps explains the effect.

CHAPTER 12

Rhythm

One of the things that characterize successful projects is that they fall into a rhythm. Actually, several rhythms. There is the overall rhythm as you move from phase to phase in the iterative development process. There is the somewhat shorter rhythm that paces the team iteration to iteration. Finally, there is the *build rhythm*, the heartbeat of the project that can be as frequent and regular as once a day. All these rhythms are healthy signs that the "project machine" is working. Of course there are setbacks from time to time, but these are unusual when set against the regular progress that the steady rhythms indicate.

In contrast, the less successful projects, to be euphemistic, have a herky-jerky feel about them. Things seem to occur in an *ad hoc* and irregular way. There seem to be long periods when nothing happens. Then a release occurs, and optimism blooms. Shortly thereafter, lots of problems reveal themselves, and discouragement sets in. Morale is very erratic, following the highly variable results profile of the project and product. As the project slips, people work harder, but things don't improve. Does any of this sound familiar?

I watched these two contrasting scenarios for many years and wondered if there was not some underlying mechanism, at least for the successful projects. I decided that there might be an infinite number of ways for the unsuccessful ones to fail, and hence an infinite number of mechanisms. Perhaps it would be easier to find the one common underlying mechanism for success.

A Physicist Looks at Project Progress

As luck would have it, I sought refuge in a simple model, that of Newton's Second Law. Because all of classical mechanics is dominated by this simple principle, perhaps there was a "Newton's Second Law" for software development projects. After all, projects tend to have a "percent completion" curve that is remarkably consistent from project to project. Could I attempt to describe the underlying forces acting on the project by considering the derivatives of this curve? While extending the laws of physics to project dynamics may be somewhat speculative, I hoped to help project managers understand the rhythm of their teams.[1]

Have You Seen This One Before?

Most of the time, progress curves reported at the end of a project look like the one shown in Figure 12.1.

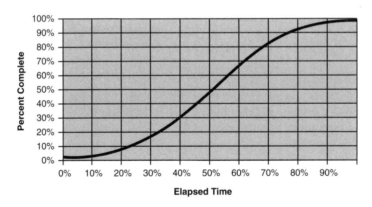

Figure 12.1 A typical project percent complete curve.

In fact, most projects are *planned* to have a progress curve that looks like this. Most wind up reporting progress that looks somewhat like the plan, with some distortion to reflect reality.

Because so many project completion curves look like this, I began to wonder if there are fundamental forces at work that cause the curve to be this way.

---

[1] This analysis also appeared in somewhat condensed form in the August 2002 issue of *Dr. Dobbs' Journal*.

It All Goes Back to Newton

Some people claim that "modern" physics started with Newton, although the first modern physicist was probably Galileo. What Newton told us in his Second Law was that the acceleration of a body was proportional to the net force applied to it, the proportionality constant being the inverse of its mass.[2] The more force, the more acceleration.

The problem is that acceleration is something we rarely experience. We experience it when our car peels out at a stoplight, when we stomp down on the brakes, or when an elevator first takes off or comes to a sharp stop. More often, we are aware of two other variables: *velocity* (speed, in common parlance) and *position* (location, or where we are). We seem to be aware of going fast or going slowly, and we are usually aware of where we are. But force is only indirectly related to these metrics.

Derivatives, Rates of Change, and the Slope of the Tangent

If you are calculus-aware, you know that velocity is the first derivative of position, and that acceleration is the first derivative of velocity, making acceleration the second derivative of position. If you never mastered calculus (or have forgotten it), substitute "rate of change" for "derivative." That is, your velocity is the rate of change of your position, and your acceleration is the rate of change of your velocity.

According to Newton, acceleration is proportional to the net force applied, so the second derivative of the position of an object is proportional to the force. Another way of saying this is that you have to take the net applied force and *integrate* twice to get information about the position. This is definitely *not* something that is intuitive for most of us. So I'll leave this integrating twice business alone for now, with the knowledge that there is sufficient mathematics to perform our integrations and differentiations once we understand the mechanisms.

If you reason or think better graphically, remember that you can find the derivative or rate of change for any curve by looking at a line tangent to the curve at the point in which you are interested. For example, in Figure 12.2—the parabola—the derivative or rate of change at the midpoint is zero. We can tell this because the tangent line to the curve there is horizontal, which has a slope—or rate of change—of zero. Prior to that, the tangent at any point has a positive slope; after the midpoint, the slope is negative.

---

[2] By *net* force, I mean the sum of all the forces acting on the mass. This is most often expressed by the formula $\mathbf{F} = m\mathbf{a}$, where $\mathbf{F}$ and $\mathbf{a}$ are in bold because they are vector quantities. I drop this vector notation to simplify things, as I am generally working in one dimension. Also, note that the more general form of the second law is $\mathbf{F} = d\mathbf{p}/dt$, where $\mathbf{p}$ is the momentum. This reduces to $\mathbf{F} = m\mathbf{a}$ if the mass is constant, something I also assume for the rest of the chapter. This is a very crucial assumption; *scope creep* corresponds to the project becoming more massive, invalidating the analysis. One must constantly guard against increases in scope; even small ones pile up in an insidious fashion.

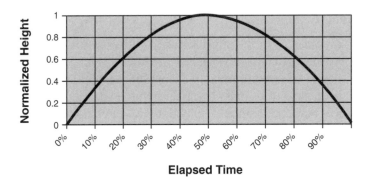

Figure 12.2 Trajectory for a vertical ball toss.

A Simple Physical Example

A ball thrown vertically up in the air has a very well-defined trajectory.[3] If I plot the height as a function of time, I get the nice parabola shown in Figure 12.2.[4]

Now if I plot the velocity of the ball,[5] I get the graph shown in Figure 12.3.

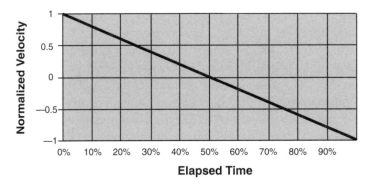

Figure 12.3 Velocity for a vertical ball toss.

---

[3] For the purposes of this example, I will ignore air resistance. As in all physics experiments that make this assumption, this has the disastrous side effect of killing the experimenter, as he has no air to breathe.

[4] A note on the graphs in this chapter: I used Excel to plot them. I took the horizontal axis—elapsed time—to run from 0 to 100 percent, and then I used mathematical formulae to generate the data values. I always normalize the vertical axis to "one"—that is, I have the height go from zero to its maximum, which I call "one." I computed all the derivatives numerically, once again using Excel to do the computations and the plots. Hence, you can replicate all of this yourself and need no knowledge of calculus to derive the results.

[5] I do this by numerically differentiating the data points from the parabolic curve. That is, I take successive differences of the values of the first curve, then multiply by a constant to get the values to fall between plus and minus one. The careful observer will notice that this causes us to "miss" the first point on the first derivative curve, and the first two points on the second derivative curve, and also causes a very slight shift (half a bin, actually) on the derivative curves. This won't become noticeable until later; it doesn't affect the arguments at all, but is just an artifact of how I am computing the derivatives.

Note that I have "normalized" the vertical axis so that the velocity falls between plus one and minus one; this helps us understand the concept by abstracting out the numbers.[6] This graph tells us that the ball starts out with a maximum velocity of one "unit," and that velocity decreases linearly until its reaches zero at the midpoint of its flight. This makes sense to us, because the midpoint of the flight is the highest point it achieves; at that instant, the ball is going neither up nor down, so its velocity is zero. Then it begins to fall, so its velocity is negative.[7] When the ball arrives at its starting point, its speed is exactly the same as when it was launched, except it is moving in the opposite direction.

Now, what about acceleration? Well, I just repeat the process one more time, obtaining the graph shown in Figure 12.4.

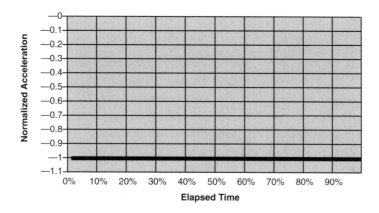

Figure 12.4   Acceleration for a vertical ball toss.

Once again, I have "normalized" the numerical value to -1.[8] What this is telling us is that there is a constant acceleration. That is consistent with our model; close to the surface of the earth, the gravitational force is constant. And it is "negative" because I have chosen "up" to be positive, so the attractive force of gravity pulls the ball "down."

Note that this acceleration is negative for the entire flight of the ball—even when the velocity is positive (upward flight), the acceleration is negative. We are "subtracting" velocity throughout the flight: We start out with some positive velocity which reduces to

---

[6] One convention is important: the "up" direction is positive. This will determine which velocities are positive and negative.

[7] Hence the difference between velocity and speed. Speed is always positive; as the ball falls, it speeds up. However, its velocity becomes more negative. The number representing speed and velocity gets larger in magnitude; however, velocity takes into account direction, so it becomes a larger negative number.

[8] Our friend Excel insists on calling zero "-0." We are smart enough to know that there is only one zero, and it doesn't have a sign.

zero at the highest point, and then we keep subtracting until the velocity is as negative at the end as it was positive at the beginning.

Whew! Newton is vindicated. I have "experimentally" verified that a parabolic position graph implies a constant acceleration, which in turn implies a constant (gravitational) force.

Can I use reasoning of this type to understand the "forces" at work on a project? As with acceleration, we do not experience these forces directly. Rather, we observe things that are indirectly related. So let's return to the percent complete curve; it describes what happened, plotting the combined results of all those forces we don't directly observe. If we assume this project completion graph is prototypical, then what would that tell us about project dynamics?

The "Project Completion" Graph: Plotting Position Against Time

As I have already pointed out, most projects can be plotted according to Figure 12.1.[9] Note that I have once again normalized things, so that the time axis goes from 0 to 100 percent, and the vertical axis also goes from 0 to 100 percent. Also note that I have somewhat arbitrarily positioned 50 percent complete at 50 percent of the elapsed time. The symmetry of the curve is a simplifying assumption, but one that is useful for this exposition. For the time being, I have no reason to assume otherwise.[10]

The Curve of Human Behavior

Generically, these curves are referred to as *S-curves* because they resemble the letter *S* if you stand back a bit and squint. They describe a wide variety of human behavior; the classic "learning curve," for instance, assumes this shape. The notion that a project completion curve mirrors a learning curve ought to tell us something.

When we begin to learn something new, we spend a lot of time fumbling around without understanding much. This corresponds to the first, *flat* part of the curve, where time goes by without much progress. Then, as we begin to understand what is going on, our progress increases; this is reflected by the second part of the curve, sometimes called *the ramp*. During this period we actually make a lot of progress per unit time, and if we could continue at this rate we would finish our task sooner. But inevitably, we enter the

---

[9] Here come the caveats. This is of course an idealization. Real-life curves are rarely so smooth. Also, projects don't uniformly move forward, although it is rare to see a *reported* percent completion curve show a dip. But the real problem is that there is no single metric we can use across the entire project to capture "percent complete." One of the largest problems on any project is figuring out how to distinguish reported progress from actual progress.

[10] You may see curves that look like this that have various other "percent completes" at 50 percent of the elapsed time. It is allowed. I don't deal with them here for simplicity.

third part of the curve, which goes flat on us again. What is happening here is that we *plateau*; we stop making dramatic progress, and the last few percent (learning all those remaining annoying details) takes a long time. This learning experience is repeatable over and over again, from domain to domain.

When the ramp is gently inclined, we talk about an easy learning curve; when the ramp goes up very fast, we talk about a *steep* learning curve. Many people cannot handle steep learning curves; they need more time to assimilate the bulk of the new knowledge.

Quick studies are interesting people; they have a very short approach period, go up a very steep ramp, and then quit without ever learning the last few percent. By truncating both flat parts and navigating steep ramps, they can radically abbreviate the time it takes them to acquire knowledge and skills. But they are rare indeed. Most of us do best with two flat parts and a moderate ramp.

Projects follow a similar rhythm. Early in the project, you make progress slowly. There is a lot of planning, organizing, and discovery that causes you to expend a lot of effort without making much tangible progress. Once you get going, you get on the ramp and progress feels (and probably is) somewhat linear (although we know it is not quite linear). Late in the project, things slow down again, which explains why finishing is hard. Once again, nailing down all the details you need to complete to deliver the product takes a relatively long time to do. That is why a project that is 90 percent complete is probably low risk from a technical point of view, but will still take awhile to finish. Things slow down at the end, and there is almost nothing you can do to fix that. Adding people at this stage, for example, will just push the end date further out, as has been shown over and over again.

What about new product acceptance in the marketplace? Same thing. Slow at first, as people have to find out about the product, understand its costs and benefits, talk to their colleagues, and go through a selection and acquisition process. These are the early adopters. Then there is a ramp, when the product "catches on" and demand seems to go through the roof. This is the point Geoffrey Moore calls *crossing the chasm*, when a product goes mainstream.[11] This goes on for a while, and then sales begin to slow. We have now hit the third part of the curve: the plateau. The product is now deemed "mature," with trailing or late adopters being the principal buyers. Very likely, another rival product is hitting its ramp at this point and taking away market share from the earlier product. So this universal curve also represents a product's sales lifecycle.

The Project Velocity Curve

Before getting into myriad debates about how "real" this curve is, let's just assume that it represents the majority of reported "percent complete" data and see what can be

[11] Moore, Geoffrey A. and Regis McKenna, *Crossing the Chasm: Marketing and Selling High-Tech Products to Mainstream Customers, Revised Edition* (New York: Harper Business, 1999).

inferred. Like many other examples in physics, we first try to understand the idealized behavior, and then modify our conclusions by adding back in the effects of air resistance and other real-world phenomena to the model.

The crucial observation is that this curve is a "position versus time" plot. In other words, this curve plots our "position" at any point in time. Now, what does the "velocity" curve look like?

Mimicking the steps used previously, we have the technology to answer that question. Taking the rate of change of our project completion curve yields the graph shown in Figure 12.5.

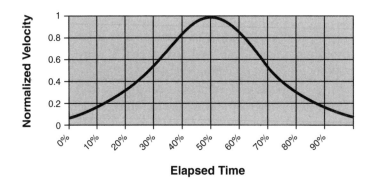

Figure 12.5   Velocity for project percent complete curve.

By now you are used to having the vertical axis normalized. What this graph tells us is that projects start off slowly and move faster for a while. Then they reach maximum velocity (in Figure 12.5, maximum velocity is achieved at the halfway point, but that is because our project completion curve is symmetric), and then start to slow down. As you cross the finish line, you are actually going fairly slowly, much as you did at the very beginning.

This is consistent with our common, everyday experience. Projects are slow to get started, they seem to "gather momentum" at some point, and then they "bog down," and things go more slowly. Finishing is hard. Getting all the fine details worked out so that you can deliver the product seems to take forever. Often it feels like you stagger across the finish line.

Once again, the exact values for this curve may vary, but the pattern, from project to project, is remarkably consistent. So what does this say about the underlying "forces" driving the project?

Well, at this point the physicist would take another derivative. Let's do that!

The Project Forces Graph

The resulting acceleration curve, which implies the forces at work, is shown in Figure 12.6.[12]

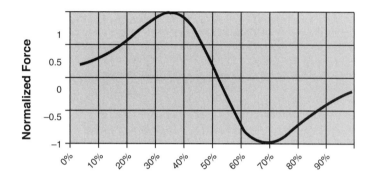

Figure 12.6   Net project forces as shown by the acceleration for project percent complete curve.

What are we to make of this?

Well, here's one interpretation: During the first third of the project, we see an increasing positive force. This corresponds to a lot of enthusiasm for the new project, the addition of new team members, and a general optimism about the chances of success. This might cynically be called the "ignorance is bliss period." It is this positive, increasing force that causes the project to gain velocity (sometimes colloquially called *momentum*, or "the big mo").[13] At about the one-third point, this positive force begins to decline. This could correspond to reality setting in; people are far enough along to start to understand what the real problems are and are beginning to feel some schedule pressure. After all, they have now used up one-third of the time but still have mountains of work left to do. Also, the team is beginning to feel the full burden of a large staff; a lot of time is spent in meetings, and communicating information to all the members of the team grows difficult.

And then we reach the halfway point. At this point, according to the previous graph, a negative force sets in. The team begins to feel the project "pushing back." Many of the really tough problems are not succumbing to solutions as quickly as we thought. People

---

[12] The slight shift mentioned in Footnote 5 is noticeable here; the forces curve should cross the axis at 50 percent. Once again, this is an artifact of the crude way in which I compute the derivative and is absolutely irrelevant to the argument.

[13] Physics seems to intrude into our language even when I don't want it to.

begin to really panic as more and more sand slips through the narrows of the hourglass. At about the two-thirds point, the force hits its maximum negative value; there is this sensation of swimming in molasses. If the project stays here for very long, it dies.

And then, when we most need it, the project "turns the corner." There is a breakthrough, and all of a sudden things don't look quite so bleak anymore.[14] While there is still a negative force at work—the knowledge that there are still a million details left to complete, and not much time in which to finish them—this negative force decreases. The main reason for this is that the team can see the finish line. The negativity decreases until we get across the finish line.

Be aware that the actual "turning points" on this curve—one-third, one-half, two-thirds—will vary from project to project, and will in turn affect the velocity curve and the project percent completion curve. There is nothing magic about the one-third, one-half, and two-thirds completion points; these result from the symmetric project completion curve I originally chose for ease of exposition. The exact points on our project are unknowable; all we can "predict" is that it will go through these phases.

This is kind of gratifying. I start with a prototypical percent complete curve, take a couple of derivatives, and infer the forces underlying the project. The data seems to empirically fit the theory. Have I really accomplished anything here?

Reality Intrudes

A physicist looks at a theory from a number of different points of view. It is always dangerous to extrapolate physical ideas like position, velocity, and acceleration to group dynamic variables like "project percent complete," "project velocity," and "project forces." We must be extremely careful not to attribute more "science" to this than can really be there. On the other hand, the analogy seems to give results that are consistent with reality. So let's move to the next step.

A physicist judges a theory by its ability to explain and predict. That is, a theory must first explain the results of all known experiments. If experimental results exist that contradict a theory, then the theory is wrong, unless you can go back and show that the experimenter made a mistake. In our example, we have seen that most projects have a similar percent complete curve, so all that will change from project to project is the details of the transition points of the derived curves.

And that brings us to the limited utility of the theory. What we would like to be able to do is to *predict* the percent complete curve while we are at some state of

---

[14] The more crusty project manager may be heard to murmur at this juncture, "We may finally have broken the back of this son of a bitch."

incompletion. Or to put it another way, we want to know when we are going to be finished. At any point in time, all we have is that portion of the curve "behind us," and some notion of the velocity curve. The "forces" curve is pretty hard to pin down quantitatively. In fact, it is often hard to understand the velocity curve, although metrics that could indicate velocity would be very, very useful. Knowing your "position" is important, but to more accurately forecast, you need both actual position and actual velocity.

Today, many of our project metrics focus exclusively on position—"Where are we?" As we can see from this discussion, having velocity metrics—rate of change of position, how fast are we going—is equally important. And should we ever get to the point of being able to understand how the velocity is changing, then we would have an even more complete picture. So we need to think about project metrics collection in this light.

What About Iterative Development?

All that I have said is somewhat introductory to the notion that we don't do projects in one fell swoop, but break them down into iterations. Each iteration has its own rhythm, so the graphs described in this chapter are really only an approximation. For example, for a project with four iterations, the percent complete curve would probably look more like Figure 12.7.

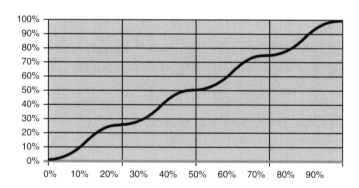

Figure 12.7   Percent complete curve for a four-iteration project.

Here what we see are four S-curves stacked one on top of another. Percent complete is cumulative, and I have made the assumption that each iteration takes 25 percent of the time and gets us 25 percent along on the completion curve. In the following sections I will depart from this simplifying assumption.

Now let's jump to the velocity and acceleration (forces) curves that correspond to this four-iteration percent complete graph (see Figure 12.8).

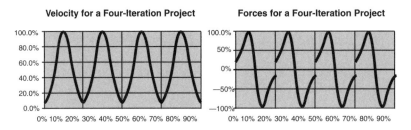

Figure 12.8   Velocity and forces in a four-iteration project.

What do these graphs of the derivatives tell us?

What we see is that the velocity curve replicates itself four times—no surprise there. The project gains and loses velocity four different times, corresponding to each iteration having a somewhat similar rhythm. The second derivative curve—acceleration[15]—has three discontinuities, which we can also "see" in the velocity curve.[16] What this means is that at the start of each iteration after the first, you need to "kick" the project out of its residual negative force from the previous iteration and impart an initial positive force. This is what causes the velocity vector to change abruptly. Without this instantaneous, discontinuous force, you won't get going again without losing time.

Most good project managers know about this and apply the requisite force at the appropriate time. We shouldn't be all that surprised by the discontinuity—after all, we started at zero with a non-zero positive force to get the project underway. All I am saying is that at the end of the iteration we still have a residual negative force, and we need to jumpstart back to that positive force we began with.

Having applied this positive force, you need to once again build it until the iteration hits its "wall," and the inevitable negative forces set in. Then it's just a question of hitting the breakthrough for that iteration, the one that again reverses the negative force curve.

So now we know how to apply our model to a multiple-iteration project. It's the same game: Plot the percent complete curve, take the derivatives, and interpret the results. The

---

[15] By now you are used to the idea that the graphs can be labeled "acceleration" or "force" interchangeably.

[16] It may be hard to see, but there is a difference between the four peaks at 100 percent on the velocity curve and the three troughs at about 10 percent. The passage through the maxima is smooth, with a zero derivative. On the other hand, the passage through the minima is not smooth; the slope changes abruptly. That is what leads to the discontinuity on the acceleration (force) curve.

only thing that has changed is that our percent complete curve is a little more complex at the outset. But the rules of the game are the same.

But all this is a bit boring when all the iterations look the same, not to mention that we have no insight regarding the real project at hand, because thus far in our analysis nothing truly mirrors reality. So let's get real.

Iterations and Phases

In real-life iterative development, we may have many iterations, divided up into distinct phases. How can I inject this sort of reality into the model?

Well, I'm not up to a multi-phase, multiple-iterations-per-phase graph. And it's not clear that we need that complexity anyway. After all, it is the phases that have the biggest difference in their characteristics, not the iterations within the phases. So, to keep things reasonably simple, let's model the phases and assume only one iteration per phase.

The *Rational Unified Process* defines four phases:[17]

- Inception

- Elaboration

- Construction

- Transition

These four phases do have different characteristics. Early in the project, we are doing a lot of discovery (new learning). In the middle of the project, we do somewhat less discovery but lots of invention; there is still a lot of learning going on. Later in the project, we are actually doing the activities that count for "completion;" some invention and lots of implementation. Learning drops off a bit as the project moves toward completion.[18]

At this point it is necessary to decouple the ideas of "learning" and "completion." Until now I have been assuming they are the same. Table 12.1 shows numbers that my colleague Philippe Kruchten[19] believes are applicable to the four phases.

---

[17] Kruchten, Philippe. *The Rational Unified Process: An Introduction, Second Edition* (Boston: Addison-Wesley, 2000).

[18] The relevant reference here is Grady Booch's *Object Solutions: Managing the Object-Oriented Project* (Menlo Park: Addison-Wesley, 1996), p. 61.

[19] The "completion" numbers come from work by Philippe Kruchten and Walker Royce in 1999 on the Rational Unified Process. See Footnote 17. The "learning" numbers are from a private communication with Philippe and represent his best estimate.

Table 12.1 Learning and Completion Metrics for Phases in the Rational Unified Process

Phase	Percent of Elapsed Time	Percent Learned	Percent Complete
Inception	0 – 10	0 – 10	0 – 5
Elaboration	10 – 40	10 – 60	5 – 25
Construction	40 – 90	60 – 90	25 – 90
Transition	90 – 100	90 – 100	90 – 100

What these numbers tell us is that we learn faster than we achieve completion when we do phased, iterative development. This accelerated learning is what helps us reduce risk. How do I introduce these ideas into our model?

I have only two modifications to make:

1. I plot "percent learned" and "percent complete" separately.

2. For each of these curves, I plot the S-curve segments according to Table 12.1, in order to model that level of reality.

Results

All the results are shown together in Figure 12.9.

Discussion of Results

There would appear to be a lot of explaining to do.

First, let's address the difference in the shapes of the learning and completion curves. Basically, you achieve 60 percent of your learning in the first 40 percent of the project, and are only 25 percent complete at that point. This reflects the notion that in iterative development we emphasize learning early to reduce risk. The counterweight is that you don't make much "visible" or "tangible" progress, because often the learning does not have many artifacts that go along with it. In any event, as a project manager you are going to have the following conversation at the 40 percent point of your project:

> Boss: "You've used up 40 percent of the time, but you show only 25 percent complete. You are in big trouble."

> You: "Not really. In iterative development, learning is important in the first half. And we have accomplished 60 percent of the learning we set out to do."

> Boss: "Really? That's great. Can you show me the 60 percent?"

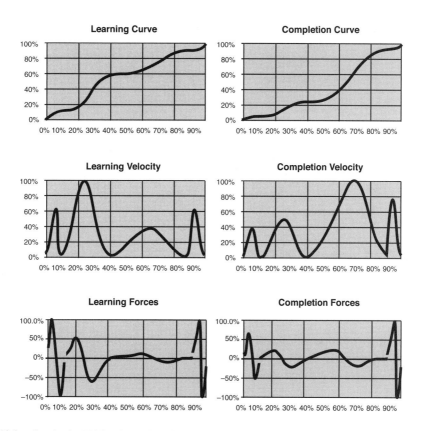

Figure 12.9   Graphs for Table 12.1— learning and completion curves.

At this point I would suggest having some additional arrows in your quiver. What I generally do is go back to the "risk list" I assembled at the beginning and show how the learning has eliminated or mitigated these risks.

Now let's look at the velocity curves. Let's defer discussion of the first and fourth phases to later, because it's more interesting to discuss these and their associated forces at the same time. For the moment, let's concentrate on the Elaboration and Construction phases, where there are interesting differences.

What we see is that learning velocity peaks during Elaboration, whereas completion velocity peaks during Construction. This is consistent with our model, in which we set out to get over the learning hump in Elaboration, sacrificing or deferring completion a bit. The idea is that the measurable artifacts of completion begin to show up only during Construction, so that is when that curve shows its peak.

You might ask why both velocity curves go down to almost zero at the 40 percent point and then back up. Wouldn't it be better if we could "keep" some of that velocity across the boundary? Yes, it would. The reason we can't is that the two S-curves join at the boundary. In fact, discontinuities in the force curve show up at the boundaries for this very same reason. The reality that corresponds to this mathematical artifact is that distinct phases cause disruption on any project. That is why many senior project managers try to blend things at the boundary; they sometimes try to get an "advance team" working on the next phase a little early (before the antecedent phase is actually done) to smooth the transition over the boundary. It is hard to pull this off. The other logical consequence of this effect is that the more phases you have, and the more iterations you have within phases, the more boundaries you create. If there is a fixed overhead at each boundary, then you increase your total overhead by increasing the number of phases and iterations.

The forces comparison for Elaboration and Construction is also pretty clear; the learning forces are stronger during Elaboration and relatively weak during Construction. On the other hand, I note that the completion forces have about the same peak values during both Elaboration and Construction, which is a good thing.

Now let's address the Inception and Transition phases. Each of these is accomplished over a short time interval—only 10 percent of the project each. Because the S-curve causes its derivative curve to have a peak, accomplishing that turnaround in a short period of time causes the peak to be bigger. Correspondingly, the force curve necessary to turn around the velocity curve in this short interval also requires large peak forces. This is why when we get to the force curve, both for learning and completion, we see maximum peak forces in these intervals. It is a result of having a very short interval. The antidote, if you will, is to not have S-curve behavior during these short periods. If the progress curve here were simply linear over the interval, then the force would be less. S-curves and their derivatives do better over longer time periods. They are perhaps the right model for long periods, and a poor model for short intervals.

On the other hand, these "large" forces may be real and not artifacts of the S-curve compressed into short intervals. It is certainly the case that we have large forces at the end of the project, during Transition. Anyone who has ever had to finish a project will attest to that; it's what makes finishing so hard—you need a big push when the team is the most tired. And, there are also large forces early in the project, during Inception, because it is at the end of Inception that we have our first "go/no go" decision to face. If people working on the project are concerned about cancellation at this early branch point, then you can be sure that there will be large forces at work.

One Last Graph

There is one other graph that is perhaps of interest. Let's assume that we can "add" the completion forces and the learning forces together. Force is a vector, so the assumption

I am making here is that the completion forces and the learning forces are co-linear, or acting in the same direction, a somewhat arbitrary assumption. However, if I make this assumption, then I can sum the forces and get the total force on the project as a function of elapsed time, as Figure 12.10 shows.

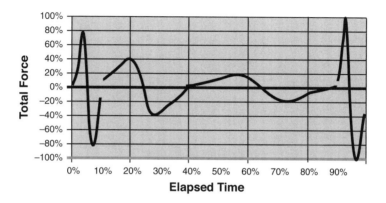

Figure 12.10   Total forces on a project (learning + completion).

Let's look at some areas under the curves in the four regions.[20] I note that all the segments have the same form, so let's look at the peak value of the total force and the length of time the segment is in play; the product of these two will be proportional to the area, as Table 12.2 shows.

Table 12.2 Product of Total Force Peak Value and Time Interval Length

Phase	Percent of Elapsed Time	Length of Time Interval	Peak Value of Total Force	Product (Impulse)
Inception	0 – 10	10	0.8	8
Elaboration	10 – 40	30	0.4	12
Construction	40 – 90	50	0.2	10
Transition	90 – 100	10	1.0	10

[20] Here I will consider all areas to be positive. That is, I take the absolute value of areas below the axis, so that there are no "negative" areas. If I didn't do this, the total area would integrate to zero.

For the mathematically and physically inclined, we know that the area is an integral, and the integral of force over time is equal to the change in momentum.[21] What we see from the table is that the change in momentum is roughly the same over the four phases. The change in momentum (or impulse) is the same during Construction and Transition—10 units. The biggest impulse is during Elaboration, 12 units. And the combined impulse of the first and second phases—20 units—is equal to the combined impulse of the third and fourth phases. Half the total impulse is applied during the first 40 percent of the elapsed time; this again expresses the idea of "front loading," which we believe is a good thing.

Note also that the discontinuity in the total force curve at the 40 percent boundary is not too large. That is probably also a good indicator. So the conclusions drawn from using Kruchten's and Royce's numbers for learning and completion percentages in the four phases are consistent with the benefits we believe we see in iterative development projects.

While I have made many assumptions and pushed the model about as far as I am comfortable with, the results do appear to be both internally consistent and consistent with observed behavior.

Recap

I have taken a simple, universal model—the S-curve—and applied it to software project management. I used simple, classical physics to infer from the S-curve the velocity and acceleration, and hence the forces, at work on the project. I extended the model to multi-phase iterative development and found results that are consistent with observation. I even attempted to separate learning from completion metrics and separately analyze those forces. Finally, I added the forces together and drew some conclusions about the total force as a function of time, and the impulse applied to the project during its various phases.

Much of this analysis is speculative, and I encourage you to ponder this and imagine alternate interpretations of the graphs I have drawn. I hope that many of you will find other nuggets in here that neither my reviewers nor I have found yet.

In the meantime, the conceptual model can make us ready to anticipate and deal with the various phases of the project as they play out. Knowing that there is some degree of "determinism" at work can sometimes be a comforting thought when a project hits its low point and you're concerned that the team may lose hope.

This chapter completes the third part of the book. I turn now to Part 4, in which I explore the human element of software development management.

---

[21] More precisely, the integral of the force over time is the impulse, which is equal to the change in momentum.

PART 4

THE HUMAN ELEMENT

The fourth part of this book moves on from a project-management perspective to a more personal one. Here I consider that software is developed by people, so it is important to understand what motivates them and demotivates them.

In Chapter 13, "Politics," I discuss the prickly problem of politics. Engineers, it turns out, generally detest this non-technical intrusion into "their" workplace. I've found that software engineers are particularly sensitive in this area.

In Chapter 14, "Negotiating," I get down to the very subject of how to talk with software people; there is a "hidden protocol" that can help grease the wheels here and prevent things from getting royally wrapped around the axle.

Ever since Tracy Kidder introduced the concept in his book, *The Soul of a New Machine,* "signing up" has been a staple of our industry. In Chapter 15, "Signing Up," I put a stake in the ground about the true meaning of commitment.

Finally, in Chapter 16, "Compensation," I broach the hairy subject of compensation. Most software people I know work for a living, and compensation is important to them. Many software managers feel stifled by the salary grades and various policies imposed on them by their human resources departments. I explore some more general and original ideas around the subject.

Once again, I endeavor to show in all these chapters what makes software people different and how to work with them effectively once you are cognizant of these differences.

CHAPTER 13

Politics

In Chapter 8, "Getting It Out the Door," I discussed putting together a repeatable build process. Some software development managers read this, in an earlier incarnation of the chapter, and took me to task for not sufficiently condemning "politics" as one of the root causes of the difficulty. This revealed to me a misunderstanding about the role of politics, not just in software development but also in the management of technical organizations in general.

Why is politics such a touchy subject? Given that it exists, can you do anything about it?

Most software managers I know have had two diametrically opposed ways of dealing with it. One group takes the position that politics is poison and attempts to remove anything that even smells "political" from their organization. This quasi-religious fervor is unhealthy in its own way. The other group pretends that politics doesn't exist. Of course, ignoring it doesn't make it go away, so they have the problem of dealing with something that they pretend isn't there. Neither group can be successful.

Of course, to deal with this in any kind of rational way requires that we have a common definition of the very word. Without a common working vocabulary, we can't make much progress. So I begin my treatment of this controversial subject by setting some context.

Context

Any time we talk about human behavior such as "politics" and political process, we enter into the minefield of cultural differences. Simply put, different behaviors are more or less acceptable in different cultural contexts. Behavior that could be considered "borderline" in one culture could be considered so offensive in another that it would never happen. When I get into "good politics" and "bad politics" later in this chapter, we need to remember that the norm I am using here is a North American standard and, even at that, susceptible to many local gradations. Some of the behaviors described might be more or less acceptable in European or Asian contexts. The part of the discussion that I believe transcends national and cultural boundaries is the difference in the way technical people (and the organizations they belong to) view the political process. Here I have observed some common tendencies that are worth noting, independent of geography and culture.

Highly competent technical people often have distaste for politics and politicians. Although I'm no psychologist, I believe this may stem from their notion that technical matters are precise (black and white) whereas politics is messy (lots of shades of gray). By training and education, scientists and engineers have a very analytic, problem-solving approach to their work, which involves invoking "first principles" and applying data in the course of various inductive and deductive processes. Often, this leads to neat, "closed-form" solutions. And because many technical managers come from the ranks of scientists and engineers, they bring along with them not only a very strong toolbox but also some of the biases that come along with it.

Politics involves a great deal of ambiguity, which makes many technical people nervous. It forces them to play on "someone else's court," as it were, a place where they feel they are at a disadvantage because their technical prowess doesn't count for much. Seasoned managers, on the other hand, have learned to deal with ambiguity and have a relatively high tolerance for it.

While this is perhaps an oversimplification, it is fairly safe to say that technical people would prefer issues to be resolved on technical merits alone, or perhaps on some mix of technical and business objectives. What they react to, often violently, is the manipulation they see in various discussions and negotiations—a manipulation they associate with the darker, uglier side of human behavior—often characterized by self-aggrandizement and personal agendas. Technical people have a tendency to broad-brush this behavior as "politics" and, in so generalizing it, give it a very negative connotation.

On the other hand, regardless of its nature, just *wishing* politics away will not make it *go* away. There is the way we would like things to be, and the way things are. Ironically, some people view bridging this gap as itself a political process.

My point is that so long as you have human beings in the loop, you are going to have politics. Human beings tend not to all think alike; in order to resolve differences of opinion, a political process is unavoidable. So, rather than condemn it, it is better to understand politics as an effective means of dealing with the inevitable need to resolve differences of opinion.

Definition

Let us note that the word "politics" refers to a category of human activity like "carpentry," "theater," or "surgery." What we really need to define is the term "political process." A *political process* is one in which you get a person or group of people to do what you want them to do. This is actually shorthand for a much more complicated set of ideas.

A political process is one in which two or more people adopt a single course of action. Typically, each individual involved in a political process maintains an agenda that is different from the group's collective agenda, or from any other individual's personal agenda. It is through the political process that an individual's agenda becomes publicized (if a free press is at work), negotiated and voted on (if a democracy), or implemented without further discussion (if the individual is the king). In every case, the individual engaged in a political process wants the group to adopt his or her agenda.[1]

By the way, getting other people to do what you want them to do is also the job of leaders and managers. But you probably have already made that observation yourself.

Note that what you are trying to convince people to do can be viewed as either good or bad; that is irrelevant to the discussion. Of course, from your point of view, you are probably trying to get them to do the right thing, but this certainly depends on your perspective. Even when purely motivated, your objectives may be viewed as wrong, bad, misguided, or even evil by some other third party.

Three Scenarios

If you are in the category of people who still find politics not their cup of tea, let me give you another way to look at it. There are, in fact, only three distinct cases to consider.

1. You are the king.

You might think that politics is irrelevant in this case. The simplistic view might be that even if you are a benevolent despot, you pretty much get to do what you want, and your vassals obey. If politicians crop up, you suppress them; dissident serfs get thrown in the oubliette,[2] so you don't have to deal in politics. In a business organization, the equivalent behavior is to fire any employee who shows political tendencies.

---

[1] Mike Perrow, my editor at *The Rational Edge*, is responsible for this excellent reformulation of my more direct but less clear articulation.

[2] A pretty awful place in the nether regions of the castle. The word derives from the French *oublier*, "to forget."

But this is an oversimplification. Even kings need to build some support amongst their circle of advisors in order to stay in power. There is a good reason today why we don't have very many absolute, powerful kings left. But, if you are the king and want complete control over your realm, you can keep politics at bay for a while. In today's world, it is just not a really good, viable, long-term strategy.

2. You are not the king.

Now you have two choices: one, convince the king to do what you want to do, or two, band together with other vassals to either reason with the king or overthrow him. I will point out that both alternatives imply a political process. If you are unclear on this concept, go back to our earlier definition of a political process.

3. There is no king.

This often occurs in organizations in which there is no strong leadership. You might even call this nascent democracy. In this instance, people have to get together and decide what to do, as there is no king telling them what to do. People will tend to have differing opinions, so we once again get to decision-making by consensus-building (also a political process).

Whether or not you consider technical organizations "democracies" (and we all know managers who strongly believe they are not!), it is important to understand that we exist in a culture that encourages participation of all its members. In fact, the strongest technical organizations are the ones that engage the talents of all, in a free marketplace of ideas. Ideally, one wants to create a *high-trust environment*[3]—that is, an environment where there is a high degree of trust among employees at every level, and where intellectual honesty reigns and politics are minimized. But we've just shown that politics is inevitable in all organizations, and technical organizations are just another form of organization. How do we deal with this apparent paradox?

Politics Is Inevitable, But…

In almost every organization, there is going to be some degree of politics. In the House of Representatives and the Senate, political context and the bartering that

---

[3] This is a very important concept, and I will return to it later in the chapter. High-trust environments are valuable to all organizations, and I have found that they are especially important in technical organizations.

accompanies it are fundamental. But as I have already pointed out, when it comes to technical organizations, most of the participants would like to minimize the political context. Why?

The answer is simple. You cannot solve technical problems by political compromise. If there are two sides to an issue, one of which is technically feasible and one of which is technically ridiculous, no political compromise will work. Imagine an absurd example: The "solidistas" want dams to be solid, while the "holeistas" want dams to look like Swiss cheese. The political compromise of having only one or two holes in the dam would make no sense whatsoever.

Most people quickly understand the issues implicit in the last paragraph, but not always. I have seen, on occasion, otherwise intelligent people falling into the trap of trying to mediate between competent and incompetent people, giving equal weight to their ideas. This never works, annoys both parties, and tends to really discourage the competent people. Another way of saying this is that "Everyone is entitled to an opinion," but technical people know that not all opinions are equally well qualified.

Another, more subtle variant of the political pitfall for technical organizations is *bartering*. In many political processes, two sides get to trade on issues: You concede on this one and I'll concede on that one. We each "win one," and we each "lose one." This is the most frequent way of avoiding deadlocks.

Well, in technical organizations this won't work in many contexts. If there are two dams to be constructed, then again it makes no sense to build Dam A according to the "solidista" philosophy and Dam B according to the "holeista" philosophy. One will hold water and the other won't. Period.

Nor does it work to give the wrong-headed side free rein in some other area. If the political compromise to achieve solid dams is to let the incompetent "holeistas" go off and design another class of structure—say fortresses—then we have once again made a really bad decision through the use of "politics."

Of course, the choices in real life are not always so clear. If it were always a choice between the "solidistas" and the "holeistas," our lives would be easier. Often the two (or more) alternatives are not so obviously differentiable, and the technical issues may be very muddy indeed. In such cases, it is not always true that both sides are willing to admit that the other side has some merit. Often, technical criteria become submerged and the discussion degenerates into politics. This is generally bad.

When Things Get Political

So what is the legitimate place for politics in technical organizations? Let's agree that *purely* technical issues need to be resolved technically. Once an issue moves out of the purely technical realm, then we admit politics. Examples of legitimate political issues include decisions on marketability, customer satisfaction, business impact, and so on. Because objective, technical criteria are harder to pin down in these areas, debate, including political debate, is necessary.[4]

However, there are good politics and bad politics. Political scientists would, of course, disagree: For them, all methods are more or less efficacious in their own ways, and they are loath to make value judgments. They might consider my categorizations naïve, but I find them useful. Let's explore "good politics" and "bad politics" a little bit further.

Good Politics

The following techniques can be considered valid, legitimate parts of a political process:

- Education
- Persuasion
- Consensus building
- Fact-finding
- Intellectually honest discussions
- Identification of common interests
- Exposure of hidden or subtle facts
- Seeking compromise
- Reasoning together

Plato could get behind this kind of politics. In fact, it has been observed that in organizations that do a good job of consensus building, decisions often are implemented more smoothly because the consensus-building process causes diverse factions to come together and exercise reason, and to participate in making a joint decision. This process in effect "pre-sells" the idea, and the eventual solution has more buy-in from the participants than if there had not been consensus building.

---

[4] There is one other exception worth mentioning. Often a better technical solution may be a poor choice, if the existing organization is very effective using the tools and methods that are deeply embedded in its culture. Although moving to a better toolset might seem obvious from a purely technical point of view, the costs in disruption may overshadow the benefits. Here is where some intelligent political compromise is useful. And it doesn't hurt to apply a good dose of empathy to the problem, either.

By the way, I'm proud to observe that one of the hallmarks of the early Rational Software culture was an emphasis on consensus building to arrive at good decisions. A little later we needed to introduce "time-bounded consensus seeking," wherein if consensus was not achieved by a certain time, a decision was made through a somewhat less democratic, more informal process by the relevant manager in the interest of moving on. Even in this case, the period during which consensus was sought did tend to give a good airing of all the alternative points of view.[5]

Neutral Politics

The following behaviors are in the gray zone. Some people admit them as part of a legitimate political process, while others abhor them. I make no value judgment here other than to put them in the "neutral" category:[6]

- Cajoling

- Ridiculing

- Lobbying

- Delaying

- Defocusing issues

- Positioning

- Not telling all the truth all the time

- You do this for me and I'll do that for you

- "Spinning"

"You do this for me and I'll do that for you" is basically yielding on one point to gain another, which is what I call *bartering* earlier in the chapter. One man's horse trade is another man's compromise. This is why I place this behavior in the gray zone.

---

[5] We need to be careful that consensus does not lead to "group think." The essence of the process is the vitality associated with competing opinions. When consensus is achieved through peer pressure, negative decisions and outcomes can result.

[6] Let's note once again for emphasis the North American bias. Some or all of the gray zone behaviors might be considered OK, acceptable, dubious, or very bad by Europeans or Asians. This is where things get very complex. But in order to frame the discussion at all, I needed to define three categories. What I put into them reflects the North American point of view, which itself is an approximation.

Bad politics

Without belaboring the neutral zone too long, I move on to those aspects of the political process that most people find unpleasant and "over the line":

- Lying or deliberately misleading
- Bribing
- Intimidating, threatening, bullying
- Undermining, conspiring, plotting
- Personal attacks, abusive behavior
- Filibustering
- Needless arguing on minor issues to exhaust time and patience
- Hidden agendas
- Committing to do something you have no intention of doing
- Committing to not do something you have every intention of doing
- Appealing to authority to subvert the process
- "The end justifies the means" or "All's fair in love and war"

Sometimes this brand of politics is labeled "Machiavellian." This does a great disservice to Machiavelli, who had a lot more to say than "The ends justify the means."[7]

What happens when you get into bad politics is that you now are dealing with people who don't view politics as an adjunct to getting their jobs done. You are dealing with people for whom the political process itself is the primary preoccupation. Winning, by political or other means, is more important to these people than getting the job done. They have their priorities reversed and, as such, are damaging to the organization. Certainly when you get to the last behavior, which basically says "There are no rules in a knife fight," you are beyond the pale.

The Engineering Mapping

The real problem with the gray zone is that many technical people have a bias toward the very high end of the integrity spectrum. They may put gray zone behaviors in their category of bad politics. For example, not telling the whole truth all the time is technically lying, yet some people admit a spectrum here, while others view it as black or white. It

---

[7] I apologize also to Sun Tzu, whom I could not work into this chapter at all.

is difficult to have a high-trust environment if there is a lot of gray zone behavior. So don't be surprised if, when you talk about politics with engineers and technical managers, they lump "neutral (gray) zone" and "bad" politics under the general, derogatory heading of "politics" and characterize the "good" politics category as "leadership" or "good management." This turns things into a black and white world where all politics is evil. As this was my starting point, I now want to make it clear that we *can* sort things out, and what remains is really a linguistic mapping issue. Table 13.1 may prove helpful:

Table 13.1 Mapping politics

	Political Scientist's View	Mainstream Usage	Engineers and Technical Managers
My "Good Politics"	All part of the political process	Legitimate	"Leadership"
My "Neutral Politics"		Doubtful	Not acceptable
My "Bad Politics"		Not acceptable	Not acceptable

One could say that the entire thrust of this chapter is reconciling the "mainstream usage" to the "engineering mapping." These are two different ways of looking at the world, but without understanding the linguistic overloading we can get into a lot of trouble—especially when those engineers think we are defending politics.[8]

High-Trust Environments

I've mentioned *high-trust environment* in the context of an organization's culture. Perhaps I should be explicit about what it is, and why it is so desirable.

In a high-trust environment, we take the following as the norm:

- We can trust each other to tell the truth.

- We can depend on each other to do whatever it takes.

---

[8] We often find some curious and contradictory manifestations of engineers' value systems. For example, it is typical for engineers to feel uncomfortable in discussions with customers if they think you are not being 100 percent honest in all your utterances. Here they apply what can sometimes be an overly rigorous standard. On the other hand, they are puzzled when their integrity seems to be impugned because they missed a schedule milestone. For them, this was just a technical problem, not an issue of a missed commitment and violation of trust. Understanding some of these characteristics is important in dealing with technical organizations, because the obvious mismatches with other parts of the organization can lead to communication problems.

- We can depend on each other to put the organization's objectives ahead of our own personal or group objectives.

- We can assume intellectual honesty in all discussions.

- We don't take commitments lightly; we view missed commitments as a violation of trust. This implies both volition and competency.

The thing that is so wonderful about high-trust environments is that they are extremely efficient. When you have trust, you have less need for verification. This means you can get more done with smaller teams. It is the equivalent of reducing friction in a machine: More of the energy goes to producing work (good stuff) and less to producing heat (bad stuff). In general, it is easier to have high trust in small, relatively homogeneous groups. As teams get larger, more dispersed, and more diverse, it becomes harder to maintain a high-trust environment. Ironically, the need doesn't diminish as the difficulty increases.

A high-trust environment is desirable in all organizations. And, while it is as important—or more important—in technical organizations than in non-technical ones, it is harder to achieve. If we go back to the engineers' view of the world in the previous table, we can see how even "neutral" politics poisons the high-trust environment. If having a high-trust environment is important to your organization, then you will need to move the bar up, and tolerate less "gray zone" behavior than you might otherwise accept.

Once you have worked in a high-trust environment, you will find it difficult to work in lower-trust environments. All your instincts can turn out to be wrong, and a trusting person in a low-trust environment is an easy target for political manipulators and can be made to suffer. On the other hand, it is crucial for people who have come from low-trust environments to learn how to trust others once they are in a high-trust environment; a lifetime of paranoia is difficult to overcome. Recent emigrants from the old Soviet Union have told me that assimilating into the less "on guard" American culture constitutes a difficult adjustment for them.

Other Variants of Bad Politics

In addition to the many items I noted in the section "Bad Politics," there are a few other negative behaviors that can crop up. I collect them here so that they don't escape unnoticed.

One particularly noxious form of bad politics is failing to "sign up." In every process, there is a period of discussion, followed by a decision. At this point, "the polls are closed." Once the decision is made, everyone must commit to it.[9] Continued whining and politicking for rejected solutions after the fact is bad politics. Instead of allowing the organization to move on and implement the solution, it continues to mire down the issue in

---

[9] I devote all of Chapter 15, "Signing Up," to the subject of commitment.

debate. Worse, failure to commit tends to undermine the leadership structure by calling decisions into question over and over again. This form of bad politics must be eradicated whenever it crops up. Managers need to send a strong signal that "If you can't sign up, get off the team." If you have a healthy political process, this is a reasonable condition.

Another symptom of bad political behavior is obvious empire building. There are still many people out there who are caught up in the trappings and symbols of success: rank in the organization, number of direct and indirect reports, size of budget, and so on. Organizations that overemphasize these statistical symbols reap what they sow; behaviors tend to follow the reward system. If, on the other hand, your organization rewards originality, contribution, "doing whatever it takes," and so on—independent of the individual's place in the hierarchy—then you are on the right track. In such organizations, the former behaviors tend to stick out like a sore thumb and can be culturally discouraged. When individuals persist in them, they are mapping to different cultures that are more politicized, in which one's opinions have value according to one's place in the hierarchy as opposed to the opinion's intrinsic value. High-trust organizations will ultimately reject such behavior, and if the behavior doesn't change, then the individuals who practice it must themselves be rejected—the sooner, the better.

Finally, there's a stylistic issue that is often characterized as political behavior, usually in a negative way. Some people turn every interaction into a negotiation; they are always "working the room." If nothing else, such individuals become tiresome, and tend to drain the energy of the group after awhile; people develop the habit of knowing that they have to "play defense" at all times with such individuals. I clearly run the risk of a libel suit if I try to give you an example here.[10] But you all know the behavior, because there are certain individuals in every organization who are annoying in just this way. You tend to just not want to have to deal with them. Try not to be one, and coach others to avoid the practice.

Recap

Political process is a part of human and organizational behavior. To disengage from it is to cede authority to those who choose to continue to play. It is morally and logically untenable to disengage out of abhorrence to politics and then later claim that you were disenfranchised.

As leaders, however, we do have an obligation to avoid the trap of letting politics intrude on purely technical decisions. Even at the national level, we have sometimes made the mistake of letting political concerns govern decisions that were untenable on technical merit. When facts are clear, we cannot ignore them, regardless of the political consequences. Try not to violate laws of physics.

---

[10] But here is a sports analogy: In tennis, this behavior is akin to always coming to the net. It applies constant pressure to the opponent.

When we engage in politics, we need to encourage good politics as indicated in this chapter. We need to become wary when we see "neutral zone" behavior starting to occur. And we need to stamp out and crush, preferably through peer pressure, bad politics.[11] Basically, bad politics corrupts the entire process by admitting as legitimate those behaviors that are clearly unethical and of low integrity.

Note that even "neutral" or "gray zone" practices will undermine a high-trust environment. The advantages of a high-trust environment are so great that one should seriously consider whether the allowance of "gray zone" practices is worth the risk.

We need to ensure that in all political processes or negotiations, the "polls close," that decisions are made, that the team "signs up," and that we move forward as one to implement the decision without continuing nonproductive debate.

It has been said that for evil to triumph, it is sufficient for good men to do nothing. If you fall back on the "all politicians are corrupt scoundrels" argument, I have only two words for you: Harry Truman. Truman was no technologist, but he was a superb politician and leader.[12] This takes us way beyond the scope of this chapter, and most likely beyond the scope of the book as well. But I am constantly (and I think legitimately) concerned that software engineers' withdrawal from a process they see as political robs the organization of important input.

On the other hand, politics is not always the issue. Many developers opt not to participate because we have discouraged them in the past. Many senior people have remarked to me that managers don't listen anyway. I think this is perhaps a somewhat jaundiced perspective, but if we want participation we do need to listen. And we certainly always need to separate technical from non-technical issues.

The separation of technical from non-technical issues is sometimes very easy. Usually, *what* we are going to do is a political decision, and *how* we are going to do it is a technical one. On the other hand, there can be interactions. For example, the time and resources it takes to implement a feature (the *how*) can affect the decision whether to do it or not, so the *how* influences the *what*. The important thing is to be sure that engineering estimates of how long things might take are honestly given, and not motivated by what people think the political consequences might be. That is a sure way to go wrong.

But sometimes even managers who are good listeners get in trouble the first time they open their mouths. How you talk with engineers is the topic of the next chapter. I've labeled it "Negotiating," because that is how it seems to both sides. In reality, it addresses communication in general between software people.

---

[11] This would be an example of good peer pressure.

[12] My point here is that Truman was a man of incredible integrity, yet he came out of one of the most corrupt political organizations in America at the time—the Pendergast machine in Kansas City. This irony has intrigued me for years.

CHAPTER 14

Negotiating

Why is it that sometimes even the simplest things seem to go wrong?

My guess is that if you go to the root of the problem in these situations, you will more often than not discover the classic "failure to communicate." "Oh, is that what you wanted? Why didn't you say so?" Exasperated, we try to control our frustration. But unless we begin to understand what is breaking down here, we will be doomed to repeat the exercise over and over again.

Now what is curious is that these miscommunications rarely happen when a negotiation takes place. As soon as there is "give and take" and resolution occurs, the odds of getting it severely wrong go way down. So perhaps there is a key there. The trick may lie in conducting a negotiation without having a negotiation, because, as we all know, negotiations are fraught with tension, and we don't want every interaction to have that flavor.

In this chapter, our friend Roscoe Leroy gives us his slant on how this might work.[1]

---

[1] Roscoe has previously appeared in Chapters 5, 10, and 11. You can refer to these chapters for background material on him.

Communication Is Everything

Roscoe and I were sitting around the pot-bellied stove, chewing the fat on a rainy Saturday. He had been working with a group of software engineers for about six months, and I was surprised that there had been no events significant enough to register on the Richter scale. Given that Roscoe is about as volatile as Vesuvius in August,[2] I figured that something was up.

"Roscoe," I ventured, "how is it that you haven't run off half that crew you inherited a while back?"

"Why should I do that?" he responded. "Buncha good hands, I'd say. Course, you gotta know how to talk with 'em."

"Oh, really," I replied. "What's the big deal? What makes talking to software engineers so special?"

"Wrong already, son. You don't talk *to* engineers; you talk *with* them. Starting off by talking *to* them can quickly degenerate into talking *at* them, and you're bound to get into trouble."

Darn! Nailed so soon, and I hadn't even gotten started. But the man had a point.

"OK, Roscoe, I get it. But really, is talking with engineers, and especially software engineers, any different from talking with other people? If so, I'd really like to understand what the secret is."

Roscoe Explains His Theory

"Well, it's like this. We could start out by saying that software engineers just want to be treated like professionals. They not only want respect, just like all human beings, but, like doctors and other professionals, they expect it. If you think of them as 'just programmers' or 'hackers,' you will get their backs up. So your 'going in' attitude is important."

"Heck," I offered, "sounds like you're talking about a bunch of *prima donnas*."

"Not really," he said, which surprised me. "You have to understand that software engineering is the newest engineering discipline on the block. Everyone knows what mechanical, civil, electrical, and chemical engineers do, and aeronautical engineers even get called 'rocket scientists' now and then. But not many people know what a software engineer actually does. Problem is, software guys often feel like the Rodney Dangerfields of engineering.[3] So I cut them some slack."

---

[2] Located immediately south of Naples, Italy, Mount Vesuvius erupted on August 24, 79 AD, completely burying the cities of Pompeii and Herculaneum in lava, ash, and mud.

[3] For our overseas friends, Rodney Dangerfield was an American comedian whose tagline was the ungrammatical "I don't get no respect!"

"OK," I said, "spare me the psychobabble about their inferiority complex. Some of them seem pretty arrogant to me at times."

"Well, do you want to communicate, or don't you?"

I swallowed hard.[4] It was time to listen some more.

I wondered, by the way, about Roscoe's classification of software developers as "engineers." There are many in the software development industry who feel as though we're a long way from becoming a true engineering discipline. But I decided to let sleeping dogs lie. Regardless of the label we use, managers still have to talk with the folks who design and write our software. And I knew that when I wanted Roscoe's opinion on the subject, he'd give it to me. Heck, when he wanted my opinion, he gave that to me, too!

The Four Steps

"Actually, there is a simple, four-step method for conversing with software engineers. Sort of like the Texas Two-Step, applied twice."

Roscoe was getting warmed up. He took a few puffs on his cigar and refilled his coffee cup.

"If you follow these four steps, you'll most of the time come out of it with a whole skin. If you make assumptions and try to skip over some steps, you will get all wrapped around the axle. So listen carefully."

Step Number One

"Now the first thing to remember is that you are dealing with an engineer. Engineers don't usually like to make small talk; they consider it a waste of their time. And boy, do they consider their time to be valuable. So, first off, they want to know what the problem is."

"You mean," I said, "that every conversation has to revolve around a problem? What if you are coming to the engineer with an opportunity?"

"Ah yes, challenges and opportunities, as you managers always call them. Well, call it an *issue* if it makes you feel any better. The fact is, engineers are problem-solvers, and they naturally assume that if you come to them, you have a problem that needs to be solved. So I usually start out by simply stating that I think there is a problem that I'd like to talk about, and then I simply state the problem."

I could see that setting up this kind of baseline for a discussion would be a good thing. Rather than beating around the bush, just come out and say why you are there. So I nodded to Roscoe to go on.

"Now sometimes you will get a grunt, and then a quick explanation of why your problem is not a problem. Sometimes you'll discover you were misinformed. Sometimes

---

[4] It reminded me of my mother-in-law's response when I criticized her for putting sugar in the peas: "Do you want the kids to eat them or not?"

you'll find out that you didn't state the problem correctly. It's OK to be persistent. Clarifying what the problem is, or isn't, will actually get you some respect from the engineer. Just remember that what the engineer is doing is qualifying you *and* your problem. Because he doesn't want to spend even one second on a problem he sees as unnecessary or unworthy. If you disagree, you'd better hash it out, because until he is convinced there's a problem, you're not gonna get anywhere."

I recalled several discussions I'd had where I jumped ahead prematurely. Sure enough, we always had to backtrack until we agreed on what the problem was. Engineers sure are funny that way.

Step Number Two

"Well, now that you have agreed that there is a problem, you need to establish ownership," Leroy continued.

Ownership? Roscoe was clearly getting comfortable with business lingo.

"You see, it comes down to this. If it's *your* problem, then what are you doing here? Seeking advice and counsel? That's OK. If you are implying that it is *his* (or *her*) problem, then he or she might actually have to do some work. So before an engineer will go further into the discussion, he wants to know: *Whose problem is it*?"

"There is another possibility," I said. "It could be neither my problem nor his problem, but a problem for some third party."

"Yeah, that's possible. In that case, you can bet the engineer will ask you something like, 'Well, why are you coming to me with it, if it's not your problem or my problem? Let him (the third party) worry about it.' So you have to explain to him why it has an effect on him. Otherwise, he'll treat the problem as either uninteresting or unworthy of his time."

I was starting to see that this was a little more complicated than I thought.

"Now, if it's your problem, the best you can hope for is some thoughtful analysis, maybe a recommendation—and then it's time to get out of Dodge.[5] An engineer is loath to spend too much of *his* time on *your* problem. That's just the way they are.

"On the other hand, if you think it is *his* problem, then you have some selling to do. Once an engineer accepts responsibility for a problem, he will act professionally and work on it. But because of that, engineers are reluctant to accept just any new problem that shows up on their doorstep. And you will be amazed at the lengths some will go to in denying that the problem is their problem. Sometimes they may even start to deny that the problem actually exists."

---

[5] Once again for our overseas friends, Dodge City was a town in the Old West that was known for violence and "frontier justice." It was generally considered to be a rather unhealthy place for the uninitiated. Hence the instruction to "Get out of Dodge" came to mean "Don't hang around too long in a dangerous place."

"Aha," I exclaimed, "that's why you need to do step one first! You have to establish that there is a problem so that it doesn't evaporate as the discussion proceeds."

"You're catching on," Roscoe said, "you're catching on."

So, I noted, the beginning was simple. Establish that there's a problem, and convince the engineer that it's *his* problem. The first Texas Two-Step was a piece of cake.

"OK," I said. "Now what about the second Two-Step?"

Step Number Three

"Well, here is where it most often goes off the rails," said Roscoe. "What you have to do is *not* suggest a solution."

Well, I'll be darned, I thought. What is so awful about suggesting a solution?

"It's the reason many software engineers bristle at the word *requirements*. In days of yore, people would come to them with preconceived ideas of how things should be implemented, and call them 'requirements.' That attitude led to lots of really unnecessary conflict.

"What the engineer always wants to know is *what* you want done. They never want you to tell them *how* to do it. After all, that is what they are getting paid for. If you come marching in with a proposed solution, there is almost certainly going to be some friction.

"And there's another problem with coming in with a solution. Often, the engineer will work backwards from your 'solution' to try to figure out what you *really* want to do. He may get it wrong. By proposing a solution, you actually add work and risk to the whole proposition."

"So," I wondered out loud, "how do you get at the solution?"

"The really smart managers," Roscoe continued, "sort of feel out the engineers to see what the possible range of solutions is. They get them to talk about what the options and trade-offs are. Exploring the 'solution space' is OK, provided the engineer is supplying most of the data. But for heaven's sake, don't tell him how to hold a pencil.

"In the software world, there is almost always more than one way to solve a problem. What engineers will do is consider alternative options, and then try to select the best one—what they call the *optimum* solution."

"Wait a minute," I interjected, "who decides what's best?"

"Good point," responded Roscoe. "'Best' could mean 'fastest,' 'cheapest,' 'lowest risk,' 'lowest maintenance,' 'best-crafted,' 'most elegant,' or a bunch of other things. So part of the exploration of the solution space with the engineer is to understand what 'best' means in your business context. Otherwise, you may get the 'best' technical solution, which may not be appropriate to your needs."

"OK," I countered, "but what if the solution is going to take too long?"

"Another valid point. The purpose of exploring the solution space with the engineer is to also give him an idea of what your *constraints* are. That way you can work with him to negotiate a solution that makes both of you only moderately unhappy. Sometimes that's the best you can do."

Well, let's see, I thought. We've defined the problem, we've got ownership, and we've got the solution space somewhat mapped out and negotiated around some alternatives. Not bad. What's left?

Roscoe, of course, read my mind.

Step Number Four

"Closure," said Roscoe. "When you are dealing with engineers, you always have to get closure. As in, 'What are the next steps?' and 'Who needs to do what and by when?' If you end the discussion without covering this ground, you will most surely come to grief."

"Why is that?" I asked.

"Well, it's like this. Engineers are busy folks. They always have more work to do than they have time to do it in. You have already taken up some of this time going through steps one through three. And it's all wasted, because if you don't do step four, nothing will happen once you leave the room."

"Huh?" I blurted out.

"Well, look, did you tell the engineer to do something? Did you tell him to actually begin work? Did you assign this new task a priority, relative to all the other things he is already working on? No. You did none of these things. So clearly you were there to discuss the problem, not get it solved.

"Now if you want the engineer to actually do something, you have to *say* so, and be clear when you do. What's that ten-dollar word? Oh yeah—you need to be *explicit*. And when he commits to do something, you will of course ask him to commit to a date. Because without a date, there is no real commitment.

"Now there may be some more work to actually complete step four. The engineer may ask you for more data, ask you to better describe the scope of work, and yes, even ask you to put it all in writing. And he may have to think about it a little more, and then the two of you may have to finally agree on the solution to be implemented. All reasonable requests. At least now you know he is engaging with you, and you may actually get a result."

Beyond the Basics

So Roscoe's formula is pretty simple:

1. Define the problem, and agree on the definition with the engineer.

2. Establish that ownership now lies with the engineer.

3. Explore the solution space, letting the engineer take the lead.

4. Make explicit and agree upon what will get done, including scope, priority, and date.

Why, I asked Roscoe, was this simple formula not followed more often?

"I think it comes down to what engineers would call an *impedance mismatch*.[6] Managers take lots of things for granted and make lots of assumptions that are just not true. Sometimes they are misinformed; often, they don't know what they don't know. But because they are smart, and they know that engineers are smart, they assume that there is a common context for the discussion. So they skip ahead. Often they jump ahead to the solution, working on steps three and four.[7] And here's the engineer, still stuck in his own mind on steps one and two. Things bog down at that point.

"Sometimes, to save time, you have to go more slowly," opined Roscoe.

"And of course, there's this other problem. Often the solution that the manager proposes is of the 'quick and dirty' variety, an expeditious way to resolve the problem. Perhaps it is a low-cost approach that involves some throw-away work. At this point, you can expect the engineer to go ballistic."

"Why's that?" I asked.

"Well, it's the nature of the beast. Engineers hate to do throw-away work. They would rather spend their time crafting the solid solution that will not need to be redone. Sometimes there is excessive intellectual purity here, rather than a careful analysis of engineering trade-offs. But it takes a really technically deep manager to argue these finer points with engineers. That's why it's best not to come in with a solution, but to let the engineer suggest options to you."

That sounded politic. Did Roscoe have any other suggestions, I wondered?

"One more. Be careful of asking software engineers to do too many things at one time. They believe that they work best when they can concentrate on one task and give it their full attention.[8] They know what multitasking is, but they don't believe that it is the optimum way of working. And you know," he winked at me, "if they believe that, it is probably true. So don't fall into the trap of even talking about piling too much different stuff on their plates. It just gets them in a really bad mood."

Sounded like a good insight. Anything else?

---

[6] A term with an interesting history. It comes from electrical engineering, and refers to trying to connect two circuits that have different capacities to absorb or transmit energy. When this is attempted, the resulting circuit is particularly "lossy." In common parlance, the term has come to mean a communication between two parties in which differences in the respective parties' contexts (or differences in the language they use to express themselves) is so great that communication is difficult and may at times break down completely. Or, to put it another way, the process generates more heat than light.

[7] Ironically, managers who have previously been engineers often make this mistake. They should know better.

[8] Word has it that some studies support this position. Roscoe couldn't cite any, though. And, to be completely correct, I should point out that there are engineers who like to work on several problems simultaneously. I have found them to be in the minority—hence, the generalization.

"You've got to be careful in all this. Remember, your objective is to improve communication. If your partner in the dialog thinks that you are patronizing or trying to manipulate him, all is lost.

"Talking with engineers is a process, not an event. The dialog needs to be ongoing. You are not going to talk with this engineer one time and then never again. That alone argues against bending him too far out of shape, doesn't it? You are going to have to talk with him again—if not on this subject, then on another one.

"So I try to establish this pattern, where the fella knows what's coming. I think of it as establishing a comfort zone. If he knows I'm first going to try to establish what the problem is and who owns it, he can be ready to discuss that. Perhaps he can get me out of his office in five minutes. Might save us both some time. Then, once we're past that, we can have the interesting part of the discussion, from his point of view. That's step three, where we discuss alternative solutions. That's where he gets to shine.

"And, of course, he needs to know that step four will always follow. That shows him I am serious, that I don't want to just talk about it, but that I want to do something about it. Once again, engineers respect that.

"And, by the way, when an engineer comes to you to talk, you can expect him to follow the four-step approach. The reason is, engineers talk to *each other* that way, more or less."

Are We Done Yet?

I had one more thing that was bothering me about Roscoe's approach.

"Roscoe," I said, "it seems to me that your four-step method is pretty waterfall in nature. I know that iterative development means that we will be having many conversations, as you have already pointed out. But isn't each conversation itself 'iterative'?"

Roscoe smiled.

"Looks like you want to be an 'advanced player,'" he said. "It would be great if I could just get most people to do the four steps. That would be progress. But you're right, son. In some cases, when you get to step four, you have to loop back to step three. That's because some implementation detail that comes up in step four causes you to reevaluate a solution proposed in step three."

"Yeah," I agreed, "but can't it loop back even further than that?"

"Sure," replied Roscoe. "It's easy to see that sometimes we might discover an alternative solution in step three that would require someone else to do some work. That would mean going back to step two, to find and convince the new owner."

"So, it is iterative after all, because I could also imagine going all the way back to step one and reformulating the problem entirely when we go and talk with the third party," I ventured.

"Be careful," said Roscoe. "Everything you say is true, but the objective of the exercise is to get closure, not to iterate forever. Some iteration is good, but your goal should always be to get to step four, and exit it with a plan. Otherwise, you might find yourself praying at the altar of Our Lady of Perpetual Revision."[9]

I recognized that trap, too. Roscoe had convinced me that I needed to change the way I interacted with software engineers. Even if I had to talk with a team of engineers, I would apply the same steps; moving from a one-on-one talk to a one-on-many conversation would require even more structure and discipline. Roscoe's formula would make it even more apparent to the group that I had an organized way of looking at—and solving—the problem at hand.

I resolved to go forth and try Roscoe's approach, and to see if I could improve my ability to communicate.

Recap

There is one other tendency of engineers that I have observed throughout the years, and it is something to watch out for. When you go to them with a problem, they tend to view it in the most general light. That is, they naturally assume you want "the whole problem" solved. Sometimes this is colloquially referred to as *DC to daylight*, because in electrical engineering, the frequency spectrum can go from zero (direct current) to infinity, which is actually well past that of visible light!

Now this is a problem for two reasons. First of all, solving a problem over the entire range of the parameter set is usually much harder than solving it over some restricted region of that same parameter set. In some cases, in fact, it may be impossible to solve generally, while being quite tractable over some limited range. So the engineer may throw up his hands in dismay until you specify that you actually only need a solution over some finite range of interest.

The second problem is more insidious. The problem may or may not be generally solvable, and the engineer may or may not be capable of that solution. In the worst case, he thinks it is solvable and tries to do it only to find out he was wrong, either because it wasn't solvable or he wasn't capable enough. This turns out to be very expensive.

Finally, there is the case where the problem is generally solvable, the engineer is capable, and he produces the golden nugget. Unfortunately, it takes way too long and is way too expensive. You just needed part of what he accomplished, one-tenth the result at one-tenth the price. He will be proud, and you will have a bittersweet taste in your mouth.

The only way to avoid this dilemma is careful discussion during step one and step three as to what the problem really is, and how much of a solution you can afford is an

---

[9] Patron saint of troubled projects.

inevitable part of step four. So you have multiple passes at avoiding this pitfall. Remember, in the business world it is usually unprofitable to build a $50 fence to keep in a $10 horse.[10]

Not every software engineer you will run across will be amenable to the protocol described in this chapter, because engineers are individuals and one size does not fit all. On the other hand, I've found that this approach works in a vast majority of cases, so it always makes a good default starting point.

In the next chapter, I turn to the follow-on to step four. In that step, we believe we have a commitment from the engineer to do something by a certain date. We will be successful or not depending on whether that commitment is met. This fundamental paradigm is further explored in Chapter 15.

---

[10] Often remarked to me by my good friend Bill Irwin. On the other hand, if you have many horses . . .

CHAPTER 15

Signing Up

Most software development projects have aggressive plans and schedules. Rare is the project that is not attempting something new or otherwise ambitious. Management always wants it as quickly as possible, and the risk element is ever-present. And most developers have previously worked on at least one project that has failed; some of them have been involved in projects that almost immediately fell behind and then seemed to painfully go on forever. So whenever a new project is proposed, developers and their managers are wary; what will be different this time?

Because a scared team is an ineffective one, it is important to overcome this initial trepidation. The wrong way to do it is to order special t-shirts and have a party. The right way to do it is to put together a reasonable plan with lots of input from the team, and then to go around to the various sub-teams and discuss it with them. Getting the *entire* team in a room and giving them a PowerPoint presentation of the plan is basically useless. This kind of dog-and-pony show will cut no ice with them; they want to talk about details and reality, and you can only do that in informal, small-group settings.

At the end of each of these smaller team meetings, you have to look around the table and ask each and every person to *sign up*. It is not sufficient that the group leader sign up; no, you need everyone on board. After you have discussed the plan with all the constituent groups and have them sign up, you can legitimately say that the entire team is on board. If anyone thought the plan was crazy, he had his day in court to say so. And, if he or she wouldn't sign up, you now have to make the decision as to whether that person should go forward with the rest of you.

But what does it really mean to "sign up"? The key notion here is one of *commitment*. In this chapter, we once again get the insights of Roscoe Leroy on the subject.[1]

Roscoe Gets His Nose Bloodied...

Roscoe and I were once again sitting around the pot-bellied stove, chewing the fat on a rainy Saturday. He had been working with a group of software engineers for about a year now and had had his first major slip. While I was not surprised that the inevitable had befallen Roscoe, I was interested in his post-mortem of this always-disappointing occurrence.

...And Immediately Cuts to the Chase

"Well," Roscoe started off, "it's really quite simple. The boys let me down."

Now Roscoe is not one to point fingers and look for opportunities to spread blame. He is one of those "the buck stops here" kind of guys. So I was curious as to what would lead him to make such a pronouncement.

"It's like this," he continued. "They committed to a deliverable by a certain date, and then they didn't deliver on that date."

I didn't inquire as to whether the slip was a small one or a large one, although I suspected the latter. What intrigued me was how "binary" Roscoe was in his judgment. It seemed to me that he was taking a black-or-white, all-or-nothing position. Wasn't the world better described in shades of gray?

"Surely," I said, "there must have been some extenuating circumstances."

Bad idea.

Vesuvius Erupts

"Bull*bleep*!" exclaimed Roscoe. "You listen here, sonny. No one on that project lost a limb between the time they made the commitment and the date on which they didn't deliver. 'Extenuating circumstances' my *bleeping bleep*!"

Well, I had obviously hit a nerve, and I shuddered to think about the effects on Roscoe's team. For, if I was surprised at his reaction as an outside observer, I could only imagine their response to what must have been a world-class butt-kicking on the

---

[1] If you still have not yet met Roscoe, see Chapters 5, 10, 11, and 14 for an introduction.

expected delivery day. As we all know, Roscoe is not exactly a shrinking violet when it comes to letting folks know how they've performed.

"Now understand, I gave them lots of rope," Roscoe continued. "They made up the estimates, and I applied my square root rule.[2] And they still came up empty. First dry hole[3] I've had in a long time.

"I suspected they were in trouble along the way. I tried to dig in and figure out what was going on. But they kept pushing me away, saying I wouldn't understand the technical issues and that everything would be fine anyway. It's my own damn fault for going along. I won't make that mistake again."

Roscoe seemed to grudgingly admit he had been too hands-off in managing this project. I guessed he had not engaged fully enough, as he normally would, because he trusted his people. It would appear that at least in this case, his trust had been misplaced.

Well, I wondered out loud, what exactly did he expect anyway? Perfection?

How They Do It in Texas

It was at that point that Roscoe introduced me to the concept of the *Texas handshake*. I was about to be educated.

"I grew up in the oil fields of Texas,"[4] Roscoe explained. "In the oil patch, a man's word is his bond. When you shake hands on something, it is a commitment. And commitments are sacred."

I asked if he could give me an example.

"Sure," he said. "Suppose I have some tubulars[5] that I need to move from one oil rig to another on short notice. What do I do? I call my local hotshot,[6] and he sends a flatbed. Within the hour, I get my stuff moved."

"Now the beauty of all this," Roscoe continued, "is that we do the whole deal with a handshake. We agree on where and when the tubulars have to move, and what the price is. His commitment is to deliver the goods promptly, and my commitment is to pay

---

[2] See Chapter 11, "Scheduling."

[3] In oil-well drilling parlance, a *dry hole* is a well that never produces any oil. It represents zero ROI, because you have no return, often on a substantial investment. Punching holes in Mother Earth is not cheap.

[4] Roscoe started out in the oil patch. Later on, he migrated into mining. If he had played golf, he would have dug his swing out of the ground, too.

[5] *Tubulars* is oil field slang for 30-foot-long sections of drill pipe or drill collars, which are cylindrical in aspect. Anything with this form factor is generically referred to as a *tubular*, regardless of any other characteristic. Tubulars can be very heavy and are always a pain to transport.

[6] Trucker for hire. These guys wait by the phone for just such business.

promptly. There's no contract, although I probably scribble my initials on some paperwork when he picks up the pieces.

"The point is, there are no lawyers. There's no need for any, nor is there time. We shake hands. If either one of us doesn't honor the spirit of the commitment, then we will never work again in the oil patch."

Really? Wow, I thought, what a concept.

"It's true. Your word is your bond, and your handshake is your word. Once the word gets around that your handshake is worthless, you become a non-person. No one will deal with you."

The Relevance to Software

So, I thought, Roscoe wanted the same kind of ironclad commitment from his software people. Seemed reasonable. What wasn't working?

"Here's the fundamental disconnect," postulated Roscoe. "In the oil field, a commitment means a 'commitment to deliver.' I think these software guys think a commitment means a 'commitment to try their best.'"

Ouch! Roscoe had ineloquently hit the nail on the head. I had often observed the failure mode he was describing. The people who had just failed to deliver would go into a long explanation of how hard they had tried, as if that would get them off the hook. In their minds, trying hard was proof that they had honorable intentions and thus should be excused.

"Commitment has two parts to it," continued Roscoe. "First there is the volition part. That means that the person will try to get the job done. Without volition, of course, it won't happen. But the second part is just as important. It's the competency part. Not only does the person have to *want* to deliver, he has to be *able* to deliver. Having the first without the second is useless from a delivery point of view.

"So, when someone makes a commitment to me," concluded Roscoe, "I assume that they both *want* to get it done and *can* get it done. Hence, they *will get it done*. Case closed. If they don't think they can get it done, then they shouldn't make the commitment."

I was starting to have to think more deeply about this than ever before.

The Dog Ate My Homework

"'Course," Roscoe went on, "there are always those varmints who come back with 'the dog ate my homework.' I have no patience for these guys, and wonder how they got in the front door in the first place. And wouldn't you know it: They always tell you the night before delivery that they are going to miss, and you know for sure that they knew they were in trouble long before that. They're just not serious people, and they need to be moved down the road as fast as possible."

That seemed fair to me. Folks who waited until the last minute to give me the bad news had always upset me. In addition to suspecting that this was a sign of cowardice on their part, I also felt it robbed me of time I could have used to find an alternate plan to cover for their failure.

"You got that right, Roscoe," I replied. "But sometimes it seems like there has just been a misunderstanding."

"Well, there are two frequent 'mechanical' failure modes. The first is not agreeing on what the commitment *is*. That is, what exactly is the deliverable? How many tubulars, and where in Notrees[7] do they have to be delivered?

"The second is being fuzzy on the 'when.' I always tell the hotshot the hour by which the goods have to be delivered in Notrees. He understands that if the delivery is late, then I'm not getting what I paid for."

"You're on the money there," I volunteered. "How does that apply to software?"

Roscoe did not hesitate. "Software guys would be well-served if they were a little more precise on what it is that's going to be delivered, and when. That would cut out a lot of the whining about whether they made it or not. It's got to be unambiguous, cut-and-dried, and not subject to endless negotiation after the fact.

"Because," he emphasized, "a commitment is a contract without the 'weasel words.' A commitment doesn't have any fine print. There are no loopholes to hide behind when you don't deliver."

I couldn't help but be amazed at what happened when simple Texas oil field logic was applied to the software business. But I had at least one concern right away.

Spec Wars?

"Wait a minute, Roscoe," I jumped in. "I've got a little problem with your desire to pin down exactly what it is that will be delivered. Walker Royce has told me over and over again that trying to achieve too much precision early in a project is a big waste of time. For instance, insisting on extremely precise delivery conditions just leads to lots of arguing about the specs."

"Actually," replied Roscoe, "I agree with Walker. Spending lots of time on the details of what you'll deliver is like lawyers arguing about the commas in their contracts. We want to avoid that at all costs. Otherwise, nothing will ever get done, and we will spend way too much time generating useless documents.

"But there is a *real* problem that does need to be addressed. Here's an example. All too often, an engineer or a programmer commits to deliver a piece of code by a week from Friday, for inclusion in a larger project build. On that date the bits arrive, but the code is buggy. It takes another week to get that settled. Then you discover that when the

---

[7] Appropriately named town in the west Texas desert.

array used in his calculation goes from 100 elements to 1,000, the algorithm takes 100 times as long to complete. So it takes another few weeks to fix that. By now all tasks that depended on that code are queued up and waiting."

Roscoe was warming to the task. He continued.

"The problem here is that the fellows never really agreed on what was to be delivered on that Friday. The programmer thought it was a piece of code. The manager wanted thoroughly debugged code that had good performance characteristics over a reasonable range of input conditions. Clearly, they didn't agree on what was to be delivered. The programmer will argue that he met his commitment by delivering the code; he will use the loophole that he didn't promise that all the bugs would be flushed out and fixed. But once you start down that slippery slope you are dead, because now you're arguing about how big a bug might 'reasonably' escape testing (if he did any testing at all, by the way). And the programmer will also argue that performance was never discussed, although his use of a quadratic algorithm[8] violates all our notions of competency and professional behavior."

Who had educated Roscoe on quadratic algorithms, I wondered?

"Now I am *not* saying that to fix this problem requires a detailed spec, down to exact performance numbers. But just like the oil field guy who reasonably expects his tubulars to get to Notrees without being twisted like a pretzel, the software project manager should reasonably expect that when he gets a piece of code, it's not just half-baked. Especially when the programmer knows it's going into a project build, where it will be used by other people.

"That's what I'm trying to get at," Roscoe said, leaning back in his chair.

The Three Most Common Excuses

I gently asked Roscoe if he had any insight into why people consistently missed their commitments. Needless to say, he had an opinion on the subject.

"Looks to me like, in the software development business, most commitments are dead the moment they're made. People just don't think enough before they commit. If they understood the consequences of committing to something, they would be a lot more careful. Let me give you some examples.

---

[8] The input array went from 100 elements to 1,000, or a factor of 10 larger; processing time went up by 100, which is 10 squared, so we say that the algorithm has quadratic characteristics. Quadratic algorithms are easy to program, but fatal to any program to be employed seriously, as we can see. We'd like algorithms to be linear with respect to their input, if possible. The competent programmer identifies quadratic (or worse) algorithms and replaces them, most often with algorithms that are at worst $n \log(n)$, which means they go as linear times the logarithm of linear. Sometimes that's the best you can do.

"One of the three most common excuses is 'I had a lot of unplanned interruptions.' Now whose problem is that? Certainly not mine. I didn't make the commitment. The person who made the commitment should have taken that into account when he made the commitment, or turned away the interruptions when they arrived. Clearly he didn't give high enough priority to the commitment he made to *me*, because he let other jobs squeeze it out. Whatever happened to the notion of 'a prior commitment' "?

"Wait a minute, Roscoe," I exclaimed. "Stuff happens. If you are digging fencepost holes and it begins to rain, you have to stop. What about that?"

"Well, it does rain," he said. "My point is that you have to take that into account in your estimate. If it rains on average 50 percent of the time, your estimate better not assume it never rains. You can't make that assumption and then complain that it rained on you."

Well, I thought, it does seem that people don't think enough about stuff like that. Many of their commitments are based on scenarios where everything goes perfectly. Not allowing for the normal things that always go wrong is one of the things that get them into trouble and cause them to miss commitments.

"OK, what's number two?" I asked Roscoe.

"Second common excuse: 'The job was harder than I thought it would be.' Once again, whose fault is that? I didn't make the estimate, he did. If he wasn't sure he could get it done, he shouldn't have committed. If he didn't understand the job well enough to make a good estimate, he shouldn't have committed. Getting blindsided midway into the job is just flat-out unprofessional. Just because you made a lousy estimate doesn't get you off the hook. You had volition, but not enough competency."

How often had I heard that one? Usually the poor guy would explain how he worked day and night to deliver, but the job was just much, much harder than he thought it would be. And he expected sympathy. I often found myself feeling bad for the guy who had just let me down. How backwards was that?

"Well, I have to admit," I said, "sometimes people seem to commit based on an idea that they know how to do it. Too often, I guess, they only figure it out once they get into it. Perhaps they should ask for a little more time to study it before they commit."

Roscoe nodded. It was clear that he would rather wait for a better estimate than get a bad commitment. What, I asked, was the third common excuse?

"And last," continued Roscoe, "is the old 'My subcontractor let me down.' In this case, the person who made the commitment farmed out part of the job to a third party, who in turn didn't deliver. Now, is that my problem? Hell no. I didn't do the farming out; in fact, I didn't even know about this third party. Although it may be true that he (the third party) failed on his commitment, that is no concern of mine. My commitment is with the first guy. I have to hold him responsible. End of story."

Well, I had to admit, I'd heard that one, too.

And Another Thing…

So, I said to Roscoe, this whole train wreck boiled down to not honoring commitments? Wasn't that a little simplistic?

"You can look at this from lots of different directions, but I always come up with the same answer," said Roscoe.

"There are these guys who draw up these PERT charts and Gantt charts and try to plan everything down to a gnat's eyelash. Now we may or may not agree that this is a worthwhile exercise, and intelligent people can have differences of opinion on the subject. One thing I know for sure: It is hard to get all the dependencies right, and there will always be new tasks introduced midstream that you didn't plan on.

"Now, these charts look like spider webs to me. If I abstract out the detail, one way to think about this is that the result is dependent on the integrity of the web. Call it a network if you want to. For me, it is a complicated set of links in a very complicated n-dimensional chain."

I was trying to figure out where Roscoe was going with this. I knew he wasn't going to give me a treatise on graph theory. But rather than interject, I bided my time.

"Now, I can try to figure out what will happen to my schedule if one link screws up. That is, if that link is on the critical path, I know for sure it will make the whole project late. If the link is not on the critical path, it may or may not make us late, depending on how late that particular activity is.

"But we all know that projects usually get late not because of one catastrophic failure—one link seriously broken—but because many, many links are a little late—or should we say, a little broken. So my idea is that the integrity of the schedule is an accumulation of the integrity of each and every one of the links.

"And what," finished Roscoe triumphantly, "is each link other than a commitment? My guess is that most projects get into trouble because of the accumulation of all the commitments that aren't delivered. That's one reason why most project managers never know why they failed. It wasn't one big screw-up; it was just lots and lots of little things that piled up. It's insidious."

Thrust, Parry, and Riposte

There was one thing about this argument that was bothering me, so I thought I'd better get it out on the table with Roscoe pronto.

"Roscoe," I volunteered, "I understand your desire to put some more realism and honesty into the process, but frankly I think you are off in the weeds here. How can you compare a simple, deterministic, closed-end task such as hotshotting a bunch of tubulars to Notrees with delivering a large, complex piece of software which, after all, is fraught with discovery, new technology, and uncertainty? That's not a fair comparison, is it?"

"Sorry, son," replied Roscoe, "but you're the one who's confused. The correct analogy is comparing the delivery of the complex software product with getting the first barrel of oil out of the well. Who ever said that was easy or deterministic? If it was, we'd never have a dry hole, would we? But I'll tell you, sure as God made little green apples, that the timely delivery of any oil at all is the accumulation of all the interdependent subtasks, including getting the tubulars to Notrees on time. What I am arguing is that all complex projects, from oil well drilling to software, are eventually decomposable into small, finite tasks. Each of them can be estimated, some with greater or less uncertainty. But in the end, each of those finite tasks and its estimate represents a commitment.

"Here's another way to look at it. We are trying, always, to work in what we call a *high-trust environment*. A high-trust environment is one in which you can depend implicitly on the other guy. Well, the 'unit of trust' is the commitment."

Why then, I argued, did people working on large projects take individual estimates and commitments so cavalierly?

Large Project Chicken

"Oh, that's easy," Roscoe replied. "The boys down at NASA relearned that one. It's called *large project chicken*. On any large project, people always think that the other guy is going to be 'more late' than they are. They depend on the notion that their small slip will be masked by the other guy's even bigger slip. The folklore at NASA was that on any launch countdown, you had to get into the single digits before someone would blink first and stop the launch. They were all waiting for the other guy to chicken out first."

Now that sounded really serious. Roscoe confirmed that it was.

"Yeah, that whole psychology is really foobarred," Roscoe finished, showing that he had learned some software lingo. "Any time you couple your 'success' to someone else's failure, you are on the road to perdition. But, in fact, that is what 'large project chicken' is all about. You are counting on the other guy to screw up worse than you. It is a very destructive force against good project morale and it totally undermines the idea of a high-trust environment."

Roscoe was right again, but I had a few more arrows in my quiver.

The End of Software Development as We Know It?

"Well, Roscoe," I said, "I've got another problem with your approach. Given this heightened sensitivity to meeting commitments, won't each individual estimate be so conservative that when you roll up all the tasks into a schedule, you'll find out that the project shouldn't go forward because it's going to take three times too long?"

"Kind of a long sentence there, Joe," winked Roscoe. "Yes, that is a problem. And I have two answers to it.

"First, you do have to get past the issue of sandbagging.[9] You have to push back on estimates that are so conservative that no task or commitment is ever missed. You need to get people to be estimating so that they make 80 to 90 percent of their commitments. Today I would guess we don't hit 50 percent, which is ridiculous.

"Second, maybe we should cancel more projects early. My problem is that I see too many schedules that are nothing more than a roll up of everyone's best case estimates on the subtasks. These aren't schedules; they are exercises in wishful thinking. These projects are doomed to failure before they ever get out of the blocks. The worker bees are telling their managers what they think they want to hear, and the managers are drinking their own bath water. Then a few months or years later, the whole charade comes crashing down around everyone's ears, and the witch-hunts begin. YOU SOFTWARE GUYS HAVE GOT TO STOP DOING THAT!!!"

The blood vessel on Roscoe's right temple looked as though it was about to burst, so I backed off a bit and made my parting shot a polite one.

Elaboration Versus Construction

"How about this," I ventured. "In the Rational Unified Process, the middle two steps, Elaboration and Construction, take most of the time.[10] I can see commitment-based schedules during Construction, when we have a pretty good handle on what we are doing. But I'm still having a problem during Elaboration, where there is still a lot of discovery and risk."

"Good point," admitted Roscoe. "Let's start with Construction. Even there we still miss wildly today because of missed commitments, so nailing that down will certainly improve our performance. Point taken.

"And, by the way, I suspect that the reason so many Construction commitments are missed is that the tasks were poorly estimated during Elaboration. Missing lots of

---

[9] *Sandbagging* is an American slang term that implies inflating an estimate so that you are sure that you will always make it with ease. Salespeople have occasionally been known to sandbag estimates of the sales potential of their territory downward in hopes of getting a sales quota they can easily exceed. Sales managers may let this slip by them once in awhile, but it is unheard of for this to happen two years in a row. The second time it happens, the salesperson is either fired or promoted to sales manager, as the case may be.

[10] Recall that the four phases are Inception, Elaboration, Construction, and Transition.

commitments during Construction is usually a sure symptom that we closed off Elaboration prematurely, perhaps because we were date-driven. We pay the piper in the next phase, of course.

"But," he continued, "let's go back to Elaboration. We still need to do a better job of scoping and estimating the research and discovery tasks which, I will remind you, can all be broken down into smaller subtasks, each with less uncertainty and susceptible to a better estimate.

"And, in fact, we do need commitments to hard dates during Elaboration, because we need a forcing function to get decisions made. Otherwise, we study the problem endlessly. Committing to a date to make a decision on some risky item is a good thing. It focuses the effort and makes sure we get closure."

I was out of counterarguments. As usual, Roscoe had thought six moves ahead, not two.

Tough Love

"So," said Roscoe, "we are going back to the woodshed. I'm going to sit down with my managers and explain the facts of life to them. We're going to have honest estimates and real commitments. And Heaven help those who don't deliver the next time.

"Oh, and by the way," he admitted sheepishly, "I won't be asleep at the switch next time, either…"

Somehow, I had the feeling that Roscoe's first slip might well be his last.

Recap

The contents of this chapter have provoked more heated discussion than the rest of the book combined. Software developers and their managers are very uncomfortable with the hard line I take on commitments. They keep trying to explain to me that "software development is different."

Well, sorry, folks, but I just don't believe it. Every area of human endeavor has risk and uncertainty. Every project ever undertaken has some new or novel element in it. All projects have schedules that are too short and resources that are inadequate. Just ask your brethren in other domains. You are not that special.

It's not that I'm unsympathetic, you understand. Software does have some peculiar problems. The most vicious of these is management's misconception that large changes can be made at the last minute through the magic of changing just one line of code. This is not reality, but fantasy. More likely, when a problem is found, it will take major rework, just like in any other area where architecture governs the result.

Another frequently heard argument is that all ambitious software development projects have new and unique aspects that make their scheduling difficult and their deliveries uncertain, that it is more fundamentally an R&D activity. I have two counterarguments.

- First, if one uses a process that constrains and contains the R&D part of the project to an "elaboration" phase (as in the Rational Unified Process), this activity can be monitored, controlled, and kept from becoming "unbounded." Risk-targeted iterative development helps a lot here.

- Second, I will wager that most software development projects are late not because the R&D activity, which after all is often but a small component of the total, was late. No, more often what happens is the project is late because of poor execution on the routine parts of the job, and then the R&D activity becomes the scapegoat. It is easier to get forgiveness for screwing up the rocket science part of the project than it is to get absolution for messing up the blocking and tackling.

What I want to crush, once and for all, is the notion that what makes software different is what makes it impossible to hold software people to their commitments. That idea is both wrong and dangerous. It gives everyone the ultimate excuse for not performing, and is at the root of a great deal of what makes software development an unprofessional activity today. Professionals take their commitments seriously, and there is always accountability. This concept is crucial both for the individuals who practice software engineering and the profession as a whole.

There is also a strong directive here for managers: Do not bully people into commitments that you want but they don't really believe are realistic. You may win the bullying war, but it will be a small consolation down the road when the commitment is not met. The only commitments that have a reasonable chance of being met are those where the compromise position between the manager and the developer makes both of them only slightly uncomfortable at the outset.

In the next chapter, I move on to a topic that is never discussed openly. This is the delicate subject of compensation. Why don't we find more help in this area? Look for some interesting new ideas on this in the pages that follow.

CHAPTER 16

Compensation

Compensation of software professionals is always controversial. Often there are tenfold differences in productivity between the best and worst performers on a development team, yet no conventional salary structure provides for this kind of dynamic range. In this chapter, I examine some new ways of looking at compensation and performance in software organizations. Although I provide no "silver bullet" for resolving the problem, I do provide a framework for thinking about it in a non-traditional way.

Here's one important conclusion: Many problems that we seek to solve with compensation are really job assignment or skills development issues that need to be attacked with tools appropriate to those domains.[1] I attempt to tie together three variables: compensation, skill level, and job difficulty. As compensation is linked to performance, the challenge is to correlate performance with skill level and job difficulty.[2]

---

[1] Disclaimer: The ideas presented here are those of the author. They do not represent the philosophy, policy, or practice of Rational Software. The author has benefited from extensive and penetrating discussions with his son Marc, who is the compensation specialist in the family.

[2] My exploration examines only one aspect of compensation: financial rewards such as salary, bonus, stock options, and so on. I will *not* consider intrinsic rewards and privileges, which might encompass "perks"—the large corner office with the window, for example—as well as visibility, power, and influence. However, I do want to emphasize that compensation does include more than just salary; management has at its disposal a wide variety of mechanisms for compensating team members and can adjust the compensation mix to fit the specific employee and organizational profile.

Going for the Flow

Let's begin by looking at the work of Mihaly Csikszentmihalyi,[3] who posits that humans have a *flow channel*, which roughly translates to the intense focus and sense of satisfaction we feel when our skill level is well matched to the challenges of our job.

If the task is too easy, boredom sets in, and people are unhappy (see Figure 16.1). If the task is—relatively speaking—very challenging compared to competence, then people become tense and anxious. When there is a reasonable match—not too easy, not too hard—then we are in the flow channel, which actually spans a broad range of competency and task difficulty. In this state of grace, achievement is high, and we experience a feeling of incredible well-being; athletes describe it as "being in the zone."[4]

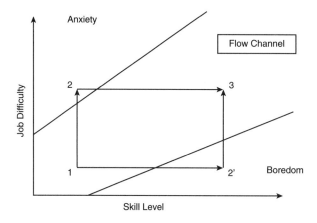

Figure 16.1   The flow model.

Note that, starting from position 1 in Figure 16.1, a person can move into an anxiety zone if the job difficulty increases without a corresponding increase in skills (position 2). To get back into the flow channel, any combination of skills improvement and decrease in difficulty will suffice, but the best move is a horizontal one, toward position 3. In a like manner, one can improve skills while job difficulty holds constant and move position 1

---

[3] Pronounced "chick-sent-me-high." See Csikszentmihalyi, Mihaly, *Flow: The Psychology of Optimal Experience*. (New York: HarperCollins, 1991).

[4] On the software development front, the person who epitomizes this state of being would have to be the legendary Howard Larsen, an early pioneer at Rational Software. Anyone who has worked with Howard will be nodding his head at this juncture; Howard is probably as far "up and to the right" as you can get in the programming flow channel. I'm sure that you either have a Howard in your organization or wish you did. And the real question is: Why are "Howards" so rare? Are "Howards" born or made, and, if made, how do we make more of them?

to position 2', where boredom sets in. Achieving flow then requires a move toward position 3—by seeking a more challenging job. Of course, then position 3 becomes the new position 1, and the cycle starts all over again. At position 3, however, there is a greater contribution to the organization than at position 1, even though they are both flow states. Clearly, moving up and to the right is a good result for both the team member and the organization. I believe the flow channel "opens up" as skill level and job difficulty increase, so individuals theoretically have more opportunities for job satisfaction.[5]

We should also state that being in the flow channel leads to *optimal* performance. One can be outside the flow channel and still perform at a level good enough to earn a "satisfactory" rating in many organizations. However, the farther from the flow channel one gets, the more performance degrades. And we should ask ourselves: *Why not set the goal of achieving optimal performance from everyone in the organization*? Would this not lead to the best possible "win-win" for both the organization and the individual?

There is obviously much, much more to Csikszentmihalyi's work, and this brief description does not do him justice. However, it does provide a basic understanding of the conceptual model I will use to frame our discussion of compensation.

Flow and Software Development Performance

Before we get deeply into the compensation discussion, however, let's look at how this idea of flow relates to productivity/performance in the software development environment. One of the most intriguing and confounding phenomena for development managers is the wide variability in productivity among team members. How do we account for these variations?

In my experience with a large number of projects and an even larger number of team members, I've seen that the productivity of architects, designers, programmers, and testers who find their flow channel vastly outstrips that of their peers who have not.[6]

Lower-productivity individuals typically exhibit one of the two characteristics Csikszentmihalyi identified: anxiety from being in over their heads (task difficulty >> skill level) or boredom because of insufficient challenge (skill level >> task difficulty). The results? Poor code—either because of inexperience and wheel reinvention in the first instance, or from procrastination and arrogance ("I can whip this thing together at the last minute if I have to") in the second.

Of course, another major factor in productivity is whether the company culture "pays" for performance rather than on the basis of how a job or a person looks on paper.

---

[5] I don't think this is part of Csikszentmihalyi's theory, but it seems like a reasonable extension to me. It is this "opening up" of the channel that leads to the three-dimensional cone I will introduce later in this chapter.

[6] In assessing productivity, I look at both quantity and quality of the software artifacts produced.

There is some confusion about what this means. In my simple view, job skills represent the *potential* to perform. Through training and experience, we attain skill levels that *should enable* high performance but do not ensure it.

In a like manner, job difficulty represents the *opportunity* to perform. That is, a particularly challenging job provides an arena in which a combination of effort and skills can produce a great result. For a highly motivated and skilled individual, the lack of a sufficient outlet is frustrating, as there is no opportunity to shine. But just as with skills, simply having the challenge by no means guarantees high performance.

So ideally, we want to pay for performance, meaning *results*, or total contribution to the organization. And that means we need to understand *all* the factors that affect performance. These include more than simply the balances and imbalances in skill and job difficulty. For example, motivation is a powerful factor. Also, people perform much better when they are engaged in activities they just enjoy doing. Yet another factor is confidence in one's abilities; good performance can generate a positive feedback loop that leads to even greater confidence and higher performance.

When one is in the flow channel, motivation and enjoyment of the job are at their highest, and confidence soars. So the concept of flow is consistent with these other factors that affect productivity/performance.

However, we should be careful not to neglect motivational factors that are independent of flow. In particular, we should not underestimate the motivational effects that come from commitment to a mission and feeling part of a great team. And, of course, individuals go through cycles of increased or decreased motivation because of other things that are occurring in their lives.

Finally, *perceived* compensation can be either a motivator or a demotivator. People who feel they are being unfairly compensated, either absolutely or relative to others, can become demotivated to the point that their performance suffers. (The problem here, of course, is that these may be to some extent *perceived* inequities; employees may overestimate their contribution and/or peer compensation.) So there is yet another feedback loop that needs to be considered.

Although all these factors affect performance, and hence compensation, in the rest of this chapter I will stick to Csikszentmihalyi's flow model, with the understanding that this oversimplifies a very complex affair. I choose to do this because I believe we can directly affect three factors—skill levels, job difficulty, and compensation—whereas some of the other factors I have mentioned are much more difficult for us to influence.

Applying the Flow Model to Compensation

In the following discussion, I will assume three zones of compensation: correct, underpaid, and overpaid. *Overpaid* means the team member in question is compensated at a level greater than the level at which he or she contributes to the organization. *Underpaid* means the team member's compensation level is lower than his level of contribution to the organization.[7] We achieve *correct compensation* when there is a balance between contribution and compensation for the team member in *this* job, and within *this* organization; all bets are off relative to other contexts.[8] And clearly, a team member who is just not doing a good job is always, by definition, being overpaid.

Skills-Based Model

Some organizations compensate by skill level, without considering job difficulty as a dominant factor. This is more common in government organizations and those that focus on seniority, where the assumption is that skills increase with time. Based on the model in *Flow*, Figure 16.2 depicts this approach.

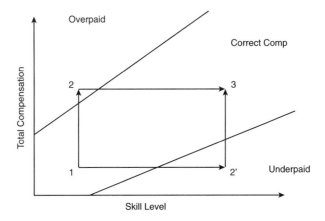

Figure 16.2   Model for skills-based compensation.

As we see, there is a zone of "correct compensation," where the compensation level is appropriate for the skill set of the team member in the job. Positions 1 and 3 are in this zone, although position 3 is clearly compensated more than position 1.

In position 2, the team member is earning more than is appropriate for his or her skill level. This may or may not be dysfunctional; for example, the team member may be doing a difficult job, one that requires more skills than the team member currently has, and is being compensated accordingly. Or, it may just be an error.

---

[7] I assume that the contribution to the organization can be objectively and consistently measured.

[8] I should note the nagging problem of "scarcity premiums" paid for certain skills when and where there is a temporary imbalance between supply and demand in the marketplace. I abstract this from the current discussion but come back to it later in the chapter.

In position 2', the team member is being underpaid for his or her skill level. Once again, there may be different reasons for this. The team member may be truly underemployed, or the job may not leverage his or her full skill set.

Job-Based Model

Some organizations worry less about skill levels and compensate according to the difficulty of the job (or, as a surrogate, responsibility). This model is more typical of entrepreneurial, start-up ventures (see Figure 16.3).[9]

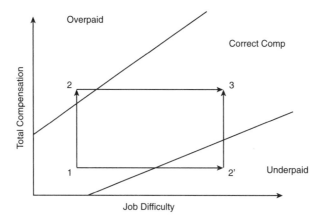

Figure 16.3   Job-based compensation model.

Once again, positions 1 and 3 represent correct compensation, and 3 is more highly compensated than 1.

In position 2, the team member is being overpaid relative to the difficulty of the job. This can occur for a variety of reasons. It may be an error, or it may be that the jobholder possesses high-level skills or credentials, but the current job assignment does not make use of those skills.

In position 2', the team member is underpaid. This is typical of a person promoted to a new and difficult job who has not yet received a corresponding compensation bump.

Note that in this model and the previous one, when someone is at 2, the remedies are to increase either skill level or job difficulty at the current compensation level. When team members are at 2', the appropriate response is to increase compensation.

---

[9] It is also generally true of executive compensation; such jobs are often benchmarked by similar positions at similarly sized firms.

No matter what the model, it is always difficult to move into the "zone" by decreasing job difficulty, skill level, or compensation. Organizations do not usually support downward changes. I will discuss this in more detail later.

Introducing the Cone of Correct Compensation

I now combine these models into a three-dimensional graph, introducing a *Cone of Correct Compensation* (see Figure 16.4).

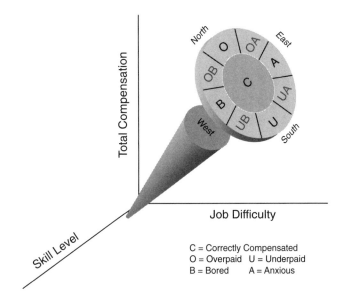

Figure 16.4   The Cone of Correct Compensation.

This cone represents the state in which skill levels, job difficulty, and compensation are all in balance. The region inside this cone, indicated by the "C" at the center of the projection, represents the classic "win-win" situation. The team member is neither bored nor anxious; he or she is in the flow channel. Compensation is also correct; the team member is neither underpaid nor overpaid. He or she operates at peak productivity, and the organization is paying a fair price for this. Note that the cone opens up because, as all variables increase, there is more latitude for getting the compensation right.[10]

---

[10] This appears to be true in actual practice; the margin for error seems to be tighter at lower levels.

The other eight zones represent "out of cone" scenarios. I have labeled them with compass directions to help navigate through the rest of the discussion.

It is possible, although sometimes challenging, to correct the problems in directions E and W. Here, team members are correctly compensated but are either bored or anxious. In these regions, productivity is suboptimal but the issues involve a skills/difficulty mismatch, so fiddling with compensation doesn't help.

The issues in the N and S directions are relatively simple to deal with. In this case, the team member is in the flow channel but is either underpaid or overpaid. An adjustment needs to be made to bring the equation back into balance, so that neither the team member nor the organization profits excessively from the team member being in the flow channel.

We will discuss the other four directions, which are somewhat more pathological, in the next section. After that, I will consider in greater detail the E, W and N, S scenarios I just described. In both discussions, I take the projection of the cone and depict it as a two-dimensional plot. The four diagonal cases become a two-by-two plot in the next section; after that, the center and eight compass directions become a three-by-three plot.

Diagonal Cases

This section focuses on the four extreme cases that involve team members who are in the wrong jobs and incorrectly compensated. These fall at the four diagonal corners of the cone—NE, NW, SE, and SW, respectively, as represented in Figure 16.5.

	Bored	Anxious	
Overpaid	Relatively easy jobs, paid by skill level; costly for the organization	Performance pay without skills development; (Peter Principle)	N
Underpaid	Underemployed	Hard jobs, over-achievers paid by skill level; long-term untenable (burnout)	S
	W	E	

Figure 16.5   Team members who are in the wrong jobs and incorrectly compensated.

Please note that team members may be "incorrectly compensated" for many reasons, including historical errors, temporary disequilibria in the marketplace between supply and demand of specialized skill sets, and so on.

The upper-left box (NW) contains team members who are being paid for their skill level but are doing relatively easy jobs that could be filled at lower cost to the organization by less skilled team members. This is a bad box: Productivity is intrinsically low relative to pay, and there is an opportunity cost to the organization because it does not exploit these team members' full potential.

The lower-left box (SW) represents the bored, underpaid team members of the world. They are at least marginally qualified, have relatively easy jobs, and are not paid a lot. Sometimes the combination of boredom and lack of compensation spurs them to seek other opportunities; often they vegetate. This class represents a waste of human capital. Some civil service workers fit into this category.[11]

The lower-right box (SE) contains the strivers in the organization: those who are doing hard jobs with relatively inadequate skills, and being underpaid in the bargain. This combination is untenable in the long term, as these team members will burn out sooner or later.

Finally, the upper-right box (NE) represents team members who are being overpaid for being overextended. They may do well temporarily but ultimately will fail unless they get some skills development. As there is a strong monetary incentive for them to continue to "get in over their heads," they are great candidates for proving the Peter Principle.[12]

The Nine Possibilities

In Figure 16.6, I consider all nine possible cases for our cone model, not just the four most pathological cases I showed in Figure 16.5.

Here the cone of correct compensation is depicted by the center bulls-eye, where flow has been achieved and the compensation level is just right. In this case, the team member is happy and productive, and the organization is getting the best productivity at a fair price.

---

[11] This is not a gratuitous swipe at civil servants, many of whom are incredibly hard-working and dedicated. Rather, it is an indictment of the kinds of jobs they are asked to do in many cases. And because we tend to have a lot of them, there is not much money to pay each of them.

[12] The *Peter Principle* asserts that people rise to their level of incompetence in any organization. One reason for this is that there is an economic benefit (better compensation) to taking on harder jobs or more responsibility. As long as they can "hang in there," the team members reason, it is better to be stressed for more compensation rather than for less. And, as most organizations do not move people backwards, there is a tendency for people to rise until it is obvious that no more upward movement is possible. This generally results in people stalling out and stagnating at least one level over their heads. This phenomenon is used to explain the perceived widespread incompetence in the management ranks of many organizations.

	Bored	In Flow	Anxious	
Overpaid	Easy job paid by skill, org loses more	Productive team members, org does slightly worse	Performance pay without skills development, Peter Principle	N
Correctly Paid	Suboptimal performance, both lose	Win-Win	Suboptimal performance, both lose	
Underpaid	Under-employed, no winners	Productive team members, org does slightly better	Hard jobs, overachievers paid by skill, burnout	S
	W		E	

Figure 16.6 Nine possibilities in and around the Cone of Correct Compensation.

In the middle row left and right (E and W), compensation is fair, but both the team member and the organization lose, because productivity is suboptimal. In this case, tinkering with compensation does nothing to address the problems that cause team member unhappiness and organizational loss of productivity. This is a pure difficulty/skills mismatch and needs to be addressed along those axes.

In the middle column, top and bottom (N and S), the team member is in flow, and productivity is maximized. Compensation should be adjusted to ensure that neither the team member nor the organization profits excessively from that situation. Clearly, this is easy to do for the underpaid case; for the overpaid case, we usually hold compensation constant while increasing both of the other variables (job difficulty and skill level) in balance.

The four corner cases were discussed in the previous section.

In the next section, I will discuss the stability of these various states, along with actions that managers can take to get team members and the organization to a win-win state.

Instability of North, South, East, and West

We know that the center in the previous figure represents an optimal condition, and once a team member is there, we need to continue to move him or her along the "body diagonal" of the cone to keep him or her in the region of correct compensation.

We also know that the four corners are potential sink states, or places where things either degenerate rapidly or are long-term costly to the team member and/or organization.

Are the four middle states stable? Although they are not as dangerous as the corner states, the problem is that they tend not to be stable over the long term if left unattended (see Figure 16.7).

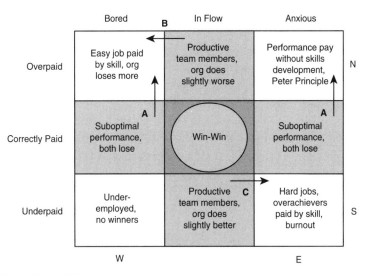

Figure 16.7   Unattended middle states move toward corners.

In both cases in the middle row (E and W), the correctly paid team member who is not in a state of flow will become less and less productive because of either anxiety or boredom. At some point, he or she will migrate upward on the chart, as indicated by the arrows labeled "A," moving into the overpaid category. This will happen without any nominal rise in compensation; it is strictly the effect of becoming less productive at constant compensation.

We have observed that in-flow team members who are overpaid (N) tend to get bored. This makes them less productive and moves them into the NW corner, as indicated by the arrow labeled "B." I have also observed that in-flow team members who are underpaid (S) tend to become anxious as a result of the inequity they see in their compensation. This has a tendency to throw them out of flow and into the SE corner, as indicated by the arrow labeled "C." (As they become less productive, they also become less underpaid.)

Getting to Win-Win

A good management objective is to get all team members to the win-win area inside the cone and to keep them there. Most organizations do not have the flexibility to easily reduce team members' job difficulty, nor are they likely to want (or be able) to reduce compensation. It is also meaningless to talk about reducing skill levels as a way to achieve equilibrium,[13] although sometimes a lateral move may have that effect—in other words,

---

[13] Lobotomies are typically frowned upon.

some of the team member's current skill set may be inapplicable in the new position, and new skills will have to be developed. But usually the only way to address an imbalance is by moving other variables in a positive direction, as opposed to changing things in a negative direction.

Most of the recommended remedies shown in Figure 16.8 are self-explanatory, but we'll examine a few special cases.

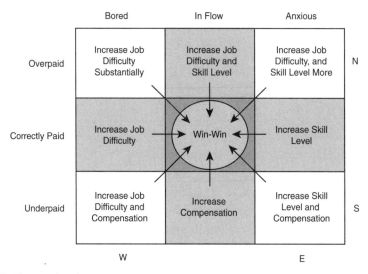

Figure 16.8   Getting to win-win.

In the NW corner, the only remedy is to dramatically increase either job difficulty or responsibility. The team member has the skills and is already being paid for a more difficult challenge.

In the N box, care must be taken to increase skill level and job difficulty in proportion so as to not violently throw the team member out of flow. In the NE box, skills must be increased *more* than the increase in job difficulty, else disaster looms.

Increasing skill level is tricky. It usually cannot be done overnight and may involve training, coaching, mentoring, and other methods that require time. Team members who have potential but need skills improvement need to be identified *early*, so that remedial action can be taken before the situation becomes so acute that the improvement cannot take place within a reasonable timeframe.

Note that of the eight suboptimal cases, only one can be addressed by solely increasing compensation. Five cases require no compensation action but do require adjustment of skill levels and job difficulty to get back into the cone. The remaining two cases require adjusting either skill levels or job difficulty in combination with compensation. So, remarkably, compensation is a partial remedy in only three out of the eight dysfunctional situations.

Mapping Current Team Members

If you are managing a team, do the following experiment. Lay out the three-by-three grid with "Win-Win" in the middle, and then assign each team member to one of the nine boxes. You will find yourself thinking about people in ways you have not previously considered. You may find people with otherwise different backgrounds clustered in the same box.

After you have finished the allocation, you will have some idea of both the development plan and the compensation strategy for each class. The exercise forces you to look at both aspects at the same time, something we sometimes forget to do. This methodology also makes discussions with team members more constructive, as you can show them that you have considered all the variables as you figure out their path forward.

Mapping New Team Members

When recruiting in a tight labor market, we sometimes have to pay somewhat more for a new hire than we would like. Equity vis à vis current team members becomes an issue. And sometimes making an attractive offer involves improving the prospective team member's situation relative to the one he already has, which may be the result of an aberration in his current organization.

One way to approach such situations is to lay out your current roster on the grid and see where the new player will fit. If it becomes clear that the salary inequity will cause not only an immediate problem but also long-term development problems, then perhaps you need to reconsider your offer.

Money Isn't Always the Answer

We might have titled this chapter, "When Is a Compensation Problem Not a Compensation Problem?" When problems arise, managers often have a knee-jerk response that leads them to focus on compensation. But many times the problem is dysfunctional behavior that might be caused in part by a compensation problem and have other root causes as well. Simply changing compensation (which always means raising it) may not achieve the desired result. Using the cone analysis method gives you a way to look at all the variables simultaneously. If you think a team member is out of the cone, the first thing to do is determine which of the eight boxes he or she is in. Then, and only then, can you proceed with a solution.

Doing this kind of analysis is also a reminder that we need to better understand the coupling between development plans for individuals and their compensation trajectories. Dealing with either of these without careful consideration of the other is worse than just solving "half the problem" at a time. Unless you take a gestalt view of the situation and

formulate a plan that considers skills progression, job difficulty, and compensation together at one time, both parts of the equation will probably come up short. The cone
methodology provides a coherent way of looking at the whole picture and helps us do a
better job of retaining and developing team members, and improving their productivity.

A very senior manager[14] read a draft of this chapter and remarked, "I think it's a great
point that needs to be made, but I'm terribly afraid that managers will misunderstand the
importance of matching assignment, skills, and motivation to optimize results. If as-
signments are made on the basis of compensation, it's a disaster. In fact, compensation
is irrelevant to making the right assignment; optimal compensation should result from
optimal assignment, and not the other way around."

So, with this order of priorities in mind, one answer to the koan[15] of correct compensation is the cone of correct compensation. Use this technique to get people in the
right jobs with the right skill levels, and motivate them for optimal performance. Once
you do that, it is easier to get their compensation right.

Recap

Some people have asked the following logical question:

> "If we go back to Csikszentmihalyi's two-dimensional plot of job difficulty versus
> skill level, we can infer that the team member is more productive when in the flow
> channel and less productive when outside it. Can we use this information to predict
> total contribution to the organization as a function of job difficulty and skill level?"

The answer is that we can try to model this information. The model would be very useful, because if we knew the contribution, we could try to make the compensation relate
more closely to it.

Recall that in our basic flow channel model (refer to Figure 16.1), the channel consists of two lines that go upward and to the right. So let us make a few simplifying assumptions. In our simplified model, these two lines are parallel and the flow channel does
not "open up." I assume that factors affecting productivity outside the flow model are
small compared to those implicit in the flow model. As I have clearly stated elsewhere,
this is a big assumption, and it should cause us to not attach more to these predictions
than the model itself justifies. Productivity affects contribution, which in turn should affect compensation, so we need to understand the factors we exclude from the model that
can materially affect productivity.

---

[14] John Lovitt, who was responsible for Rational Software's Field organization for many years.

[15] The Concise Oxford Dictionary defines a koan as follows: "Riddle used in Zen to teach inadequacy of
logical reasoning. [Jap., = public plan]." The atrocious pun notwithstanding, I hope I have shown that
correct compensation does not have to be a riddle immune to logical reasoning.

Next, I'll assume that contribution—the "performance" we are paying for—is the product of job difficulty and productivity. That is, for equally productive people, those doing harder jobs are contributing more.

I'll also assume that, at a given level of job difficulty, all skill levels within the flow channel have equal productivity, arbitrarily set to 1. This seems reasonable, as team members can be optimally productive anywhere within the flow channel. In the example we will see next, the flow channel is fairly wide; this is part of the model. Setting the breadth of the channel relative to other factors is one way to "tune" the model.

Then, I will assume that, at the same level of job difficulty (a horizontal line on the plot), productivity tails off as we move farther and farther away from the flow channel, both in the anxiety region and the boredom region. In our example, I have made this productivity degradation fairly rapid once outside the channel. At one skill level outside the channel, productivity drops to 0.75; at the second, to 0.50; at the third, to 0.25; and at the fourth to zero. If we choose a different rate at which productivity decreases, we will get a different profile. This is another way to "tune" the model.

The plot in Figure 16.9 shows the contribution measured in arbitrary units; I center the plot on 100 units of contribution. The level of difficulty of the job changes by 10 units in the flow channel for each step up or down. Please remember that this is a very simple model. Yet it may capture the effective contribution to first order, if Csikszentmihalyi's theory is valid. If we agree on the model, then we also have a notion for how compensation should go as a function of skill level and job difficulty.

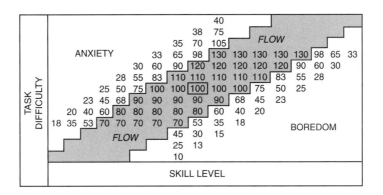

Figure 16.9   Effective contribution using Csikszentmihalyi's flow model.

As an example, consider the person represented by the boxed "100". He or she has a contribution level of 100 and is in the flow channel. Assume this person is being paid 100 units for his 100 units of contribution. Compare this with the person outside the channel at the same task level with a contribution equal to 75 units; that person could be outside and at 75 either to the left or the right of the flow channel. If that person's compensation is greater than 75 units, we would consider him overpaid according to this model, as his pay is greater than his contribution. Or, to put it another way, if the person in the channel contributing 100 units and the person outside the channel contributing 75 units are both being paid 85 units, then one is underpaid and the other is overpaid.

This is an interesting way to make comparisons, and one that I have not seen elsewhere.

This ends Part 4. I now move on to "thinking laterally."

Part 5

THINKING LATERALLY

We've been through some pretty tough sledding in the last two parts. Both the project-management view and the human-element chapters asked that you think hard about some of the thornier parts of our craft. In this section, there's a bit of a respite. Before I work up to the crescendo of the symphony in Part 6, "Advanced Topics," I have a quiet interlude for you.

The theme of this section is that software people think differently. Some of their ideas are speculative, maybe a little off the beaten track. It's helpful to gain the insight of seeing some of the various ways in which they look at problems. Much as sports have been referred to as the "toy department of life," you can take this section as the toy department of this book.

In Chapter 17, "History Lesson," I discuss an interesting episode in naval architecture. The sinking of the Swedish warship Vasa on its maiden voyage centuries ago can provide some valuable lessons for software developers.

Chapter 18, "Bad Analogies," confronts the issue of pseudoscience. Using bad scientific analogies to "explain" software to non-practitioners gets us into trouble, so this topic is worth exploring.

In Chapter 19, "The Refresh Problem," I look at an interesting problem in a new light—how should we go about updating software in an installed base? The answer I propose may surprise you.

Finally, in Chapter 20, "Not So Random Numbers," we have our last visit with Roscoe Leroy. Therein he relates to us some calculations he once made on a desert island, without the benefit of any computers. This tale shows us how to analyze a problem that starts out simple but turns out to be more complex than we thought.

CHAPTER 17

History Lesson

In 1993 and 1994, I lived in Stockholm, on assignment at one of our largest and most important customers. Jaak Urmi, my friend and temporary boss, insisted that I spend an afternoon at the Vasa Museum in Stockholm Harbor. The museum is "one of a kind."[1] The Vasa was the pride of the Swedish Royal Navy, launched in August 1628. Twenty minutes into her maiden voyage, she caught a small gust and sank to the bottom of Stockholm Harbor. She was raised 333 years later and today is meticulously restored and on display. Because there have been centuries to work on a post-mortem, and because naval architecture has made significant advances during this time, we now know a lot about why the Vasa sank. Some interesting lessons can be learned from this fiasco, and some of them apply to software development.[2]

---

[1] See http://www.vasamuseet.se.

[2] Tom Love and I independently made the connection between software and the Vasa at about the same time. See Tom Love, *Object Lessons: Lessons Learned in Object-Oriented Development Projects* (New York: SIGS Books, 1993), p. 1-6. This material was originally written in February 1994 and was published in the Rational technical newsletter as "What Can We Learn from the Vasa?" *The Sheep* (#40, June 1995), p. 7-8. It also appeared, with permission and attribution, in Pierre Robillard and Philippe Kruchten, *Software Engineering Processes: With the UPEDU* (Boston: Pearson Education, 2002), p. 151-152.

Don't Let the King Be Your Architect

One of the Vasa's problems was that she was specified and re-specified by the king himself. The boat was midway between the "small boat" design and the "large boat" design of the day. The keel was originally laid for a small boat, and then lengthened somewhat. This inhibited the builders from making her appropriately wider, although they tried. In the end, the Vasa became a tall, narrow boat.

Additionally, she had two gun decks. Originally, she was designed to have only one. But the king heard that a boat was being built in rival Denmark with two gun decks, and he wanted to be competitive. The late addition of the second gun deck made the boat top-heavy.

Software people have a term for this. It's called a *kludge*.

Things Aren't Always as They Seem

When you see the Vasa today, your first impression is "No way!" The boat looks tall, narrow, and top-heavy. However, it turns out that boats of that epoch were all of this design, and most of them were stable. Calculations conducted today on the resurrected ship show that the numbers were off, but not by as much as you might think; the center of stability is only several *inches* too high. This is actually a surprising result.[3]

Checking the Design

There are no surviving plans for the Vasa, because there never were any! Today we would be scandalized by this lack of documentation, but it was not common in those days to have detailed drawings; the naval architect had a few carefully guarded calculation tables and rules of thumb, but most of the boat was built on-the-fly. Although this was the common practice in those days, and certainly not to be condoned as reasonable practice today, one can only speculate on whether having detailed drawings would have altered subsequent events.

Knowing What You Don't Know

The state of the practice in those days was very rudimentary. Calculations of center of mass and the like were not known or performed. It was basically impossible, given the

---

[3] Much of the technical information on the Vasa is drawn from the most authoritative book (in English) on the subject, *Why Wasa Capsized* (ISBN 91-85268-23-2), by Curt Borgenstam and Anders Sandström, around 1984. This thin book (80 pages) is published by the National Maritime Museum, Stockholm. My copy is one of 2,000 printed.

intellectual and practical tools of the day, to know if a design was stable or not. There was very little ability to predict anything. It is amazing more boats didn't sink.

This situation is not unlike bridge-building in America in the 1800s. Many, many bridges collapsed simply because engineers of the day didn't know how to calculate well enough. John Roebling, the builder of the Brooklyn Bridge, knew he didn't know how to do the calculations, so he built in very large safety factors. Smart man.

Continuity of Leadership

The principal builder, Henrik Hybertsson, died midway through the project, and there was a period before he died when both he and his assistant, Hein Jacobsson, were in charge. This didn't work very well—a good example of what happens when you lose a strong, single point of leadership.

In a Hurry, As Usual

The Vasa was built in about two years, and there was a lot of schedule pressure. This no doubt also contributed to some bad decision-making.

Focusing on the Wrong Features

It's very easy to be impressed by the ornate carvings and decorations that were accomplished in time for the launch. Clearly a lot of resources went into this work. It turns out that this was not just a matter of decoration; the function of this artwork was to impress and overawe Sweden's Baltic neighbors. And they might have served this function had the ship stayed afloat. This detail is a good example of "featuritis" defeating robustness.

When the Design Is Bad…

One of the criticisms of the day was that they didn't load enough ballast into the hold to make the boat more stable. Actually, they crammed as much in as they could, but there wasn't enough room. And, even if there had been, making the boat ride lower wouldn't have helped, because in the face of swells, water would have started pouring through the portals of the lower of the two gun decks. Of course, had there been only one gun deck…

The Relevance of Testing

Several days before the launch, the designers performed a very pragmatic stability test on the Vasa—they had 30 sailors run from one side of the boat to the other and back. After three iterations, they had to stop because the boat was heeling over too much. The test was a dismal failure.

However, the king was out of the country at the time, and no one else dared postpone the launch. The rest, as they say, is history.

Ironically, the notion that you can "test in" quality in software is equally fallacious. Once the boat (or software) is built, testing can only *characterize* what is there. On the other hand, if it is possible to do tests early and often, one can detect flaws that may be corrected in time. In this case, it is unlikely that this would have been possible. On the other hand, in most software development projects, early testing should be *de rigueur* as part of the iterative development process.

Prototype Versus Product

Given her (accidentally) experimental design, the Vasa should be considered a prototype, not a product. When they discovered she was unstable during test, they should have put her in the museum 333 years early. However, it was the king's boat, it cost 4 percent of the GNP that year, and it was needed in a hurry for an ongoing war. So they declared it a product and launched it.

The Inquest

Of the 150 people on board, between 30 and 50 lost their lives. Immediately after the tragedy, the surviving captain was arrested and put in prison. Of course there was an investigation. But as soon as competent people realized that so many of the problems could be traced back to the king himself, a lot of obfuscation took place. Nothing much ever came of the inquiries; no one was found guilty. The masts protruding above the surface of the water were sawn off, and the rest of the event was silently buried at sea.

We tend not to want to dig into our failures in software. I doubt there will ever be a museum dedicated to one of our more spectacular sinkings.

Recap

Software engineers could learn a lesson or two from the Vasa.

CHAPTER 18

Bad Analogies

Explaining software and software development by analogy can be a dangerous enterprise. The problem is that while certain aspects of the analogy hold, others are misleading or often just plain wrong. For example, no one would claim that building a piece of software in the early 2000s is anything like building a warship for the Swedish navy in the 1600s—yet we used that very comparison in the last chapter. The point is that there are valuable lessons to be learned, so long as we don't take the analogy too far.

In a similar vein, we find many instances these days of scientific language used to "explain" common phenomena. Unfortunately, these usages are often metaphorically or analogically incorrect, devoid of meaning, or just plain silly. In this chapter, we choose some common examples, show the improper application, and then try to illustrate a better way of saying what the author would like to say, stripped of the jargon intended to impress the layperson.

Houston, We Have a Problem

Plato was the first philosopher to point out that achieving a conceptual understanding of the physical world is trickier than we might think at first. In more recent times, Immanuel Kant should be given credit for trying to figure out what knowledge can be known with and without the "filtering of reality." That is, we have a notion that there is an "objective" reality, but in some sense we can never get to it, because it is filtered through our human apparatus for experiencing it—our senses, minds, and emotions. What we are capable of experiencing, both as individuals and as a species, is a "subjective" reality—and that limitation introduces lots of doubt as to what "reality" is. This doubt has permeated our thinking, and sometimes its effects can be less than subtle, or even subconscious. Consider how often we say, "Things are not always what they seem."

Our knowledge of physics, in some sense, compounds the problem. As far back as Galileo and then Newton, scientists have been formulating theories that seemed, in their time, *very* counterintuitive—for example, that bodies in motion, left to their own devices, would continue in motion forever. As the centuries passed, however, many (but not all) of these counterintuitive ideas became accepted by educated people as reasonable; the ideas became common knowledge and were assimilated as accepted doctrine. Another trendy way of saying this is that certain ideas achieved *mind share*—that is, they became part of our collective consciousness.

But "modern" physics is only about 100 years old. Although the rate at which the general population accepts new scientific ideas has accelerated, many of these ideas have not actually been absorbed. There are some very good reasons for this. For one, "new" theories such as relativity and quantum mechanics deal with realms of reality outside our everyday experience—velocities near the speed of light and subatomic distances—and turn out to be governed by laws that are very counterintuitive, even to our "modern" way of thinking. Both physicists and non-physicists alike recognize that it is very hard to explain these fundamental theories, in part because the mathematical apparatus that makes them clear to the practitioner is simply not accessible to most people. So physicists have a problem: Although their theories are correct and powerful, they are not explainable in any detail to the non-physicist.

Nonetheless, people want to understand. So what happens in most cases is that popularizers attempt to explain by analogy. This is perfectly valid. But throughout the years, the analogies themselves acquire the status of fundamental truth for the lay public and are bandied about as common clichés. Each time this happens, people like me who have some understanding of the underlying science become baffled by these overused analogies because we don't see the applicability.

Because of my training as a physicist, I want to be sure to state up front that I don't think physics, or science and mathematics in general, is the exclusive province of some exalted priesthood, and that the layperson "shouldn't talk about what they don't understand." I would like everyone to understand science and technology better. But I am also a realist about the magnitude of the problem. What I would settle for is a better understanding of what those scientific clichés actually mean so that people can either use them only when they are appropriate or replace them with better arguments. In particular, I would like to discourage the practice of smugly quoting scientific jargon to impress an audience with the correctness of one's position. This is akin to the "appeal to authority" school of persuasion. And, for my money, the best way to do this is to point out when the popular analogies actually apply and when they don't.

So here goes. See if you can spot the *faux pas* as we proceed. Let's start with some leftovers from classical physics—that is, ideas that are still poorly understood, even after a few centuries of simmering in the intellectual pot.

Fig Newtons

Newton's Laws of Motion (or The Three Laws of Motion) are liberally quoted. Here are some of the things one hears from time to time.

From people in general:

"That object is in equilibrium, so by Newton's First Law, there must be no forces acting on it."

From a project manager, remarking on someone else's project:

"That project is definitely in free fall."

From a manager in response to observing a backlash to a recent business initiative:

"We should have known that would happen. Newton's Third Law predicts that for every action, there is an equal and opposite reaction."

Let's look at these one by one.

Misapplication of the First Law

Newton's First Law of Motion says:

> A body at rest or in a state of uniform motion (constant velocity) will stay that way unless acted upon by an external force.

Note that this means there are no *net* external forces acting on the body unless precisely stated. Or, to put it another way, there *may* be external forces acting on the body, but they (the multiple external forces) cancel exactly. When these external forces balance each other, the object is in equilibrium: static equilibrium if the body is at rest, or else equilibrium in uniform motion—that is, in a straight line at constant velocity. So remember: Equilibrium does not mean "no forces acting." Equilibrium means "all external forces balance exactly." Of course, *internal* forces have no effect, as they cancel in pairs by Newton's Third Law, as we shall soon see.

Let us assume that a lump of coal is moving at constant velocity along the surface of a level table. Ignore for a moment how it came to be in motion, but let's assume it is moving at one inch per hour toward the west. Newton's first law tells us that unless we impose some other horizontal force on the lump, it will continue to move at one inch per hour toward the west *forever*.

Now, as I pointed out earlier, this defies common sense. In our real world, we would expect the lump of coal to slow down and eventually stop for at least two reasons. One, there is air resistance; and two, there is friction with the table's surface. Both of these will tend to retard the uniform westward motion. But of course, there is no violation of Newton's First Law here at all: Both air resistance and friction are external forces acting on the lump of coal, and the first law states very precisely that the rule does *not* apply if external (net) forces are acting on the body in question. Now a physicist, used to thinking about and stating conditions precisely, would understand that a force is a force and you can't neglect any of them. To describe the case precisely, you would have to state: "The lump of coal will continue to move at one inch per hour to the west in a perfect vacuum on a perfectly level, frictionless table." The problem is, most of us are not so precise in describing daily phenomena, so it's easy to understand how ordinary folks might misapply Newton's First Law.

A member of the younger generation of physicists recently pointed out to me that, these days, students use deep space as a theoretical framework for working out problems, so that they can quickly dispense with the effects of air resistance, friction, "tables," and the gravitational pull of nearby massive bodies. Although this idealized context simplifies the requirements for understanding mechanics, one wonders what will happen when these students are called on to solve real problems "back on Earth."

Misapplication of the Second Law

The Second Law says:

> A body will be accelerated by an external force in direct proportion to the force and inversely proportionally to its mass.

This one is often quoted as simply "$F = ma$," which is just a formulaic restatement.[1] It is an unbelievably simple and elegant result that applies over an incredible range of phenomena.

But what does it mean to talk about a project "in free fall?" I think managers mean that it is accelerating under the influence of gravity, which means that it is gaining speed and will inevitably collide, inelastically and catastrophically, with Mother Earth. Splat!

---

[1] While "$F = ma$" is the commonly quoted formula, the more general equation is "$F = dp/dt$," which says that the force is proportional to the rate of change of momentum. This only matters if the mass of the system does not remain constant, as in the problem of a rocket becoming lighter as it burns its fuel and thus loses mass during its flight. "$F = dp/dt$" is more general than "$F = ma$," but the latter formulation is the one you hear the most. Just remember when you hear it that it contains the assumption that the mass doesn't change.

I understand the notion that there are no parachutes and no brakes, thus a sense of rapidly impending doom. Yet I see here a misuse of the physics analogy. Projects are subject to constraints just as surely as they have mass (inertia); the notion that management is so absent that we have effectively yanked the table out from under the lump of coal is certainly disheartening, to say the least.

Misapplication of the Third Law

The Third Law says:

> Whenever two bodies interact, the force on the second body due to the first is equal and opposite to the force on the first due to the second.

When something happens in the business world in reaction to an event, someone is sure to bleat out, "For every action there is an equal and opposite reaction." In fact, it is that person who is having a knee-jerk "reaction." Rather than applying any thought to the situation, he quotes Newton to justify or validate whatever backlash has taken place. The reaction is postulated as something that had to happen according to the laws of physics. In truth, however, what goes on has nothing to do with physics. Not only is the typical reaction unequal to the effect that produced it; often it is not even delivered in the opposite direction but is rather off at some tangent. Moreover, it may not have been a result of the original action at all.

Once again, Newton's Law is correct, but we must be precise about the force and the body. Often the "equal and opposite" forces people cite in business situations are really an internal force pair that does not exert *any* external net force on the body. So whenever you hear someone intone, "For every action there is an equal and opposite reaction," my advice is to check to see what the forces are and what bodies these forces are being applied to.

Everything's Relative

Now that we understand the gravity of mistreating Newton, let's try a couple more popular idioms on for size. Two people disagree on something, and one says:

> "Well, it all depends on your frame of reference."

Or, someone wants to make the point that "the old accepted laws of nature are no longer true." The usual expression of this is along the lines of:

> "Einstein showed that Newton was wrong."

Well, as they say in the Hertz commercial, not exactly. Einstein did a hell of a job with relativity, but his theory has spawned some strange notions.

Frame of Reference

With respect to the first example, it's true that things can appear different depending on your perspective or point of view. But as Galileo first stated, things are *not* different depending on your frame of reference. When you are within a framework that's moving at constant velocity, you cannot know your velocity as perceived by a stationary observer, because everything else inside your framework behaves according to the laws of physics, and all appears to *you* just as it would if you were stationary. Einstein's work cleared up an apparent contradiction between Galileo's principle and Maxwell's electrodynamics. In a similar fashion, you also cannot distinguish between acceleration and space-time curvature.

Einstein Proved Newton Wrong?

As for the second claim, Newton's Laws are perfectly valid at velocities that we encounter in our daily lives. Change comes only when things are moving at or near the speed of light. Then you need to apply different rules. And that's where Einstein comes in. Newton works at low speed (that is, most of the time), and Einstein's Relativity Theory kicks in when you start to go very fast. If you use "just Newton" for too long, then you will get progressively more incorrect results as you approach the speed of light, and your answers will be *completely* wrong when you actually *reach* the speed of light. Just remember that, relative to our daily experience, the speed of light is a very, very big number.

The effects of relativity are completely negligible in our common experience. You can compute them if you'd like, using Einstein's Theory of Special Relativity, but you will find that your results don't change at all.

That is because the speed of light is so great. On the other hand, the speed of sound is something we relate to daily. You can observe that the speed of light and the speed of sound are very different by doing this experiment the next time you are playing golf. When you are about 250 yards or more down the fairway (you have just hit your second shot and are walking toward the green), look back and watch (and listen) for the next group's tee shots. You will see the club hit the ball, and then a split second later you will hear the impact. You can compute this discernible interval by using the speed of sound in dry air at sea level[2] and by assuming that the speed of light is infinite; that is, it takes zero time for the light to travel from the golf club to your eyes. This will give you the right answer.[3] If you do the calculation using the actual

---

[2] Notice how precision just starts to creep into our language when we want to be careful about using physics. The speed of sound depends on a lot of things, including the temperature, which I did not specify.

[3] I hope you were curious enough to do the calculation yourself. If not, here it is. At 68 degrees Fahrenheit, the speed of sound is 1127.3 ft/sec. Two hundred fifty yards is 750 feet, so the sound will reach you in 0.665 seconds, or roughly two-thirds of a second. This is a noticeable interval. And by the way, I used English units here, not metric, because golfers, by and large, are "calibrated" in yards, not meters.

speed of light, then you will get basically the same answer.[4] So although you can legitimately apply Einstein's Theory of Relativity here by using a finite speed for light, it won't buy you much.

There is a real-life situation in which you can experience the speed of light as finite. When making an international phone call, you are sometimes unlucky enough to go up to a geostationary satellite and back down to Earth, and that takes about a half-second. That's long enough to give you the impression that your interlocutor is pausing; you might misinterpret that pause as dissent, hesitation, apprehension, or the like, depending on the conversation.

And Another Thing...

When it comes to Einstein, we have just scratched the surface. All the phenomena we've just discussed are manifestations of his Special Theory of Relativity, which holds only for bodies moving at constant velocity. When bodies actually accelerate relativistically, then you have to use his General Theory, with consequent additional heavyweight mathematical baggage. Yet popularizers invoke the General Theory with equal impunity. In fact, there are only a small number of experimental tests that we know of to test the General Theory, all of them involving very, very small effects.[5]

None of this diminishes the magnitude of Einstein's accomplishments. However, applying his brilliant discoveries to situations in which they do not really apply in a sense cheapens them.

Quantum Nonsense

Let's move on from relativity to quantum mechanics. Recently I had someone who was unwilling to make a forecast say to me:

"It's just like quantum mechanics. All I can give you is a probability."

Although the second part of his claim was most assuredly true, I am certain that it had absolutely nothing to do with quantum mechanics.

---

[4] Another common example of this calculation is determining how far away a lightning bolt is by timing how long it takes to hear the thunderclap after you see the lightning. Same idea.

[5] When I was doing physics around 30 years ago, there were only three tests. They were the precession of the perihelion of the orbit of Mercury, the gravitational bending of light as it passes by a massive object, and the gravitational red shift of light as it climbs out of the gravitational field of a mass. My sources tell me that, since then, several more have been added; one involves measurements on binary pulsars. Until recently, all these effects have been extremely small and hard to measure and have had very little connection to our everyday lives. However, today the clocks in GPS satellites have to be corrected for effects that are purely due to General Relativity, so technology has now brought even this realm into our daily lives.

About 20 years after the relativity revolution, circa 1927, quantum mechanics burst upon the human race with equally momentous and unsettling effect.[6]

All you have to remember about quantum mechanics is all you have to remember about relativity. Neither theory replaces Newton's Laws. Whereas Einstein's Relativity Theory extends Newton's Laws into the domain of the very fast (velocities near the speed of light), quantum mechanics extends classical physics into the domain of the very small. That is, when we get down to subatomic dimensions, new rules come into play. That's when we need to use quantum mechanics. For everything else, the rules of quantum mechanics still apply, but the effects are so small that they are irrelevant.

It's important to realize that quantum mechanics is one of the most successful theories of all time. It has been able to explain a vast array of very counterintuitive things that we now take for granted in our everyday lives. Without it, we wouldn't understand how semiconductors work, which would make my use of a Pentium processor to write this book somewhat moot. It goes right to the matter of explaining why atoms are stable, without which, as John Walker points out, your whole day would be ruined. So while we daily deal with technology that derives from quantum mechanics, we rarely see phenomena that directly exhibit quantum effects. It's a subtle point, perhaps.

The reason it took so long to discover both bodies of knowledge is that we could not measure either stuff that went really fast or things that were really small much before the second half of the 19th century. Actually, it was the invention and perfection of the vacuum pump—an engineering feat—that facilitated measurement in both arenas. This also explains why the effects that required the application of either Einstein's theory or quantum mechanics were not observed; except for the conundrum about the wave-particle duality of light—known even in Newton's time—nothing in our plodding macroscopic world hinted that anything was "wrong."

The "It's just like quantum mechanics" quote reveals another interesting misconception. Because quantum theory depends on calculations involving probabilities, many people think that predictions based on quantum mechanics are somehow imprecise. The reality is just the opposite.

For example, we can determine α, the fine structure constant,[7] experimentally. Now this number is quintessentially a "modern" physics number: It is made up of, among

---

[6] Some date the origin of quantum mechanics back to Planck's work in the early 1900s, which was contemporaneous with that of Einstein. I use 1927, because the papers that Schrödinger published in 1926 were publicized in early 1927, giving us Schrödinger's Equation. That formalized things and really launched the revolution.

[7] The fine structure constant comes up when considering the separation of lines observed when doing spectroscopy on the atoms of an element. Quantum mechanics evolved as physicists tried to explain the various separations for different elements; later, quantum theory was used to predict higher-order effects on the spectra when, for example, the atom in question was subjected to an electrical or magnetic field.

other things, the charge on the electron, Planck's constant (see more on this later), and the speed of light. When you are measuring it by any method, you are doing quantum mechanics, and the theoretical predictions of the number involve some of the deepest applications of quantum theory we know. Yet we can do experiments that measure its value to about one part in 10^8. Now that is pretty good in anybody's book.

By contrast, G, the universal gravitational constant—a perfectly "classical" quantity known since the time of Newton—has been experimentally measured to only about one part in 10^4. That's not bad either; it corresponds to 0.01 percent precision. Yet we know α with several thousand times *more* precision. Somewhat ironic, isn't it?

So much for the probabilistic nature of quantum mechanics and its relation to making predictions.

More Quantum Nonsense

Actually, my pet peeve is the frequent misuse of "Heisenberg's Uncertainty Principle." If you are interested in a particularly droll example of this, see Freddy Riedenschneider's monolog in the Coen brothers' movie, "The Man Who Wasn't There."[8] It is easy to see why Billy Bob Thornton got the chair after his lawyer tried to use the principle to convince (or confuse) a jury.

I hear a common lament when someone is asked to make a difficult measurement:

"We're screwed. Heisenberg tells us we can't measure something without disturbing it."

Here's another example: Software people now talk about "Heisenbugs."

"Man, it took us weeks to track down that defect. Turned out to be a Heisenbug."

These are bugs that are very hard to eliminate because, in the process of trying to do so, we change the working of the program, and our original bug is further hidden by the actions of the debugging apparatus.

What is really going on here?

Measuring Stuff

The fundamental issue is this: Can you measure something without at the same time disturbing the thing you are trying to measure? That is, when you perform the measurement, do you influence in some way the very thing that you are trying to determine? If so, then

[8] USA Films, 2001.

you have a problem, because your measurement will be contaminated by your perturbation of the system you are trying to measure.

Now, this is not an extremely "deep" problem. Medical diagnosticians have to deal with it all the time. They spend a lot of time and energy making assessment procedures as minimally invasive as possible. Yet we know that some people's blood pressure goes up the minute a cuff is put on their arm. Ergo, their measured blood pressure is higher than their normal resting blood pressure.

In software, we work very hard to make debuggers "non-intrusive." Nonetheless, sometimes the act of debugging changes *something* that causes the program to behave differently from when it is running without the debugger. Whether this is the fault of the program or the debugger is somewhat moot; in either case, the programmer has a big problem.

And in the 1920s, Elton Mayo discovered the *Hawthorne Effect*—he demonstrated that in studies involving human behavior, it is difficult to disentangle the behavior under investigation from the changes that invariably occur when the group under study *knows* it is being studied. That is why medical experiments today are performed using a double-blind methodology: neither the patients nor the administering doctors know who is getting the treatment and who is getting the placebo.

Note that these phenomena are perfectly "classical;" you don't need quantum mechanics or the Heisenberg Uncertainty Principle to explain them.

Before we delve more into Heisenberg, we might ask the following question: Is it possible to do any measurement, even a macroscopic one, which is totally "non-intrusive"? If I can find just one example, then I can debunk the idea that it is impossible.

So here's my example. I wake up in a hospital bed in a room I have never seen before. I want to figure out how large the room is. So I count the ceiling tiles. There are 16 running along the length, and 12 along the width. I know that ceiling tiles are standardized to be 1 foot by 1 foot. Hence, I know that the room measures 16 feet by 12 feet for an area of 192 square feet. Bingo! I have performed a measurement without even getting off my back, and I claim that I have not disturbed the room at all.[9]

Applying Heisenberg

Where the Heisenberg Uncertainty Principle applies is in the atomic and subatomic realm. Basically, it posits that it is impossible, quantum-mechanically, to specify both the position and the momentum of a particle to arbitrary precision. If you want to make your

---

[9] If you're a semanticist, you may claim that I have made an *estimate,* not a *measurement*. I respond by pointing out that every measurement is an estimate, in that it has uncertainty attached to it. For example, when you "measure" one of those ceiling tiles with a ruler and determine that it is "12 inches by 12 inches," do you really believe it is exactly so?

knowledge of the particle's position more exact, then you will have less precision on its momentum, and vice versa.

To observe said particle, you have to "shine a light on it." But when you do so, the light itself affects the particle's momentum and therefore makes it impossible to know the particle's position exactly. So "non-intrusiveness" is impossible at quantum dimensions, and Heisenberg supplies you a formula to compute just how much the intrusion will affect your measurement.

One caution: Heisenberg's Uncertainty Principle uses Planck's constant, which is very, very small. So small, in fact, that the Heisenberg Uncertainty Principle yields nonsensical results once you investigate anything greater than atomic and subatomic distances. That is, if you shine a light on an electron, you will affect it measurably. On the other hand, if you shine a light on the ceiling tiles of the hospital room, you affect them not at all. So using the Heisenberg Uncertainty Principle for macroscopic objects is just nonsense.

Heat Death

On to the last misuse. Some say that there have been only four or five fundamental watersheds in physics. Sandwiched in between Newton and the 20th century behemoths of relativity and quantum mechanics is the science of thermodynamics.[10]

Thermodynamics really shook things up. Here is where our modern ideas of energy conservation come from. Here is where the relationship between work and heat becomes clear. Here is where we show that perpetual motion machines are impossible. But most intriguing of all, here is where we get an entirely new concept: *entropy*.

So today we hear statements such as this:

"Large companies are doomed to failure, because entropy inevitably takes over."

Entropy is a measure of disorderliness. And one of the key tenets of thermodynamics is that entropy is always increasing. The most common example given to students is intuitively very appealing. Take a box that has a partition down the middle, and fill one side with oxygen molecules and the other side with nitrogen molecules. Remove the

---

[10] We might mention in passing that, around the time of the American Civil War, our friend James Clerk Maxwell, building on the empirical work of Michael Faraday before him, recast electromagnetism in a beautiful mathematical formulation. It made electricity and magnetism understandable as aspects of one theory, and it is stunning. It enabled, in some sense, modern telecommunications to be born; for example, Marconi and his radio came after. So it is not to be downplayed. Yet to me Maxwell's equations are a mathematical *tour de force*; much of the physics and phenomenology was well understood at the time of Maxwell's work. For example, we know that the laying of the transatlantic cable was interrupted by the Civil War, so that telegraphy was in place well before Maxwell's Equations.

partition, and the molecules will continue to move about spontaneously. After some time, we observe that there is a uniform mixture of oxygen and nitrogen in the box. We can wait forever, and the molecules will *never*, of their own accord, find themselves back in the state with all the oxygen on one side and all the nitrogen on the other.[11] The mixed state is considered to be more "random" or disordered; the segregated system more ordered. The entropy of the final system is greater than that of the initial system.

In any closed system, entropy spontaneously and naturally increases. Eventually the system reaches maximum entropy, or total randomness. In applying this phenomenon to the universe, physicists refer to it as *heat death*—hence, the title of this section.

Seems logical, and by and large it is. Most systems, left alone, will tend to a more disorderly state. Just look at my desktop.

But somewhere along the line, lay people started extending the concept to economic and social systems. And this is where I think it took a wrong turn. Note that the previous quotation is not entirely without merit. It is certainly true that the larger an organization becomes, the more communications links it must support; as Kenneth Arrow pointed out many years ago,[12] this may eventually limit its growth. Certainly it becomes harder for large organizations to coordinate activities, and even more difficult for them to respond quickly to changing circumstances. On the other hand, it is a mistake to assume that entropy must inevitably win.

Although it's certainly true that a *closed* system, left alone, will tend to a state of maximum entropy, economic systems—such as the company you work for—are not "closed." They are open to the flow of matter and energy. And we don't tend to leave our companies alone. We add raw materials to them all the time; we do work on the system; we expend energy to combat entropy. Just as I work to clean off my desktop and make it more orderly (less entropic), I can invest work in the communications channels and mechanisms in my company to reduce the disorder.

Now this work is roughly equivalent to the energy a machine might expend to overcome friction; it is not, in some sense, "useful" work. On the other hand, it does provide us with a rationale for continuing human enterprise. With the correct balance, we can at least hold off entropy while we make progress on the "real" objectives. One philosopher, long since forgotten, pointed out that we spend our whole lives combating entropy. It's how human beings and societies survive. In effect, the social organizations—countries and enterprises—that do a better job of beating back entropy ultimately win over those that are less successful in this fundamental enterprise.

The key thing to ask when someone refers to the inevitability of entropic disorder is: "Is it a closed system?" If not, then the spontaneous and inevitable increase in entropy is not a given.

---

[11] Theoretically, you can compute the probability that this will happen. It is very close to zero, believe me.

[12] Arrow, Kenneth, *The Limits of Organization* (New York: W. W. Norton & Company, 1974).

Other Examples

There are, unfortunately, lots of other examples I could delve into. Each one would require a few paragraphs, and this chapter grows long already. I have heard numerous misstatements concerning the dual nature (wave-particle) of light. The discoveries within the last 40 years in Chaos Theory have been incorrectly quoted to (once again) invalidate Newton's Laws. Gödel's Incompleteness Theorem, around 70 years old, is sometimes used to justify our inability to prove something. And in the computer science arena, Turing's Machine is frequently used to demonstrate undecidability[13] in areas where it has no applicability at all. The late scientist Stephen Jay Gould wrote extensively on how Darwin's Theory of Evolution has been widely quoted and generally misunderstood. All of these fundamental theorems are profound, and all of them are betrayed when used in situations in which they absolutely don't apply.

Good Science

Scientists and mathematicians have given us some incredibly powerful tools to help us understand our physical world. These tools are wonderful triumphs of human intellect, allowing us to start with first principles and explain a wide variety of phenomena, right down to the existence and behavior of elementary particles. As the phenomena get farther and farther away from our common experience, however, the theories become more abstract and require more esoteric mathematics for their exposition. It is at this point that we sacrifice to inaccessibility much of what we stand to gain in fundamental understanding. Nevertheless, although the average Joe[14] cannot really appreciate all of the subtleties, he can certainly benefit from the trickle-down effects of these discoveries, embodied in practical products that come into his life. In this sense, it is all "good science."

What is *not* good science is using shibboleths from science to explain things that are clearly unrelated to the physical principles that underlie those shibboleths. Human beings are *not* just like fundamental particles; there is no reason to believe that they obey quantum mechanical laws as macroscopic beings. Such analogies really are misleading, and we should be wary of those who would use them to convince us that their positions are valid.

Likewise, we should all be careful about using pseudoscientific jargon in our daily communications with others. The least harmful result is that they will believe us without thinking, because we have "snowed" them with technical lingo. A more harmful result,

---

[13] The notion of "undecidability" refers to the impossibility of writing a computer program to determine the result of a problem or class of problems.

[14] This one included.

which you should carefully consider, is that they will nod in agreement and secretly conclude that you are a carnival huckster. And you will never know that you have lost credibility when you thought you were gaining it.

Recap

This chapter is dedicated to my dear friend Mark Sadler (1945–2002), who passed away after a valiant struggle with ALS. Mark went to Oxford, and his college (Balliol) inspired him to be "effortlessly superior." He was, in so many ways. We often talked about the material in this chapter, and he encouraged me to propagate these ideas more widely.

CHAPTER 19

The Refresh Problem

As a group, we spend proportionately way too much time talking about new software development. Although those are the projects people prefer to work on—the "green field" development we hear so much about—the plain fact of the matter is that software lives for a very long time. As a result, we spend a lot of time maintaining and upgrading legacy code. It is not uncommon for systems' lives to be measured in decades, not years. Now one might ask, in a field that changes so rapidly, why does software hang around for so long?

There are a few reasons. First, initial development costs are usually much higher than forecast, so the "sunk cost" of a newly deployed system is already more than was anticipated at the origination of the project. At each subsequent decision point, the cost of an update must be weighed against the cost of a replacement, either by acquisition or by rewrite. Usually these update costs are small compared with replacement, and minor upgrades to functionality can usually be accommodated if the original architecture was robust. Error rates go through a relatively predictable pattern.

Let's talk about error rates a bit more. Early in the lifecycle of a new software product, reported error rates are usually relatively high. These are the errors that have escaped detection during testing and have been discovered by the first wave of customers using the product. We could compare these bugs to the "infant mortality" failures in hardware. These are discovered and flushed from the system relatively quickly.

Then, just like hardware, we enter into a relatively long period when there are few bugs or failures. In the hardware world, we attribute this to parts that have been *burned in*; in software, it corresponds to a mature product that has usage patterns which are fairly commonly repeated. Most of the code that is being exercised is the same code, over and over again; remember that many parts of a software system are infrequently called—rare error cases, for example.

Finally, we enter into an "end-of-life" period. In hardware, this corresponds to parts failing through fatigue. It is almost the mirror image of the infant mortality problem; these are the critters that are dying of old age. In software, we see a similar problem: In older systems, bug rates go up again. There are two reasons for this:

- First, statistically infrequent paths begin to be explored in the code, and a bug that may have been present from Day 1 is triggered because some unusual combination of circumstances finally arose.

- Second, the cumulative effects of years of maintenance take their toll. All the patches and fixes put in by generations of maintenance programmers have so degraded the initial architecture that "code rot" is taking over. Make one more fix and the whole house of cards may come tumbling down around you. It is at this point that a replacement system makes more technical and economic sense than even one additional upgrade cycle.

The total lifecycle cost of most software systems is large when compared to the initial development cost. But this cost is rarely even estimated when new systems are proposed. The right cost metric for any new system should be its total lifecycle cost, but we rarely see this number at proposal time. It is another manifestation of the immaturity of our discipline.

Refreshing Embedded Software

Now that we understand that software is "out there" for long periods of time, we need to confront the problem of how to refresh it. This is a particularly perplexing problem for embedded software. In the remainder of this chapter, I address the pesky problem of upgrading software in a certain class of device: those that are handheld, mobile, wireless, and fairly lightweight. In this class, we find cell phones, personal organizers, GPS receivers, digital cameras, and various combinations thereof. They all have embedded software, some programmable memory, and batteries. They may or may not communicate with other devices.

This class of device is increasingly important, and its members are proliferating, for at least two reasons. In the first place, every product that is designed for personal portability tends to get smaller over time; and as the benefits of their functions (for instance, the transferability of digital photographs) become widely understood in the marketplace, their decreasing size makes them more attractive as well. In the second place, we are constantly seeking ways to free ourselves from detestable tethers. Wireless communication does that nicely because there's no landline to fuss with, and batteries do away with the other tether, the power cord.

My notion is that upgrading software for these devices should be made as simple as possible. The proposed solution is speculative, but I believe it merits further discussion.

The Current Situation

When you buy one of these products today, you *think* you are buying a device. Actually, there is a basic shell of a device, but all the good stuff is in the software. Any software person knows when he turns on his cell phone, for example, that he has to wait for it to "boot up." And that numeric keypad you use to dial phone numbers is also the keyboard you use to "program the software." By that I mean it is one of the mechanisms by which you can put various information (such as stored phone numbers) into the phone's memory.

Effectively, this device consists of three parts:

- The "hardware"
- Embedded "software"
- The batteries, without which, I hasten to add, nothing will work

Today, this device is packaged as two parts: the phone, which contains both the hardware and the software, and the batteries. That is just the way things have evolved.

Now this poses an interesting dilemma.

All the intelligence is in the software. So when you want to upgrade the phone, you have two options:

- Somehow upgrade the software which, today, means either replacing or reprogramming the chip in the phone.
- Depending on the economics, replace the whole phone with a new one which, in turn, might be exactly the same shell with a newer version of the chip.

Other devices take a slightly different tack: You can hook them up to your PC, get on the vendor's Web site, and download a new version of the software. Sometimes called an *oil change*, this operation allows you to replace the software with a more recent version. The oil change analogy is a little dangerous for some people, because it implies that your software could be replaced for you automatically at regular intervals without revealing what internal changes the vendor made, and they find that notion scary. For others, the whole process of using the PC to accomplish the objective seems more akin to changing an engine instead of just the oil in it. That is, they do not view it as a simple task.

The Software Upgrade Game

Software vendors are under continual pressure to make their products better. This means that, at fairly regular intervals, they issue upgrades to their software. New purchasers get the latest and greatest when they buy. And, to spread the development costs and keep existing customers happy, vendors would like to encourage current users to acquire the latest version, too, albeit at a modest price point.

So, how do they get people to upgrade their software?

The industry is wrestling with this issue as we speak. People tend to get used to their software, and getting them to upgrade to the latest and greatest version is a bit of a problem. You have to convince them to pry open their wallets and spend some of their discretionary income to replace something that already works pretty well. Vendors have tried various mechanisms, most of them based on a subscription model; TiVo's oil change and AOL's online upgrades, for example, both depend on users paying for their software (and, implicitly, the upgrades) as part of a monthly service.

It has been noted in some parts that major software vendors have been tinkering with all sorts of pricing ideas, including subscriptions, to guarantee a steady revenue stream into the foreseeable future.

But once we get past the economic problem, we still have the quasi-technical problem: How do we make the upgrade as easy and user-friendly as possible?

A Modest Proposal

What we ought to do—for cell phones and, by extension, all devices with embedded software—is to *package the software with the battery*, not with the device. You would buy the basic device without batteries or software, although it wouldn't be worth much—not even as a doorstop, because it's so lightweight. But at least it could be commoditized down to the lowest unit cost manufacturing efficiencies will allow.

Then, to power it up, you would buy batteries.[1] Each device would have its own type of battery. The software would come along, piggybacked onto the battery. I abstract the technical implementation details here. Think of it as a "battery pack" if you like; I prefer, for marketing reasons, just to think of it as a "smarter" battery.

This would cause a vast diversification in the battery business, but we have seen industrial transformations of this type before. Today, we tend to think of batteries as a commodity. Actually, they already exist in many sizes and varieties, depending on electrical requirements and how much you want to spend; rechargeable costs more, for instance. You might think that turning such a commodity business into a more variegated

---

[1] Of course, these batteries could be packaged with the device at the time you buy it.

"marketplace" is counterintuitive. But not really; as an analog, just think of the infinite variety of tires (such as car, truck, tractor, snow, racing, and high-performance, not to mention a dizzying array of sizes and form factors) that are currently stocked for mass consumption today. Yet most people think of tires as a commodity. And a hundred years ago, they were.

Needless to say, the battery distribution business would change; there would still be the "dumb batteries" we have today, along with the "smart batteries" that would have piggybacked software. Not all corner grocery stores, souvenir shops, and convenience stores would carry both kinds. We would expect, though, that over time more and more stores would stock and carry smart batteries as the demand for them increased. The free market has a wonderful way of working all that out.

This transformation would lend another layer of meaning to the phrase, "power it up." When you turned on a device, you'd be feeding it *electrical* power by virtue of the battery; you'd also be giving it *intellectual* power by virtue of the software on the battery. Power to the hardware, in both senses!

Software Upgrades, Revisited

Under this new regime, when you purchased your software with your batteries, you would upgrade as you go. When your batteries ran out, you would replace them. And when you did, you would get the latest version of the software applicable to your device.

Notice that this has an interesting property: It couples the shelf life of the battery to the useful life of the software, so we wouldn't have to worry about obsolete versions of software lying around.

What about the cost of the upgrade or, more generically, the cost of the software? No one in his right mind thinks that the batteries for his cell phone should be free. So your batteries would cost a little more, of course, because you'd have to cover the software development expenses. But those expenses would be spread over the cost of all the batteries onto which the software is piggybacked.

There is also this wonderful coincidence. Someone who used his device sparingly would replace batteries infrequently. However, whenever he did, he would automatically be upgraded to a recent version of his software. On the other hand, someone who used his device constantly would go through a lot of batteries and would therefore typically be replacing his software with identical copies of what he had been using. The intensive user would see little or no change over time, and the infrequent user would see "step" changes in his software when he swapped out his batteries, something he would do rarely. So there would be a really good match between upgrades and the respective usage patterns.

As the software that goes onto the battery would have to be completely self-contained, we would forever do away with the notion of patching old software. You would throw away your old software with your dead battery, and your fresh battery would start over again. Manufacturers would have to be clever to ensure that features wouldn't change abruptly. At the worst, there might have to be some release notes for your new batteries. I think marketing folks could put the appropriate spin on this and turn it into an attractive feature.

The big advantage of this model is that it saves users from having to download software upgrades from the Internet. Which is easier: doing a download and installation of software from the Internet, or just changing the batteries? Ask your mom.

Some Nice Things Come for Free

Devices with embedded software should be easy to use. To paraphrase the late Jef Raskin, "There's no Maytag Users' Group, because there doesn't have to be." Many people think we should adopt an "appliance" model for these devices.[2]

Unfortunately, software sometimes gets in the way of this.

But consider some of the benefits of packaging batteries and software together. Want to install your software? Plug in the *batterychip*.[3] This would bring new meaning to the term "plug and play." Want to move your software from one device to another (compatible) device? Just move your batterychip from one device to the other. If the devices weren't compatible, then you would have the equivalent of trying to use the wrong battery. Most people would understand that.

Note that for this scheme to work, the batterychip would have to contain some kind of writeable memory in order to store user-specific information (such as settings and files), otherwise it wouldn't be too useful to plug the batterychip into another device. The memory could be PROM or NVRAM, but because it would be integrated with the battery, it could even be normal RAM. One reason you might want to upgrade the batterychip would be to get more memory.

Our European friends have already started down this path. My friend and colleague Pascal Leroy writes from France:

> "The GSM phone system in Europe relies on a chip called the SIM card, which contains (1) information about your rights, subscription, phone number, and so on, and (2) your settings. People have gotten used to plugging their SIM card into just about any phone to place a call: I was on the train the other day next to two girls, one of whom had a cell phone with a dead battery; she just borrowed her friend's phone, plugged in her own SIM card, and was able to chat on the

---

[2] I acknowledge that a Maytag washing machine is not a handheld device.

[3] I thank Kate Jones for this improvement over my original made-up word, *softerry*.

phone for the entire trip. And they didn't exactly look like nerds, so this kind of technology is probably usable by just about anybody."

This "ease of use" example demonstrates some of the potential benefits of the batterychip, which would take the idea one step further.

Do you have multiple devices, each of which needs the same software? Well, in the old days, software manufacturers might have worried about you. In many cases it was rather easy, although technically illegal, to purchase a licensed copy of the software and install it on multiple machines. With the batterychip, the question would become moot for both you and the manufacturer. You could either buy multiple batterychips to use simultaneously, or you could put a batterychip into the device you wanted to use right away, and then transfer it to another device later if you wished. As with ordinary batteries, it would be your choice: cost versus convenience. Here we see the instantiation of the ideal model that maps one copy of the software to one physical device. By making these batterychips simple and cheap enough, we would reduce the incentive to copy software illegally.

Why This Will Work

Economics.

People don't like subscriptions. They don't like to be locked into recurring charges. As the economy tightens, we see people cut back, and the first thing they cut back on, if they are smart, are those silent monthly charges. If software vendors decide to go in the direction of subscription pricing, my guess is that they will prosper in good times and get pinched in hard times. I think this is basic economics and psychology at work.

The fundamental dynamic here is that people will always fear that they will not get enough for their money with a subscription. That is, they will always be concerned that their usage will be below average, and hence that they are funding (subsidizing) other "free riders" who use the service more at their implicit expense.

On the other hand, people are used to paying for batteries. Batteries are a consumable, and *you pay for them according to how much energy you use*. Use the device more, deplete your batteries more. No one complains about that. To most people, that seems fair.

To illustrate my point, look at the consumption of inkjet cartridges in low-cost color printers. These cartridges are relatively expensive, but the market tolerates this because they are viewed as a consumable. In fact, there are all sorts of after-market vendors whose existence attests to this basic usage model; their only function is to lower the unit cost.

So by putting the software into the batteries, you would transform it into a consumable that gets thrown away with the dead battery. You would factor the software cost into the price of the battery. Spread over many, many units, the added cost would be pretty low. Coupling software usage to battery usage might ultimately be the simplest algorithm we could ever devise for charging (no pun intended) for software based on a usage model.

Will people (electrically) recharge their software batteries? They could, assuming we have piggybacked our software onto rechargeable batteries. In this case, they would retain their old software, perhaps indefinitely. But it wouldn't invalidate the basic model. And someone could always upgrade their software, if they wanted to, by throwing away a perfectly "good" battery and replacing it with a newer one. Who knows, there might spring up a secondary market for "old" batteries that still hold a charge. Maybe there will be battery exchanges. I could ring up a lot of changes on the basic model. The important concept here is that the free market and its economics would drive things appropriately.

Refinement

There are a few additional details to consider, which might appeal to you if you're a techno-junkie. Coupling software and batteries will open up some new horizons.

One refinement, suggested by Philippe Kruchten, would be to take advantage of large memory capacities to store the software for multiple devices on a single batterychip. This would ease the distribution problem somewhat, as one physical unit could then serve several different devices. So you might imagine a generic "cell phone" battery, and so on. What this would mean is that you could replace your Motorola cell phone with a Nokia cell phone, plug in the batterychip you used with the Motorola, and everything would still work. Of course, this would require that the various cell phone manufacturers agree on some standards, and that is always tricky.

Conversely, one could imagine a vertically integrated company putting the software for several different device types on one batterychip. Then one could purchase, for example, an Ericsson batterychip, which would power (both from an electrical and a software point of view) devices of different types made by Ericsson.

Today you can, of course, introduce all sorts of power-saving algorithms in the software to economize as much as possible on battery usage. We already do this in laptops, whose software ships with the device. Under our proposal, we would put these same power-saving algorithms where they more logically should reside: into the laptop battery.

Also, consider a generation "n" battery with generation "n" software. Let's say that, in the next revision of the software, you improve your algorithms and so on, so that you can get the same amount of work accomplished in the same amount of time with less electrical power. That means you can now ship generation "n+1" software on a battery that has less electrical output and still achieve the same result. So the price of the battery could come down, your profit could go up, or some combination of both.

These possibilities are all definitely within the realm of current technology but are not essential. They are refinements of the original idea, and I want to obey the KISS[4] principle as much as possible.

What About Software Piracy?

Fundamentally, I want to eliminate piracy by making the batterychip the most persuasive economic choice for the majority of users. As with all other schemes, when we try to build a better technical mousetrap, we just incite smarter mice. Better to figure out a way to make them buy the cheese of their own accord. Perhaps the batterychip's memory will be programmed at the factory, using a device that is relatively expensive and not generally available to the public. Then it would be cheaper just to buy a new batterychip instead of copying the software from an existing one and trying to "reburn" it onto an older batterychip. But, fundamentally, I am not trying to address software piracy with this proposal. It may have some fortuitous side effects, but that is incidental.

Until the Sun Takes Over

Today lots of money is spent making batteries better (smaller, more powerful, longer lasting, and so on) so that we can become mobile. Some day, there might be solar-recharged capacitors capable of replacing batteries entirely. This technology depends on getting the form factor small enough, the capacitance large enough, and the solar panel interface nearly perfect. We would use the capacitor as a virtual battery. It would be just another way of storing energy for use at a later time. However, unlike batteries, the capacitor/solar panel combination would not have to be replaced periodically. Until that day comes, we will be replacing or recharging batteries. So why not marry them to our software?

It would be foolhardy of me to claim that I have stumbled upon the next great vertical integration of our time: batteries and software. On the other hand, the idea intrigues me. I enjoy exploring the pluses and minuses of such schemes, without any terminal effects.

Batterychips would solve the software upgrade problem for electronic devices by making the operation as simple as changing batteries. They would alter pricing dynamics by making software more of a consumable than a capital item. As the devices that the embedded software resides in are themselves becoming commodities, this makes sense. There may ultimately be interesting distribution issues for batterychips, but I'm confident that these could be addressed effectively.

---

[4] *KISS* stands for Keep It Simple, Stupid!

Recap

In the few short years since I originally floated this proposal, there has not been a groundswell of enthusiasm for the notion of batterychips. But sometimes these things take time to catch on. The biggest objection seems to come from people who use only rechargeable batteries; their claim is that because they never swap out their batteries, they would never get new software, and that this raises the per-copy price on the software included with the battery.

I'm not sure that this is a valid issue. First of all, today we see a broad mixture of people who use replaceable batteries and rechargeable ones. It is a price/convenience trade-off for most of them, and the market adjusts the prices so that neither side goes out of business. Similarly, I think the price of the software piggybacked onto each kind of battery will be priced according to the expected life of the battery. So the same software piggybacked onto a rechargeable battery will be more expensive on a per-unit basis than the same software piggybacked onto a non-rechargeable battery, because it has a longer life. It's just a pricing issue, and the market will decide.

The key notion, from my point of view, is getting software into the consumable category and out of the capital expense category. Once you do that, usage-based pricing becomes logical, and in the end I believe that is what serves the market best.

See you at the batterychip store!

CHAPTER 20

Not So Random Numbers

When it comes to calculating things these days, we have a bewildering array of tools in front of us. Unfortunately, we often don't use the most powerful one of all—our brain. What I'm trying to say here is that we sometimes jump into the middle of figuring something out by opening a blank spreadsheet when what we really need to do is consider what it is we are trying to accomplish. Don't let the tool govern the method of solution. The old adage applies: To the man with only a hammer, everything looks like a nail.

There's a good antidote to this reflex, one I have used for many years. I imagine that I have the problem and am stranded on a desert island. How would I approach the solution using only the tools of Archimedes—my brain and a stick to draw diagrams in the sand? (Of course, it would help to have Archimedes' brain, but that is not an option.) So the rules are simple: I can do whatever calculations I want, but I have to be able to write them in the sand.[1] What problems can still be countenanced?

Of course, the answer is that we can do some pretty interesting things. And surprisingly, sometimes problems that appear to be quite simple at the outset require more thought and calculation than evident at first blush. The rest of this chapter tells the story

---

[1] I do get to use as much sand as I want, sort of like having an infinite supply of paper. This basically means I don't have to remember all my intermediate results, but can "store" them for future use.

of Roscoe Leroy and such a problem.[2] I do give him the additional crutches of pencil and paper and his trusty slide rule; but as I point out later, these are really a luxury.

Roscoe Sets the Stage

"Remember the time I got shipwrecked in the South Pacific with my pal named Monday?" Roscoe began. Monday, it should be noted, was Roscoe's answer to Robinson Crusoe's Friday—his traveling companion and overall helper. Roscoe and Monday had spent many a night under the stars and, if two guys had to be marooned, those two had a chance of surviving together without killing each other.

"Yeah," I replied. "You guys were really lucky; as I recall, you were the only survivors. The island was tropical; there was plenty of food, and you had shelter from the elements. All you had to do was wait to be rescued."

"Well," snapped back Roscoe, "all we *could* do was wait. There was no way we could accelerate anything. Our biggest problem was boredom; there were no books in the flotsam and jetsam, and we desperately needed a way to pass the time without going bonkers."

It turns out that in going through their salvage inventory, Roscoe and Monday discovered a mint set of baseball cards. After awhile, Monday, an inveterate and incurable baseball fanatic, suggested they use the statistics on the baseball cards to construct two teams so that they could conduct some "fantasy" baseball games to pass the time. Fortunately, they had an ample supply of pencils and paper. Roscoe had even rescued his pocket slide rule.

"As soon as Monday came up with the idea," said Roscoe, "I was keen on it. It would give us something to do, and it would be a harmless form of competition. So I set about figuring out how to create the game.

"And that is how the thorny problem came about."

Simulating the Batter

"In all these simulations," continued Roscoe, "you need to devise a sort of random number generator."

"Well," I said, "what devices did you have at your disposal?"

"Not much," responded Roscoe. "All we had were three identical dice of the usual variety, with one to six spots on each. Still, I figured it would be easy to simulate probabilities with them, because that was really what we needed to do. We decided that the simplest thing to do was roll the three dice simultaneously, add up the number of spots, and use that total to determine success or failure."

"Probabilities? I'm not sure I understand," I said.

---

[2] We have previously dealt with Roscoe in Chapters 5, 10, 11, 14, and 15.

"Sure, probabilities! That's how the fantasy baseball concept works. For example, assume you have a hitter at the plate with a batting average of .250. At the lowest level of sophistication (forget, for a minute, about walks) we need a way of randomly deciding if he gets a hit for this at-bat, so we need to create a random event that has a probability of occurring 250 times out of 1,000." I had never known Roscoe to be that interested in probability and statistics, but I was about to be impressed.

"Now in reality, it's more complicated. In our game, for example, we ignored the quality of the pitcher, and complicated situations like sacrifice flies and so on."

"Well, assuming you have made these simplifications, how do you actually simulate a batter's appearance at the plate?" I asked.

"We have only two things to think about," Roscoe replied. "Plate appearances and official at-bats. When a player gets a walk, it counts as a plate appearance, but not as an official at-bat. So basically, you need two numbers: the percentage of plate appearances that yield official at-bats for that player, and then his batting average. Suppose, for example, that a player walks in one out of every 10 plate appearances.[3] What you would do is then first determine if the player walks by asking for a successful trial of an event with probability 0.1. With the three dice, you'd need to know what combined number on a given throw has that probability. So imagine that you roll the dice, and you get that total—then, bingo! The batter walks to first base, and you're done.

"On the other hand, if you don't roll that total, then the player does not walk; instead, he has an official at-bat. Now you take his batting average, say .250, and you roll for that probability. If you're successful, he makes a hit; if not, he is out. Then, of course, you can roll for what kind of hit (single, double, triple, home run) by using those statistics per at-bat. And so on. I used batting average as the generic example, but basically you can refine the simulation to your heart's content, depending on how many of the 'corner cases' you want to include.[4] It will always, however, come down to simulating an event with a certain probability. And, because sometimes we will need probabilities for things other than batting average, we need to be able to cover the entire range from zero (total failure) to 1 (certain success.)"

"Fair enough. I get the gist of it. So what's the problem?" I replied in turn.

---

[3] We note here that statistics such as official at-bats and walks (from which plate appearances can be calculated) are the kinds of numbers that appear on the baseball cards mentioned in the salvage inventory.

[4] Another example of a "corner case" would be the probability, in the case of an out, that the batter hits into a double play if there is a man on first base. People actually construct these kinds of fantasy simulations for a living; as baseball mavens record almost every kind of statistic imaginable, this is a natural result. It should also be noted that our scheme for simulating the batter's plate appearance is certainly not unique; there are many ways to achieve the same result. For example, you could recompute the batting average based on plate appearances, and then compute walks, singles, doubles, triples, and home runs from renormalized statistics. There are many, many alternative formulations of which we have picked just one as an example. However, regardless of the formulation, one of the big challenges before the widespread availability of computers was figuring out how to conduct the probability simulation using simple, low-cost devices available to most people.

"The problem," said Roscoe, "is this: Can we figure out how to simulate probabilities using a device as simple as three dice, and still have enough granularity to make the simulation reasonable? For example, if we can only simulate .250, .500, and .750, we don't have enough values to do a good simulation."

"Well, if you throw all three dice simultaneously, you get totals that range from 3 to 18; that's 16 different outcomes, so that's a start," I responded.

"Indeed," said Roscoe, "that is exactly how we proceeded."

First Steps

"Monday got right on the basic combinatorics. With three six-sided dice, there were 6 × 6 × 6 possible outcomes, or 216 possibilities, but only 16 different totals. So Monday constructed Table 20.1.

Table 20.1 Ways to Form Various Totals

Total	Number of Ways to Roll that Total
3	1
4	3
5	6
6	10
7	15
8	21
9	25
10	27
11	27
12	25
13	21
14	15
15	10
16	6
17	3
18	1
Sum	**216**

"Looks good to me," I replied. "There is some obvious symmetry. For example, both 3 and 18 come up exactly once, as you would expect. And 4 and 17 are the same, and so on. The most frequent occurrences are 10 and 11, as there are lots of combinations that will yield those totals. And the number of total ways adds up to 216, so you can't be too far off the mark. But it looks like there are, so far, only eight distinct probabilities in the offing."

"Appearances can be deceiving," said Roscoe. "But let's add in the probabilities we have so far to double-check our work." He then produced Table 20.2.[5]

Table 20.2 Probabilities Corresponding to Each Total

Total "N"	Number of Ways to Roll that Total	Probability of "N"
3	1	0.00463
4	3	0.01389
5	6	0.02778
6	10	0.04630
7	15	0.06944
8	21	0.09722
9	25	0.11574
10	27	0.12500
11	27	0.12500
12	25	0.11574
13	21	0.09722
14	15	0.06944
15	10	0.04630
16	6	0.02778
17	3	0.01389
18	1	0.00463
Sum	**216**	**1.00000**

[5] Note that the probabilities have, in some cases, five significant figures. On his desert island, Roscoe and his slide rule could do three at best. 0.00463 represents three significant figures; the others should be appropriately rounded. Even though the decimal probability is infinitely precise, being the quotient of two integers, Roscoe can only achieve three places with his slide rule; on the other hand, if he does long division by hand, he can get as many as he has the time and patience for.

"Whoop-de-do!" I exclaimed. "Roscoe can divide by 216."

"Calm down, Sonny," said Roscoe. "The fun is only beginning."

Second Steps

"Well, of course, it should be obvious that if you want to simulate a probability of 0.00463, all you require to be successful is that the shooter roll a 3. You could ask him to roll an 18, which is the symmetrical result; however, we are looking for distinct probabilities, so we pick one or the other. We pick 3." Roscoe waited a second, and then sprang his first surprise.

"But what happens if you define 'success' as rolling either a 3 or a 4? Now the probability of rolling a 3 is 0.00463, and the probability of rolling a 4 is 0.01389, so the probability of rolling either a 3 or a 4 is simply 0.00463 + 0.01389, or 0.01852. So you can see that we can create some new distinct probabilities by considering multiple totals as 'successful.'"

"Let me see if I get this," I replied. "To simulate 0.00463, I demand that the shooter roll a 3. To simulate 0.01389, I require that he roll a 4. And to simulate 0.01852, I ask that he roll either a 3 or a 4. Is it that simple?"

"Yeah, you've got the hang of it. But how do you start to figure out all the other possibilities?" Roscoe smiled that smile that bordered on a smirk. I started to crank up my "thinking on my feet" engine.

Generating More Probabilities

"Hmm," I said. "Let's add a column to your table. We can generate some new probabilities by considering more 'cumulative' outcomes." So I augmented Roscoe's table to produce Table 20.3.

"Well, you're on the right track," Roscoe offered. "Your fourth column definitely adds some new probabilities. For example, the probability of shooting either a 3 or a 4 is 0.00463 + 0.01389, which you have calculated to be 0.01852. You express this '3 or 4' as the probability of '4 or less.' By '5 or less' you mean that rolling a total of either 3, 4, or 5 defines a successful outcome.

"In fact, that's exactly how Monday and I proceeded. Problem is, you haven't gone nearly far enough."

"Before you jump ahead," I said, "let's look at how many probabilities we have so far. I'll shade the non-redundant ones in the table." I added some shading to produce Table 20.4.

Table 20.3 Augmented Probability Table

Total "N"	Number of Ways to Roll that Total	Probability of "N"	Probability of "N or Less"
3	1	0.00463	0.00463
4	3	0.01389	0.01852
5	6	0.02778	0.04630
6	10	0.04630	0.09259
7	15	0.06944	0.16204
8	21	0.09722	0.25926
9	25	0.11574	0.37500
10	27	0.12500	0.50000
11	27	0.12500	0.62500
12	25	0.11574	0.74074
13	21	0.09722	0.83796
14	15	0.06944	0.90741
15	10	0.04630	0.95370
16	6	0.02778	0.98148
17	3	0.01389	0.99537
18	1	0.00463	1.00000
Sum	**216**	**1.00000**	

"So I count 8 in the first column and 14 in the second column, for a total of 22. Is that what you get?" I asked.

"Not exactly," said Roscoe. "We have what might be called an *accidental degeneracy*. Note that the probability of rolling a 6 is identical to the probability of rolling a '5 or less.' That's because there are 10 ways to make a 6, and (1 + 3 + 6 = 10) ways to make a 3 or 4 or 5, which is 5 or less. So I guess you have 21 distinct probabilities so far.

"But, as I said, you haven't gone far enough. There are lots more combinations."

Table 20.4 Augmented Probability Table with Shading

Total "N"	Number of Ways to Roll that Total	Probability of "N"	Probability of "N or Less"
3	1	0.00463	0.00463
4	3	0.01389	0.01852
5	6	0.02778	**0.04630**
6	10	**0.04630**	0.09259
7	15	0.06944	0.16204
8	21	0.09722	0.25926
9	25	0.11574	0.37500
10	27	0.12500	0.50000
11	27	0.12500	0.62500
12	25	0.11574	0.74074
13	21	0.09722	0.83796
14	15	0.06944	0.90741
15	10	0.04630	0.95370
16	6	0.02778	0.98148
17	3	0.01389	0.99537
18	1	0.00463	1.00000
Sum	**216**	**1.00000**	

Of Course, We've Already Left the World of Baseball

Things were getting a little hairy. "What did you guys do next?" I asked Roscoe.

"Well, a couple of things became apparent," replied Roscoe. "In fact, Monday sat me down for a chat, and what he said made a lot of sense.

"First thing he told me was that if we wanted to generate baseball probabilities, this was not the best way to proceed. He came up with a scheme whereby we could roll a single die several times and generate what we needed for baseball in three rolls. I had to agree with him on that," Roscoe continued.

"But he also said that the problem of creating probabilities out of the total of three identical dice rolled simultaneously was interesting, in and of itself. He was now more interested in that than in the original problem. So we decided that we would concentrate our focus on seeing if we could figure that one out in all its generality.

"This sometimes happens in the real world, by the way," remarked Roscoe. "We start out trying to solve one problem, only to discover a new, more interesting problem in the process. I think it is called serendipity, or something like that."

Reality Is Ugly

"The next thing we decided was that figuring out all the combinations was going to be laborious. We started making some tables but quickly gave up. Monday said he wanted to sleep on it a bit." Roscoe lit up a stogie, and I figured the rest of the tale would come out now.

"Wouldn't you know it, Monday came back with the answer the next day," continued Roscoe.[6]

"Monday concluded that the first thing to do was decide how many probabilities were possible as an upper limit. Because there were only 216 different ways to roll the dice, that had to be the maximum. So the best we could possibly do was to cover the interval from zero to 1 in 216 steps. From a granularity point of view, the optimum solution would be to have equal steps of 1/216, or 0.00463."

"Well," I said, "we know we can generate the first one!"

Roscoe grinned.

"Why was it important to try to determine the maximum possible number of probabilities?" I asked.

"Well," said Roscoe, "if you don't do that, you have a problem. Suppose you muck around and find 87 distinct probabilities, up from the 21 we have found so far.[7] How do you know if you've got them all, and not missed some? Once you know the maximum possible, you can stop if you attain it. If not, you have to figure out why you couldn't get the others.

"Actually, all we have to do is figure out if we can do 108 possibilities up to a probability of 0.5. Then we can get the other 108 by taking the complementary solution," said Roscoe.

---

[6] Some of you may have come to the conclusion that Roscoe is an avatar for your humble author. If that is true, then Monday is an avatar for our son, David, who figured out the solution to this problem. I may be good at discovering interesting problems, but David is even better at solving them, and he's an avid baseball aficionado as well. And the name of the avatar is Monday, because that is the day we come to work.

[7] As Roscoe himself did in an early attempt to solve this problem.

That made sense. This is a common "trick" in this domain. If you know that rolling a 3 has a probability of 0.00463, then rolling anything but a 3 will have a probability of (1 - 0.00463), or 0.99537. So getting to a probability of 0.5 is always good enough.

Monday's Solution

"Monday started out systematically. First, he worked with the number of ways a total could be rolled, knowing that we can always convert to probabilities by dividing the number of ways by 216. That, it turns out, is easier to think about than decimal numbers.

"His first approach," continued Roscoe, "was to see if all of the first nine 'ways' could be constructed. He came up with Table 20.5.

Table 20.5 How to Get the First Nine Ways

Ways	Need to Roll
1	3
2	3 or 18
3	4
4	3 or 4
5	3 or 4 or 18
6	5
7	3 or 5
8	3 or 5 or 18
9	4 or 5

"I'm beginning to see," I said. "What Monday is going to try to do is see if he can cover the entire set of 'ways' up to 108, using the elements in the 'ways' column of 1, 3, 6, 10, 15, 21, 25, and 27. Very clever."

"Yes," replied Roscoe, "that's the idea. But remember, he can only use each element twice. The symmetry of the problem is helpful, but notice that 'ways' get used up, so we need to be careful. As an example, suppose we used 3 and 18, and needed one more 'way.' We would be stuck. So there are constraints we have to watch out for."

"Wow," I said, "so the answer is still in doubt."

"Monday was equal to the task, it turns out," said Roscoe. "Here is the rest of his logic: To get 10 ways, you just use a roll of 6. By using 6 and its companion of 15, we have two '10s' to work with, so we can now get from 1 to 29. We can now add 1 to 29 to anything, provided we don't need any additional totals of 3, 4, 5, 6, 15, 16, 17, or 18. We have basically used up the 'ways' elements corresponding to 1, 3, 6, and 10."

"Well, 29 is still a long way from 108," I said.

Roscoe completed Monday's solution. "If you now use one of the '21s,' say 8, you extend the range from 29 to 50. And you still have both '15s', both '25s', and both '27s' to work with. Using the second 21 extends the range from 50 to 71. The pair of '27s' takes us to 125, well past the 108 we needed. So it is possible."

"What you are saying, then," I responded, "is that every way is possible, so that we can uniformly cover the interval in steps of 1/216. That is pretty amazing. Did you actually construct the table?"

"It was easy, once we knew it could be done," said Roscoe. "Table 20.6 is the final result."

Table 20.6 The Solution to the Problem

Ways	Probability	Roll Any of These Totals to Get This Probability					
1	0.00463	3					
2	0.00926	3	18				
3	0.01389	4					
4	0.01852	3	4				
5	0.02315	3	4	18			
6	0.02778	5					
7	0.03241	3	5				
8	0.03704	3	5	18			
9	0.04167	4	5				
10	0.04630	6					
11	0.05093	3	6				
12	0.05556	3	6	18			
13	0.06019	4	6				
14	0.06481	3	4	6			
15	0.06944	7					
16	0.07407	3	7				
17	0.07870	3	7	18			
18	0.08333	4	7				
19	0.08796	3	4	7			

continues

Table 20.6 The Solution to the Problem (continued)

Ways	Probability	Roll Any of These Totals to Get This Probability				
20	0.09259	6	15			
21	0.09722	8				
22	0.10185	3	8			
23	0.10648	3	8	18		
24	0.11111	4	8			
25	0.11574	9				
26	0.12037	3	9			
27	0.12500	10				
28	0.12963	3	10			
29	0.13426	3	10	18		
30	0.13889	4	10			
31	0.14352	6	8			
32	0.14815	3	6	8		
33	0.15278	3	6	8	18	
34	0.15741	4	6	8		
35	0.16204	6	9			
36	0.16667	3	6	9		
37	0.17130	3	6	9	18	
38	0.17593	3	6	10		
39	0.18056	3	6	10	18	
40	0.18519	7	9			
41	0.18981	3	7	9		
42	0.19444	8	13			
43	0.19907	3	8	13		
44	0.20370	3	8	13	18	
45	0.20833	6	9	15		
46	0.21296	8	9			
47	0.21759	3	8	9		
48	0.22222	8	10			
49	0.22685	3	8	10		

Ways	Probability	Roll Any of These Totals to Get This Probability					
50	0.23148	9	12				
51	0.23611	3	9	12			
52	0.24074	9	10				
53	0.24537	3	9	10			
54	0.25000	10	11				
55	0.25463	3	10	11			
56	0.25926	3	10	11	18		
57	0.26389	4	10	11			
58	0.26852	6	8	10			
59	0.27315	3	6	8	10		
60	0.27778	5	10	11			
61	0.28241	3	5	10	11		
62	0.28704	6	9	10			
63	0.29167	3	6	9	10		
64	0.29630	6	10	11			
65	0.30093	3	6	10	11		
66	0.30556	3	7	9	12		
67	0.31019	7	9	10			
68	0.31481	3	7	9	10		
69	0.31944	7	10	11			
70	0.32407	3	7	10	11		
71	0.32870	8	9	12			
72	0.33333	3	8	9	12		
73	0.33796	3	8	9	12	18	
74	0.34259	3	8	9	10		
75	0.34722	8	10	11			
76	0.35185	3	8	10	11		
77	0.35648	9	10	12			
78	0.36111	3	9	10	12		
79	0.36574	9	10	11			
80	0.37037	7	9	12	14		

continues

Table 20.6 The Solution to the Problem (continued)

Ways	Probability	Roll Any of These Totals to Get This Probability					
81	0.37500	3	7	9	12	14	
82	0.37963	3	7	9	12	14	18
83	0.38426	3	4	9	10	11	
84	0.38889	7	10	11	14		
85	0.39352	3	7	10	11	14	
86	0.39815	3	7	10	11	14	18
87	0.40278	4	7	10	11	14	
88	0.40741	3	4	7	10	11	14
89	0.41204	6	9	10	11		
90	0.41667	3	6	9	10	11	
91	0.42130	3	6	9	10	11	18
92	0.42593	8	9	12	13		
93	0.43056	3	8	9	12	13	
94	0.43519	3	8	9	12	13	18
95	0.43981	4	8	9	12	13	
96	0.44444	8	10	11	13		
97	0.44907	3	8	10	11	13	
98	0.45370	3	8	10	11	13	18
99	0.45833	4	8	10	11	13	
100	0.46296	6	7	9	12	14	15
101	0.46759	3	8	9	10	11	
102	0.47222	4	8	10	11	13	17
103	0.47685	3	5	8	10	11	13
104	0.48148	9	10	11	12		
105	0.48611	3	9	10	11	12	
106	0.49074	3	9	10	11	12	18
107	0.49537	4	9	10	11	12	
108	0.50000	3	4	9	10	11	12

"Note," said Roscoe, "that for some of these the answer is not unique. But remember also that it doesn't have to be. We just need to find one set of totals that gives us the right number of 'ways' to get there."

Lessons Learned

Roscoe seemed less than totally happy at the end of the story. "What's bugging you, Roscoe?" I ventured.

"Well, first of all," he replied, "I got suckered once again. I thought I had a baby problem on my hands, and it turned out to be much more complex than I first thought. That's always annoying.

"Second, one of my time-honored techniques washed out on me," he continued. "Usually when a problem starts to grow teeth, I revert to a simpler instance of the problem to gain insight. But in this case, the simpler case of the sum of two dice was totally useless.

"Third, Monday's solution is convincing, especially when you finally have the table in hand. But even there, it seems like he used some heuristics instead of a logical proof. Although I am the last guy in the world to criticize anyone for getting the answer any way he can. Never let it be said that I was an advocate of excess purity, let alone elegance."

Now, I take a much more clement approach. Roscoe, and especially his buddy Monday, had done a great job using pencil, paper, slide rule, and common sense. In fact, had Roscoe lost his slide rule in the shipwreck, Monday still could have solved the problem, as the division by 216 is a purely cosmetic event—we can state probabilities as 67/216 if we want to.[8] That the problem can be solved on a desert island, with no computers, no Microsoft Excel, and no pivot tables by using just time, energy, and intellectual curiosity, is wonderful. It also means that Blaise Pascal could have solved the problem in the 17th century; he had all the tools he needed back then. And he didn't lack for intelligence or intellectual curiosity, either. Ironically, Hamming notes that sometime before the year 1642 Galileo was asked about the ratio of the probabilities of three dice having either a sum of 9 or else a sum of 10. He got at least as far as constructing our Table 20.1, correctly deducing that rolling a 10 was slightly more probable than rolling a 9. So people were thinking about these things long before baseball.

Roscoe and Monday wound up being able to extract a uniform probability distribution with a granularity of about *half a percent* [9] by simply rolling three dice and looking at the total, so long as they used the algorithm of specifying the probability first and then

---

[8] Or Roscoe could do long division by hand if he had to.

[9] One part in 216 is slightly better than half a percent; one part in 200 would be exactly half a percent.

deciding whether the roll was successful or not. In the original baseball example, it meant they could get batting averages to within five points.[10]

Recap

"And here's the last laugh," Roscoe concluded. "Monday showed he really understood the problem with the following observation. If you do the same experiment with *four* dice, you can prove that it is *impossible* to cover the interval from zero to one uniformly, as you could with three. That is, you can generate many more probabilities, but you cannot have them spread out equally. Now *that* is an interesting result, and it is true not only for four dice, but for any number of dice greater than three. Put that in your pipe and smoke it!"

I encourage readers to see if they can rediscover Monday's impossibility proof for four or more dice.

This is about as far afield as I am going to go in the direction of "thinking laterally." This section has been less about software development and more about opening up your mind to different ways of looking at the kinds of challenging problems we come across all the time.

I now move on to the last part of the book, one I call "Advanced Topics."

---

[10] The late Ted Williams hit .406 in 1941 and is the last player to have batted over .400 for a season. Hence, Table 20.6 is more than adequate for batting averages. For other probabilities greater than 0.500, one needs to extend the table symmetrically, using the complementarity principle mentioned earlier.

PART 6

ADVANCED TOPICS

We're rounding the final turn and coming into the home stretch. In this section, I address topics that will be important to you as you hone your software development management skills. For example, every good manager sooner or later is asked to take over an in-progress project that is in trouble.

Chapter 21, "Crisis," allegorically deals with jumping into the middle of the mess and getting on the road to recovery.

In Chapter 22, "Growth," I address the issues that crop up when you are asked to grow your organization. Perhaps you have just come off a successful project, and your boss wants you to take on a bigger one. Can you increase the size of your team and still be effective?

As you begin to manage enterprises that are larger than a single project, your thoughts will turn to what kind of organization you want to build. Chapter 23, "Culture," tackles the issues of culture and values, those intangibles that govern from on high and create the environment in which all the teams must function.

Finally, Chapter 24, "Putting It All Together," closes out the book with a philosophical piece on the very nature of people as they move through their careers.

CHAPTER 21

Crisis

Every successful manager is "rewarded" by being asked to do harder and harder things. The path to professional growth entails taking on new and different challenges. Among the most difficult of these is jumping into the middle of someone else's project.

Management is usually very reluctant to change managers in the middle of a software development project. The manager usually has so much "context" in his head that the replacement costs are prohibitive. But sometimes there is no choice. A change must be made, and you have been selected to go in and set things right.

First, you need to realize that you have a sick patient on your hands. If the situation weren't grave, they wouldn't be changing doctors, so don't expect that things will be wonderful when you get there. Second, for the project to be in this situation, a lot of things were probably done wrong. Third, assume that the problem is even worse than your manager thinks it is; usually more bad news is yet to be revealed. Every time you turn over a rock, you are more likely than not to find slimy things that make you shudder.

At least you don't have to pussyfoot around. Because the patient is sick, he can't complain too much about the medicine. You need to assess quickly, make decisions, and go forward. Do not be afraid to make changes. The characteristics of a crisis include a scarcity of time. But even if there is abundant time left, the road to salvation rarely consists of continuing down the current path. A different course needs to be established, and that needs to happen quickly.

But what do you do, and in what order?

The Five Days of the Fish

A dead fish begins to smell bad on the second day after it dies; we say something "stinks like three-day-old fish." Business problems are a lot like dead fish. Typically, people perceive them only when they start to stink—after they have been fermenting for some time. When you are asked to intervene in a decomposing situation, time is of the essence. Here's some guidance, in allegorical form, to help you analyze and resolve these crises.

The Fish Market

Let's imagine an exotic fish market, where fish are kept alive in a display tank until just before they are sold so that they can be eaten when fresh. The store has high prices, high overhead, and low volume, leading to very thin profit margins.

This market has in its employ a small but very vocal group of Cassandras who periodically announce that a fish is about to die, although all the fish are cruising around the tank as usual. This group consists of:

- Employees who don't have enough to do and are always looking for things that are not quite right. They are never taken to task if their predictions don't come true. So they predict all kinds of things with great abandon, hitting it right every once in awhile just because of statistical probability. The signal-to-noise ratio for these people is very low, so usually the owner can safely ignore them.

- A few individuals who actually *can* see what's coming and aren't afraid to speak up. Provided that the owner can distinguish these folks from the first subgroup, they can be useful to him, but they are not always right, either.

Day 1: Unaware

That very week, a fish *does* die, but very few people take notice. One or two clueless employees poke around and discuss whether it's normal for fish to float on the top of the tank. Later, they will remark that they suspected something was wrong but weren't sure.

Day 2: Avoiding the Issue

The following day, more people perceive that something is wrong, although some speculate that the fish is just tired. There is not yet enough stink in the air to arouse them to action. Although customer traffic has dropped off a bit, the head clerk delays telling the owner, who is notorious for flying into a rage upon receipt of bad news.

Day 3: Enter "The Fixer"

Some time during the third day, when the dead fish really begins to smell, the clerk finally summons the owner who, in turn, calls in an outside specialist. This "Fixer" arrives on the scene and pronounces the fish legally dead. The owner, in complete denial, scolds the Fixer for not employing mouth-to-mouth resuscitation. When the Fixer points out the futility of such an action, citing the fish's odor, the owner then commands him to "fix the fish problem."

What does this mean?

- Banishing the odor?
- Keeping any more fish in the tank from dying?
- Working with suppliers to get healthier fish in the first place?
- Finding someone who wants to buy the dead, putrefying fish?
- All of the above?

Knowing that the owner does not yet know what he wants—and that his idea of "fix" will probably change a few times before the Fixer is done—the Fixer rolls up his sleeves and gets to work. In the meantime, business continues to fall off.

No one can ignore the odor, and customers are staying away. Rumors spread throughout the bazaar that many fish in the store have died and were surreptitiously thrown away. The Cassandras are abuzz with "I told you so," and employees are putting as much distance as possible between themselves and the dead fish. The owner assures everyone that the Fixer is working on the problem and will soon have a solution.

Meanwhile, the Fixer is up to his elbows in stinking fish guts, feeling dirty, lonely, and desperate. The owner tells him what a prince he is. Because this is not the first time he has been called in on a "dead fish" problem, the Fixer is mildly upset and concerned about the extent to which he is being "managed." But he knows that to be successful, he must keep his head down and solve the problem.

Day 4: The Turning Point

By Day 4, the stench is so bad that the employees are clamoring for the Fixer's head. Some even blame him for the fish's death. Moreover, the health department arrives and threatens to close the store, sending the owner into a full panic.

The Fixer is prepared for all of this. He knows that Day 4 is his moment of truth—the get-rolling-or-smell-horrible-forever day. That is why he wasted no time trying to resuscitate the dead fish on Day 3, knowing from experience that he would need time to examine the entrails and formulate a solution. Today, he has several crucial tasks:

- Close out the preliminary analysis phase

- Formulate a plan for going forward

- Announce the plan internally

- Begin implementation

- Calm down the team

This is a tall order, and it is more than enough to accomplish on Day 4.

He makes no attempt to control the odor (focus on public relations) yet, understanding that doing so before a true solution is underway would invite catastrophe. Privately, the Fixer thanks his lucky stars that the remaining fish appear to be hanging in there, because another dead fish at this point could push the whole thing over the cliff.

Day 5: Two Critical Paths

Day 5 is as critical as Day 4. It has been a long time since the fish died. Even though the corpse has been removed, the smell still lingers. The Fixer knows that if the odor doesn't disappear quickly, things will take a dramatic turn for the worse. It is time to get out the Lysol. So he divides his efforts between two tasks: continuing to resolve the problem and getting rid of the odor. The Fixer must balance the two tasks carefully.

If he neglects diligently continuing his problem-solving work, more fish may die. If he ignores the continuing bad odor, the owner might mistakenly interpret the ongoing stench as a lack of progress and jettison the Fixer's proposed solution—tossing the baby out with the bathwater, so to speak.

If the Fixer can survive Day 5, things will get better. Both employees and customers will quickly forget about the problem, and he can finish resolving it without all the pressure. He will succeed by making steady, regular progress and ensuring that no new fish die on his watch. Until the problem is fully resolved, ongoing vigilance is critical.

Moral of the Story

Fixers of the world, remember that in a crisis you have three days to prove yourself:

1. Fish start to stink on Day 2, but you will rarely be called that early.

2. Don't waste Day 3 fooling around. Open up the fish and conceive a plan. The stink will be bad, and it will linger.

3. Announce your plan internally and begin executing it on Day 4.

4. Devote Day 5 to working on the problem *and* eliminating the odor.

Good luck! Work on keeping your fish alive, and may all your dead fish be little ones.

Recap

Of course you are not going to solve all your crises in three days, but the allegory is useful in describing how you have to stage your work. Remember, everyone around you, including perhaps your boss, may be in a high state of panic when you arrive on the scene. Take the point of view of the Texas Ranger who got off the train alone, to the consternation of the townspeople he had been sent to help. "We wired that there was an insurrection—where are the others?" asked the elder statesman of the group. "One insurrection, one Texas Ranger," was the reply. You must remain calm while everyone else is up in arms.

The "odor" on the project can take many forms. The rumor mill will make sure of that. In the early days, one of your jobs is to understand the root causes of the odor. Is the software simply late? Are large parts not working? Is the user interface clumsy? Is the build process broken? Has sufficient testing been done? What's the state of the documentation? Is the team in open revolt? Have the marketing people gone ballistic? All these and other smells will be in the air.

Getting rid of the odor means doing the "public relations" part of the job to stem the tide of negative opinion now surrounding the project. This means you need to be able to calmly respond that certain problems reputed to exist really don't or are not critical. And, for the other legitimate causes of odor, you need to freshen the atmosphere by publicly explaining what the "get-well" plan is.

So your first and most important task is *assessment*. You must get first-hand data on what's going on, and you need to make quick and accurate judgments about the people you talk to. Some of them are going to be instrumental in helping you out of the mess, but don't forget that some of them are the reason for the mess in the first place. So think in terms of who stays and who gets moved down the road. You must have team players who will get on board with the new plan; those who seem especially resistant to change are going to be too high overhead to be useful.

As you assess, you need to be moving as rapidly as possible into figuring out and beginning implementation of the new plan. This must be done before any attempts at damage control are undertaken. Until you can explain how you are going to do things differently, you really have nothing to say. Resist at all costs going public with opinions until you are confident of your assessment and have at least the outline of a plan ready to talk about. There will be a lot of pressure, because people want reassurances that "things will get better." Well, you can't do that until your get-well plan is underway.

Once the new plan is underway, then you can turn some of your attention to the damage control part of the job. It is important, don't get me wrong. But you can only do it effectively once you have done the other two activities to the best of your ability.

CHAPTER 22

Growth

There is an important interaction between growth and productivity. A very simple model can enable managers to better understand what occurs as new team members are integrated into an existing organization. While straightforward, the model also permits some interesting predictions; and with some simple graphs, I can show how the various factors interact.

There are no clear answers to all the problems that growth presents, but I believe good managers can learn to manipulate the parameters that define the model. It can pay big dividends to balance organizational development ("OD," with its focus on growth) with project management ("PM," with its focus on productivity). The organization needs to cope with the problems of growth in order to prosper, while the projects it works on need to be concerned with productivity and cost. These two are often seen to be in conflict, requiring delicate trade-offs. I attempt in this chapter to show areas of commonality and ways in which both objectives can be achieved.

Growth Issues

Healthy organizations have a tendency to grow over time. Plainly speaking, those that are successful in getting done what needs to get done are called upon to do more. Usually this translates into growth, as measured by the addition of new people to the team.

A significant challenge facing any successful organization is how to stay successful as it grows. This is harder than it looks. The organization needs to continue to do well what it has been doing in the past; it needs to also succeed at the new challenges that are put before it; and, last but certainly not least, it needs to do both these things while assimilating new team members. And, issues of *scaling* become important; what was relatively easy to do when the team was small becomes more difficult to do as the team grows larger.

Even in periods of zero growth, there are the challenges associated with new hires. Those organizations that don't acquire periodic introductions of "new blood" tend to stagnate and succumb to group think; and there is always the addition of team members just to offset attrition, which I'll discuss briefly at the end of this chapter.

In Silicon Valley, in the arena of software development, we have seen a different problem: Organizations have a variety of reasons to attempt what I would call excessive growth. Management sees windows of opportunity as fleeting, and the addition of contractors or consultants can't always help. In an attempt to capitalize on a leadership situation or a beachhead established in a new market, organizations rush pell-mell to solidify their position through ultra-rapid growth; middle managers are asked to grow their organizations as fast as they can. The result is usually less than optimal. Certainly, when growth rates exceed 50 percent a year, one must understand that something very difficult is being attempted.

As early as 1972, in less politically correct times, Fred Brooks talked about adding people to software projects that were late, enunciating Brooks' First Law in his classic *The Mythical Man-Month*:[1]

Adding manpower to a late software project makes it later.

We examine a variant of the same idea. What is new here is a quantitative generalization to other provocations for growth in organizations, not just as a knee-jerk reaction to being late. In other words, we look at Brooks's notion of the lack of interchangeability of "men" for "months."

There are two interesting data points in Brooks' notes. Vyssotsky, on page 179, estimates that large projects can sustain growth rates of no more than 30 percent a year without suffering. Yet, in the very same note, Corbató is quoted as pointing out that long projects must anticipate a turnover of 20 percent a year; this means a significant need to integrate new people, just as with growth. Clearly, given this narrow band of approximately 10 percent between what must occur and what is difficult to accomplish in long, large efforts, we need to better understand, in a quantitative fashion, the dynamics of adding people to projects.

Other previous work in this area is usually qualitative and anecdotal, probably because the hard data needed to validate models of this type is difficult to come by.

---

[1] Brooks, Frederick P. *The Mythical Man-Month: Essays on Software Engineering*. 2nd ed. (Boston: Addison-Wesley, 1995), 25.

Shooman is one of the rare exceptions; his treatment is more complex than mine, but a good starting point.[2]

The Naïve Model

The model is a very simple "one-period" model, with the following assumptions:

- At the beginning of the period, we have an organization in place that is well integrated, well trained, and firing on all cylinders. We take the productivity of its team members to be the baseline for comparison.

- During the period, we add new team members of the same average quality as those already in place.

- At the end of the period, we have a "new" organization with more people and a greater capacity to get work done, because we have more people with the same average productivity as when we started.

What we deal with here is what happens to productivity *during the period of transition*.

Note an important assumption: We assume that the overall *per capita* productivity does not decrease because the organization gets larger. While this is often *not* the case, we naïvely assume that once we are done with the transition, the organization has gained productivity in direct proportion to the growth.

For organizations that are constantly growing, we can still use this model. We just sequence a series of one-period models one after the other. By superposition, we can make predictions for this case. It is mathematically a little more complex, but nothing new needs to be added conceptually.

Effect of New Hires During Transition: Contribution

Even during transition, we should add useful productive hours to the current total. Even an employee who is only 10 percent effective during his ramp-up period is still adding, for his or her part, four hours of "useful" work per week. We must view the remaining 36 hours as "training," "ramp up," or "investment in the future." We pay for those hours, but they do not show up in the current product.[3]

---

[2] Shooman, Martin L. *Software Engineering: Design, Reliability, and Management* (New York: McGraw-Hill, 1983), p 469-479.

[3] I use product development as the main focus. However, the analysis applies to other types of organizations as well. For example, in a sales organization, substitute the words "hours spent in direct selling" for "hours worked on the product." Everything else follows in parallel fashion. When we add new salespeople, our revenues go up, but so does our cost of sales on a per employee basis.

So, in this most naïve model, we gain hours but lose overall productivity during the transition period. That's a reasonable tradeoff, and we should quantify it so that we know what we are trading off for what. However, there is a secondary effect that we should add to the model to increase its fidelity: drag.

Effect of the New Hires on the Existing Team: Drag

It turns out that while new employees add hours by being productive at some marginal rate, they actually detract from the total by being there as well. That is because others in the organization lose productive time in working with the new, less productive employees. This can be time lost in supervision, explanation, "showing them the ropes" and any other manner of bringing the new employee up to speed, *or correcting their mistakes.* These are very costly hours, because the in-place employees are, by definition relative to the newbies, 100 percent productive. Another way of saying this is that the new employees place a drag on the organization because otherwise fully productive, in-place employees must interact with them.

I should point out some obvious exceptions to this rule. If we recruit a new team member who has a skill set that is needed and otherwise absent, there can be a spontaneous increase in overall productivity. Similarly, if we recruit a superior manager, we may turn around an otherwise dysfunctional team. Both these instances are examples of almost immediate improvement and represent "negative drag," as it were. But, generally speaking, these are exceptional cases.

The Model and Its Assumptions

As with all models, we make some simplifying assumptions, which I collect and enumerate here for clarity. Note that we can make successively more complicated models to increase fidelity, but at some point we hit the law of diminishing returns. The best models are the simplest.

Our assumptions are as follows:

- **Existing in-place team members are "100 percent productive."** We ignore any loss of productivity due to *their* training and overhead. Basically we are using the existing people as the productivity benchmark, and everything is relative to them. We assume that the organization has a total productivity equal to the product of the average productivity of the existing team members times the number of them in steady state. Thus we do not assume that all existing employees have the same productivity but rather have some distribution that we can characterize with an average productivity.

- **During the ramp-up period (one year), new employees are characterized by an average fractional productivity P, with $0 \leq P \leq 1$.** We make the simplifying assumption that they are hired "en masse" at the beginning of the year. For example, P = 0.6 indicates that, during the ramp-up year, the average productivity of the new team members will be 60 percent of that of the existing team members; 60 percent of their hours go to "useful" work on the product, and 40 percent of their hours go to "getting up to speed." You can, of course, choose the ramp-up period to be anything you like without loss of generality; my observation is that it is usually longer than managers think it is.

A simple extension of the model could allow for "learning curve" behavior. That is, we could model the typical S-Curve that characterizes new-hire learning ramp-up during the period using a spreadsheet. In the interest of simplicity, I choose instead to assume a constant average productivity during the entire period.

- **We measure the annual growth of the team by the fraction G of new employees, usually between 0 and 1.** For example, G = 0.1 indicates a 10-percent growth rate, or the addition of one new team member for each existing 10. G = 1.0 would correspond to 100 percent growth or attempting to add one new person for each existing person. As we will see later, growth rates of this magnitude are highly risky. Once again, we make the simplifying assumption that new team members are hired "en masse" at the beginning of the year. More complex models would stage, or phase, the arrival of the new hires; once again, this leads to more complicated math, but nothing that is conceptually novel. Once again, this could be built into a spreadsheet model.

- **The effect of new hires is characterized by a drag ratio D, with $0 \le D \le 1$.** For example, a D of 1.0 means that for every hour spent in non-productive work by a new team member, there is an associated loss of an hour of an existing team member. The smaller the D, the better for the organization; for example, a D of 0.2 means that we lose only two hours of work by existing team members for every 10 hours of lost work by newbies.

- **New team members have the same average hourly pay rate as the existing team members.** This is reasonable, because we are assuming that once the ramp-up period is complete, the new team members will be just as productive as the existing ones; that is, we assume they will attain "100 percent productivity." Another way of saying this is that we assume that the newly hired people are of the same average quality as those already in place; hence, they are paid at the same average rate.

Consequences of the Model

I first consider whether we are achieving the result of making more hours available for the product. There are two competing factors:

- On the one hand, we add hours due to the productivity, however small, of the new team members.

- On the other hand, training them costs us in productivity on the part of the existing team members.

The equation that relates H, the number of useful hours, to G, P, and D is:

$$H = 1 + G[P - (1 - P)D].$$

Note some quick checks:

- With $G = 0$, we have $H = 1$. There is no difference in useful hours.
- If $P = 0$, we have $H = 1 - DG$. Useful hours are decreased by the training drag on the rest of the organization.
- If $P = 1$, we have $H = 1 + G$. Useful hours increase as fast as we grow.
- If $D = 0$, we have $H = 1 + PG$. The gain in productive hours equals the growth times the productivity of the new team members.
- Finally, when $D = 1$, we see that $H = 1 + G(2P - 1)$. Every hour new team members consume ramping up must be matched by an hour from an existing team member. Unless P is at least 0.5, we don't recoup the hour lost by the existing team member with a new-hire productive hour.

In fact, one can see that we increase the number of useful hours on the product if and only if

$$P > (1 - P)D.$$

Note this condition is *independent* of the growth rate G. That is, you can always get more useful hours by growing faster if you observe this condition on P and D.

Nailing the Multiplier

We can rewrite the equation

$$H = 1 + G[P - (1 - P)D]$$

as

$$H = 1 + GM,$$

where

$$M = P - (1 - P)D.$$

In Figure 22.1, I display the quantity M, which, when multiplied by the growth rate G, will give us the percent increase in useful hours on the product. (Because we are using 1 as the baseline, the term "GM" actually represents the increase "over one," so it is actually a percent increase.)

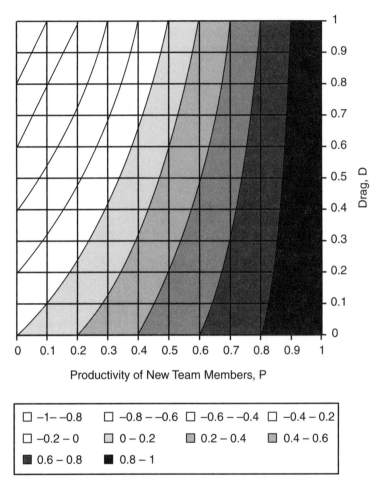

Figure 22.1   Contour plot of the multiplier M as a function of drag D and productivity P.

- The five white bands to the left correspond to *negative* multipliers. In this region we see a *decrease* in the number of useful hours per unit of growth; growing faster in this case actually results in fewer and fewer hours devoted to the product.

- The other shaded bands represent progressively better scenarios; for example, the first band next to the white region corresponds to an M between 0 and 0.2. In this region we get an average of 0.1 times the growth rate in incremental useful hours; with 30 percent growth, for example, we will achieve 0.1 times 30 percent or 3 percent in incremental useful hours.

- At the opposite extreme, the dark band at the very right of the chart corresponds to an M between 0.8 and 1.0, so in this region we can assume an average value of around 0.9. For the same 30 percent growth rate, we now attain 0.9 times 30 percent or 27 percent more useful hours on the product.

To summarize, we see that this multiplier depends on two factors in a non-linear way:

- P is characteristic of the population of new hires; it estimates their relative productivity during ramp-up.

- D characterizes our existing organization; it is a measure of our ability to integrate new people efficiently.

What the chart tells us is that if we can keep D small, we can tolerate fairly low P. On the other hand, the higher the value of D, the more sensitive we are to P. This agrees with our intuition.

Useful Hours Added to Product

Now that we understand the multiplier effect, we can plot a simple graph, shown in Figure 22.2, illustrating the percentage increase in useful hours as a function of growth. This

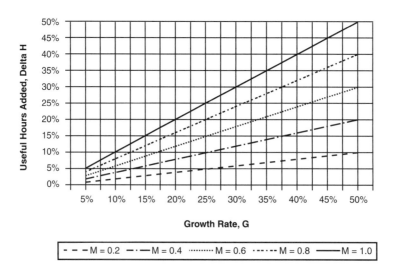

Figure 22.2   Useful hours added to product, ΔH, as a function of growth rate G, for various values of the multiplier M.

is simply linear in the multiplier. Once you know M, you can read off the percentage increase in useful hours by looking up G on the horizontal axis and using the appropriate sloped line for M. The result is read off the vertical axis. Or you can do the reverse: For a required percentage increase in useful hours, you can read off the growth rate required for your calculated value of M.

What About Cost?

Remember that you have to pay for all hours, productive or not. As soon as you have hours that are non-productive, due either to the new team members or to the drag that they cause, the overall productivity of the organization *decreases.*

What management must consider is what constitutes a reasonable trade-off. You produce your product *faster* because you are devoting more hours to it, but in doing so you are making the product *more costly to produce*, because the overall productivity of the organization is lower due to training the added team members. The management balancing act consists of deciding how much time is worth how much cost. For many projects, especially in software, *the labor content represents the preponderance of the cost*, so these arguments are cogent.[4]

The total number of useful hours that one has dedicated to the product is

$$H = 1 + GM.$$

On the other hand, the new total number of hours we are paying for is

$$T = 1 + G.$$

So the new overall productivity of the organization is just

$$N = H / T,$$

or

$$N = (1 + GM) / (1 + G).$$

We can plot this relationship to see how the overall productivity varies as a function of M and G. This is shown in Figure 22.3.

The zone to the right is "good." That is, we have a productivity that is between 95 − 100 percent of our base productivity. At the other extreme, our overall productivity has dropped to between 70 and 75 percent of the baseline. Note that the best way to guard against precipitous drops in productivity is to grow slowly, say no more than 20 percent.

---

[4] And, of course, one has to be sure that all this happens under conditions of "equal or better quality." A more costly product brought to market faster may not be a good thing if the overall quality suffers.

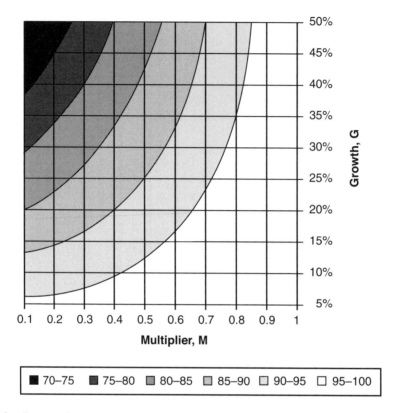

Figure 22.3 Contour plot of new overall productivity (as a percentage of baseline) as a function of the growth rate G and the multiplier M.

If we stay under 20 percent growth, we can guarantee that overall productivity will not drop below 85 percent regardless of the multiplier; it won't fall below 90 percent so long as M is at least 0.4. On the other hand, at 20 percent growth or more, we start to become very sensitive to M.

As a side note, if you can keep your M at 0.85 or higher, you can also stay in the 95 percent productivity zone regardless of the growth rate. Achieving an M of 0.85 is a real challenge, as you can see from Figure 22.1.

What about the labor cost to produce the product? If we are putting H useful hours into the product per unit time, then the product will be completed in 1/H the time. But each unit of time is now costing us $(1 + G)$ dollars, so the new total cost is $(1 + G) / H$. This is just the inverse of the overall productivity. The idea that cost and productivity are in inverse proportion to each other appeals to our notions of good sense.

Figure 22.4 shows how product cost increases with M and G.

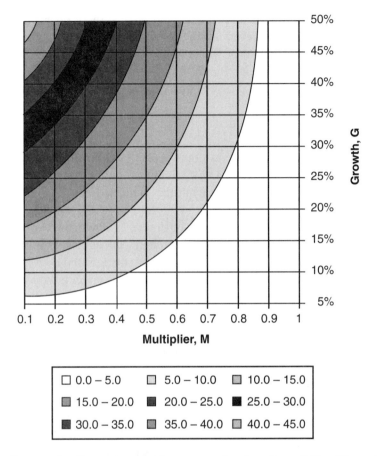

Figure 22.4   Contour plot of percentage cost increase as a function of growth G and the multiplier M.

An Illustrative Example

Suppose that we currently are spending $1 million in labor costs a year, and that we assume we can get out our new product at the end of the year with the current team in place. Our management would like to get the product out in 10 months instead of 12. We assume that any new team members we recruit will be only 60 percent productive during the year, and that our organization has a medium drag, with a D of 0.5. The two numbers we need to come up with are the following:

- How many new people do we need to hire?
- What does this do to the cost of developing the product?

To produce in 10 months what would have been produced in 12 means that we need 20 percent more useful hours devoted to the product. (Check: 10 months times 1.2 hours/month equals the equivalent of what would have previously been produced in 12 months.) So H = 1.2, which means that GM = 0.2. But M = P − (1 − P)D = 0.6 − (0.4)(0.5) = 0.6 − 0.2 = 0.4. That means that G must equal 0.2/0.4, or 0.5, which is a 50 percent growth rate.

The labor cost of the product per unit time goes up by 50 percent, because G = 0.5. We do produce it in only (10/12) of the time it would have taken, so the total cost goes up by 25 percent. That is, we are now spending $1.5 million per year in labor, but produce the product in (10/12) of a year, so that its total cost is $1.25 million. Note that this 25 percent increase is exactly what the increased cost graph of Figure 22.4 predicts.

Note from the overall productivity chart of Figure 22.3 with an M of 0.4 and a G of 0.5 we achieve an overall productivity of 80 percent. This agrees with the idea that we are devoting 1.2 useful hours to the product but paying for 1.5 total hours; 1.2 divided by 1.5 is 80 percent. The inverse of 0.8 is 1.25, which squares up with the idea that the cost to produce the product has gone up by 25 percent.

Here's the bottom line: To gain two months on the 12-month schedule, we must grow at 50 percent and increase our product cost by 25 percent. This is a result of having only 60 percent productivity on the part of the new team members, and having a training drag of one hour of current team-member time for each two hours of new team-member training time. Also, we are undertaking substantial increased risk due to the 50-percent growth rate.

We leave it to the reader to compute the implications of a management desire to reduce the time to market from 12 months to 9 months. It is interesting to consider how much additional cost and risk are added to the project in this attempt to gain yet another additional month in the schedule.

Non-Linearity

We tend to have good intuition about things when there is a linear relationship between the controlling variables. For example, all other things being held equal, we expect that if we have three times as much work, it will take us three times as long to get the job done. However, our intuition starts to work less well when the variables involved have a non-linear relationship.

With the problem at hand, we note that once we have computed the multiplier, M, there is a linear relationship between the number of useful additional hours devoted to the product and the growth rate, G. That is, we gain useful hours in direct proportion to growth rate, with M as the constant of proportionality. Unfortunately, this is the only linear relationship in the whole model.

To compute the key ingredient M, the multiplier, we used a relationship that is non-linear in the variables P and D:

$$M = P - (1 - P) D.$$

This leads to Figure 22.1, where different bands correspond to different ranges of M. Note that we have only weak intuition as to how those bands come out as a function of P and D; we know that low P and high D are bad in combination, but it is hard to judge just how bad. That is why the graph is so helpful.

Similarly, both the overall productivity and increased cost to produce the product are non-linear in M and G. Recall that the relationship for the new overall productivity is

$$N = (1 + GM) / (1 + G).$$

This is clearly once again a non-linear relationship. We don't have a good feel for how overall productivity goes, other than the notion that large G and small M must be bad. The increase in cost is just the inverse of N, so that relationship is non-linear as well. The two graphs for these quantities, Figures 22.3 and 22.4, show a banded structure similar to that when computing M. And, as M is non-linear in P and D, we have a non-linearity on top of a non-linearity! So trying to infer what N might be as a function of P, D, and G is a difficult leap indeed; the relationship we are trying to intuit is

$$N = (1 + G [P - (1 - P) D]) / (1 + G).$$

Most of us would freely admit that we have little or no intuition for N as a function of these three variables. Yet that is implicitly the task we start out with.

The moral of the story is:

Even simple natural phenomena are sometimes *non-linear.*

When this occurs, our intuition can be weak. In order to understand what is really happening and make intelligent predictions, having a simple mathematical model and some graphical visualization tools can be invaluable.

Call to Action

Now that we understand how the various factors interact to affect productivity during periods of growth, we are faced with the question of doing something about it. I have three suggestions:

- **Whenever possible, use real data to estimate the parameters P and D.** These are the ingredients in computing the multiplier M, on which everything else depends. Pulling numbers for them out of the air will likely lead you astray. Not all organizations keep records that are detailed enough to help. On the other hand, you can look at hours explicitly devoted to training, for example. These go into both P and D, as both new employees and old are involved. All meetings should be looked at to see whether they are primarily product-related or focused on getting the new hires up to speed. The better you can estimate P and D, the better the numbers you will get coming out at the other end.

- **Think hard about P when evaluating new hire candidates.** The model is most sensitive to P, and nothing can overcome a low value for it.

    - Selecting fast learners is always a good thing; slow learners have low P and should be avoided.

    - Look out for a "missing skill," such as specific knowledge about a programming language or technique that allegedly can be picked up easily. Even very bright people take time to learn new things; if these things are to be learned on the job, you are agreeing to reduce P for that person.

    - Avoid hiring people who come from a company culture that is radically different from yours. There is an implicit and somewhat large decrease in P (and a corresponding increase in D) for hires who have the additional learning burden of adapting to "how we do it here."

    - If the new hire has a tendency toward inflexibility, these factors will be magnified still further.

- **Think of D as amplifying the effects of a low P.** Ironically, smaller organizations may have larger D than more mature organizations. This is because they have most of their organizational memory stored in the brains of a few people. When new people are brought on board, there is no way to get them up-to-speed other than one-on-one dialogs with these key people. A few things are obvious:

    - Hire and train new people in batches, so you can get some economy of scale in the adaptation process.

    - To the extent possible, invest in documenting "how things get done," so that new hires can read materials instead of having to take time from existing team members every time a question arises.

    - For software development organizations, having well-written and well-documented source code can dramatically diminish D, as well as help to increase P.

There is no "silver bullet" here, but understanding the importance of both P and D can help managers keep the damages to a minimum. It also allows us to estimate the return on investment of things like documentation. Reducing D by a few tenths can tell us how much we will improve the overall productivity and reduce our incremental cost during our next growth period. We can then compare the cost of reducing D in this way with the benefits that would accrue.

Conclusions

I have explored a very simple three-parameter model for growth and productivity in organizations during the transition period when we are assimilating new hires. I have modeled "useful hours" and "overall organizational productivity" as a function of growth rate, new team-member productivity, and organizational assimilation effectiveness. While the model is simple, it shows that high growth rates are risky and that the combination of high growth and low new-employee productivity can be disastrous. Note that this occurs even under the assumption that the steady-state productivity of the new employees equals that of the existing ones. Add to that an organization that is inefficient in assimilating new team members, and you have the recipe for a perfect storm.

Even if the new hires are as good as the people already in place, there is yet another danger: The new, larger organization may be less productive, *per capita,* than before. Overall productivity may suffer due to size and scaling effects, such as the increased overhead of more communication links, and so on. Our model ignored these effects.

What happens in reality is often even more insidious: In our attempt to grow faster, we often lower our recruiting standards. When this happens, not only is the combined "growth + training hit" large, but there is a dilution of the talent pool, leading to a permanent lowering of productivity even after the ramp-up is complete. The problem for the organization is a difficult one: During the ramp-up period, we attribute the decrease in productivity to ramp-up activities; it is only after that period is completed that we observe that our overall productivity has suffered. By then, of course, it is too late. A long-term problem has escaped us under the guise of being a transitional or short-term one; there has been "masking." That is why it is crucial when hiring to always bring people on board who, in steady state, will raise the average productivity of the group.

Along the way we made an interesting observation: Although our model was very simple, it led to several non-linear relationships. We have poor instincts for things that are non-linear. The graphs that we produced to illustrate the interdependencies amongst the variables revealed structures that we had not foreseen. It is these "hidden" structures that cause otherwise good managers to be surprised; things diverge on them more rapidly than they expect because of non-linearities. Cutting just one more month off a schedule by adding people sometimes has disastrous consequences if you are already in the "yellow zone" without knowing it. That last seemingly small step pushes you over the cliff and into the abyss. Better to draw some graphs and understand where you really are than to scream loudly on the way down.

Attention should be paid to the suggestions I made to improve the parameters P and D that govern everything else. This is the "call to action." Models are useful only to the extent that we use them to understand nature and then work on changing the values of the parameters that negatively affect our performance.

The model made several simplifying assumptions about which I prudently tried to warn you. If, based on these assumptions, the model predicts productivity and cost effects that are unpleasant, it behooves the manager to proceed with caution. The reason is simple: Nature is rarely as kind to us as the mathematical model. When Mr. Murphy (of "Murphy's Law" fame) adds his contribution to the mix, one can be sure that the results will in general be *worse* than what our models predict. One needs to have a margin for error. So "taking the model with a grain of salt" means this: If the model says you are OK, proceed with caution; if the model says you might have a problem or be in a high-risk situation, back off and reconsider. In most situations, managers are too optimistic in estimating the parameters that go into the model, and that, coupled with some of the "ideal" assumptions that go into it, can lead to project Hell.

Nomograph

It would be nice to be able to do the calculations presented in the illustrative example quickly, and even better to get results without having to plug numbers into equations. Though the relationships are simple, even I must admit that working with equations is not a favorite activity of most managers these days. All is not lost, however.

Back in the days of ships of wood and men of iron, there was a simple solution to capturing relationships among variables: graphical methods, in particular, the device known as the *nomograph*.[5] The user simply laid a straightedge across some specially arranged and calibrated scales. If serial calculations were required, multiple instances of this technique could be chained together, all on one sheet of paper. An engineer did the non-trivial mathematical work behind the nomograph, and a master nomographer produced a chart that was ridiculously simple to use. This technique, documented by d'Ocagne around 1900, was highly developed by the worldwide engineering community from around 1925 to 1975, when the advent of pocket calculators and computers caused it to go out of fashion. A quarter of a century later, as is frequently the case of useful things that fall by the wayside, we await its worthy replacement. In vain, I'm afraid.

I've created such a nomograph for the equations in this chapter. It is displayed as Figure 22.5. As with all good nomographs, a usage example is included right on the chart. Note that this is our illustrative example from earlier.

Nomographs have the interesting property of solving equations both explicitly and implicitly. You can find any missing variable or combination of variables by "working backwards." Experiment a little with this. For example, start with an "allowable" increase in cost and percentage increase in useful hours desired to find the growth rate

---

[5] From the Greek *nomos* (law) and *graphein* (to write). *Nomogram* is also used synonymously.

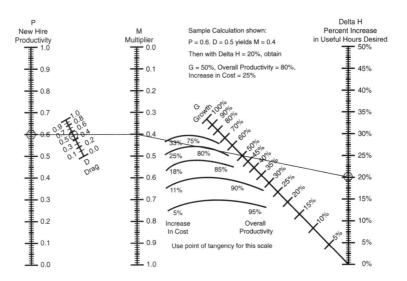

Figure 22.5   Growth and productivity nomograph.

needed and the multiplier this implies. Then see which combinations of P and D give you that M. Often this type of exploration is useful in seeing whether your constraints can be met.

Let me explain how I constructed the nomograph. Moving left to right, the first part is done by observing that the relationship between P, D, and M is a standard form that is amenable to a "Z-type" nomograph; the non-linear scale for D is constructed manually by finding appropriate common intersection points. Then the M, Delta H, and G nomograph is added, using the notion that useful hours derive from growth G times the multiplier M. Once again, a slightly different "Z-type" nomograph is appropriate, and the non-linear G scale is determined by the method of intersections. Finally, once we know the Delta H we want and the multiplier M we have already determined, both overall productivity and its inverse, the increase in cost, are determined. These, however, turn out to be envelopes, not simple intersections. These envelopes were constructed graphically by using many pairs of values for Delta H and M corresponding to each value of overall productivity; adding the increase in cost is just a labeling exercise at that point.

Spreadsheet

The more modern approach to simplifying the calculations is to use a spreadsheet. Figure 22.6 is a snapshot of one that I constructed in far less time than it took to create the nomograph.

		Example
Enter values in cells that look like this:		
Results appear in cells that look like this:		
Enter number of manhours for project here:	7,000	7,000

Baseline:

Enter number of current team here:	5	5
Enter average wage rate in $/hour here:	50	50

Based on 40 hours per week,   40

The project will take	35 weeks,		35
and the total cost will be	$ 350,000	$	350,000

New Hires:

Enter number of new hires here:	1	1
Enter average wage rate in $/hr here:	50	50
Enter relative productivity P here:	0.6	0.6
Enter drag D here:	0.1	0.1

Results:

The growth rate is:	20%	20%
Useful hours/week added by new hires:	24	24
Hours/week lost due to drag:	1.6	1.6
Net hours/week added by new hires:	22.4	22.4
Total hours/week available for project:	222.4	222.4
Overall productivity is:	92.7%	92.7%

The project will now take	31.5 weeks,	31.5
which represents a savings of	3.5 weeks.	3.5
The schedule has been cut by	10.1%	10%

The project cost is now	$ 377,698	$	377,698
The increased cost is	$ 27,698	$	27,698
The cost has increased by	7.9%		7.9%

The multiplier M is	0.56	0.56

Figure 22.6   Growth and productivity spreadsheet.

Starting from this very simple spreadsheet, you can easily develop some of the more sophisticated enhancements talked about earlier in the chapter. For example, I have already allowed for using a different wage rate for the new hires, although the example has them equal so that you can compare the spreadsheet result with your own calculation using the equations or nomograph. Moreover, once the model is cast in spreadsheet form, you can use tools such as Goal Seeking to implicitly solve, or work backwards, as you see fit.

Recap

The material in this chapter originally appeared in *The UMAP Journal*, 25 (4), (2004) 357-374.

Here's a quick note on attrition: Its effects can be insidious. Assume, for example, that you have 20 people in your group, and four of them quit. You have suffered 20 percent attrition. To get back to your starting point, you have to hire four people. However, that corresponds to a growth rate of *25 percent*, because you have to add four to an existing team of 16. When thinking about attrition, it is important to remember that the growth factor G that you are going to have to use in computing new overall productivity is always higher than the attrition rate, because of this effect.

CHAPTER 23

Culture

We are seeing a renaissance of interest in culture and values in business these days,[1] which I view as another example of nature abhorring a vacuum: Culture and values are coming into focus now because we simply haven't given them much consideration in recent times. While revelations about errant companies and company officers continue to multiply, those who have hewn to the true path seem to be forgotten. It's always that way: The foibles and follies of rascals sell newspapers and media air time, and the honest folks don't get much publicity—even if they represent the majority.

In this chapter, we'll delve into the relationship between "culture" and "values." I'm proud to have worked for a company that has a strong culture, coupled with the right values. But this is not an accident. In mapping out the territory from my own perspective, it goes without saying that my own set of values aligns pretty closely with those of Rational Software; otherwise, I would not have spent more than 16 years there.

We'll start by examining what a culture is and then see how values play into defining and supporting culture.

---

[1] For example, see Amy C. Edmondson and Sandra E. Cha, "When Company Values Backfire." *Harvard Business Review*, November 2002, or Patrick Lencione, "Make Your Values Mean Something." *Harvard Business Review*, July 2002.

What Is a Culture?

I define a *culture* as a set of characteristics that sets one group of people apart from another. For example, we sometimes regard differences in the way the English act as opposed to the French as the result of cultural differences. In doing so, we take a vast number of differences and agglomerate them under one umbrella.

Some characteristics are transcultural, though. For example, we more or less expect that all children, everywhere, will grow up to love their parents. The way they express that love may depend a lot on the culture in which they are raised, but the loving feelings are culturally agnostic.

Another way to think about this is that a culture defines how a set of abstract principles is translated into day-to-day behavior. That is, we all have a set of nearly instinctive "default behaviors," programmed into us from infancy, which represent accepted norms and modes within our local environment. Of course, we can consciously choose to behave outside these norms, which we may well do in unusual situations. For example, if we live in a culture that believes violence is bad, then when disagreements arise, our default behavior, according to that cultural norm, is to use our words and not our fists—to resolve conflict verbally. However, if it becomes clear that someone who is threatening another person's life will not listen to reason, then the culture admits violence as a last resort for the potential victim—or a law enforcement officer. But this is an exceptional case. In general, there are sanctions, both formal and informal, for violating cultural norms when exceptional circumstances do not apply.

Perhaps my colleague Philippe Kruchten said it best when he wrote the following (in an unpublished paper):

Our behavior is driven by three forces:

- *Human nature:* This is inherited and is universally shared across all human cultures.

- *Culture:* Our collective programming, which is learned, not inherited.

- *Personality:* The component that is the additional unique set of mental programs not shared with other human beings; it's partly inherited and partly learned.

If we're not exposed to other cultures, we have a difficult time distinguishing culture from human nature. We naturally assume that all these aspects are universal, but they are not. It is also important to distinguish those characteristics that are cultural—that is, generic to a group of individuals—as opposed to attributing such characteristics to individual personality quirks. It is somehow easier to condone someone for not having surmounted a cultural barrier than it is to forgive what we perceive as a personal deviance.

Strong and Weak Cultures

Continuing down the same path, I believe there are two different kinds of cultures: *strong* and *weak*. This speaks to how a culture translates its underlying principles, or values, into everyday life.

In a strong culture, the abstract principles (values) are translated very directly into people's day-to-day lives. The military, for example, has a definite set of values and a very strong culture. Whether or not you agree with these values, you have to admit that they are translated into daily use very rigorously and consistently; they are enforced through external rules and regulations, as well as through education that is absorbed internally. The prevailing culture of the 1960s was also a strong one, characterized by distrust for authority and a desire to question all social conventions. Once again, whether you agree with these values or not, you have to acknowledge their powerful influence on people's behavior at the time. I remember, for example, how difficult it was to "organize" a peace march, because the participants were so anti-authority—leaders had to explain and justify every "request" they made,[2] and "enforcement" came almost entirely from peer pressure.

Not all cultures are that strong, though. Some have a set of generally accepted abstract values, yet these do not really inform daily life. In Western culture, for example, the degree to which churchgoers apply their religious values to daily life varies widely. Some churches and sects have a very strong culture and strive to place religious tenets at the core of every act and thought, day in and day out. Other sects, in contrast, are much more *laissez faire* with respect to regulating daily behavior and treat faith as the most important value.

The strength of a culture depends, finally, on two factors. One is the degree to which the values of the culture are codified and effectively transmitted to all. The second is the degree of pain people suffer for straying outside the cultural norms. The strongest cultures, obviously, are those in which all members clearly know and understand the "code," and also recognize that the penalties for violation are harsh. Whereas strong cultures are successful at translating their abstract principles into daily actions, weak cultures do this much less predictably and effectively.

Defining Corporate Values

We'll return to strong and weak cultures later, but first I want to plant a stake in the ground on the way we define values.

---

[2] Yet, ironically, some members of this culture had "non-negotiable" demands. We lived in interesting times.

We sometimes refer to *core values*, as though these particular values transcended other, less worthy, values. But then I get lost when I read that a company has 17 core values. This does not make sense to me. There can't be that much room at the "core."

Still, I believe that some values do transcend others, and we get to pick which ones run our lives. Maybe some people can keep a hierarchy of values straight in their minds and hearts, but I'm too simple for that. I have a very small set that I try to hold myself to and evaluate others by. I keep the set small so that I don't have to worry about order and priority, or about balancing one value against another.

I've also learned that it's not helpful to label as "values" those qualities that everyone endorses. Take "citizenship," for example; who is going to argue that we *shouldn't* be good citizens? The problem is, this word is always interpreted according to more "local" values that define the behavior of a good citizen within a given culture. So, paradoxically, the more general and vague the term, the closer it gets to being a universal "value," but the narrower and more culture-bound its interpretation becomes.[3] The value of such a value is really very small.

In defining a set of desirable values for a corporate culture, then, I will choose terms *not* for their relative popularity, but rather for their utility in describing a company that is worth working for. I want to work with people who share these values. If others don't, I hope they will gravitate to another organization that has values more to their liking. We will all be happier in the long run.

My list has three items, few enough that I can keep them in "registers" at all times.[4] They are integrity, customer focus, and results.

Integrity

The cornerstone of all that is honorable, *integrity* is a value that requires us—in all our relationships, both internally and externally, with colleagues and customers—to conduct ourselves in an honest, truthful, and straightforward way. There may be dishonest people in the world, but we don't have to admit them into our company. We can choose to associate only with those whose conduct meets our standards.

Integrity is a high standard, but it is exceedingly easy to know whether or not you have acted with integrity. It is as easy as knowing right from wrong. It is not complicated.

Many desirable characteristics of corporate culture that I have written about in previous chapters[5] are based on integrity: a high-trust environment, honoring commitments,

---

[3] It is sometimes said that it is impossible to be all things to all people, but some values are bland enough to fit that bill. The American colloquialism for such values is "apple pie and motherhood"— things everyone is in favor of.

[4] In the olden days of programming, we could specify things we wanted to keep in fast memory so we could access them rapidly, on the principle that we would be using them often. Such locations were called *registers*.

[5] See, for example, Chapters 13, 14, and 15.

an absence of noxious politics, true teamwork, and an open interchange of ideas. Without integrity, we cannot hope to achieve or implement any of these. Later, I will discuss why these characteristics are so crucial in a software development organization.

Customer Focus

Anyone working in the business world is torn over and over again by having to make difficult choices. Sometimes the choice is obvious; we usually have no problem doing something that is clearly required or rejecting behaviors that are clearly wrong. It gets tricky, however, when there are conflicting requirements, a gray area, or something that involves reasoning on the margin. At these times, success means getting a higher percentage of these choices right than we might otherwise do by flipping a coin.

I'm not talking about technical decisions here. Instead, these are judgment calls such as, "Do we ship the product today or work on it for a few more weeks to get it to a better state?" There is usually no single, unambiguous answer. But is there a simple criterion you can use to help frame the decision?

I believe there is. The question I always ask is, "What is right for the customer?"

To further complicate matters, however, there is rarely a single customer.[6] So you must visualize the customer base as a distribution, and try to reason what is best for the mainstream group of customers—the greatest good for the greatest number. If you can put yourself in the customers' shoes and reason through what is right for them, my belief is that you will get many more of these decisions right.

Note that doing the right thing for the customer may sometimes cause a great deal of internal pain. But if you don't do that, then all you are doing is deferring the pain to a later date. And, most likely, that deferred pain will be far worse than the pain you'd have to bear early on to create a responsible, responsive solution.

Customer focus has many cultural manifestations: a drive to release products on time, a passion for creativity and quality, and products that are genuinely fit for use. But it all starts with having the courage to ask the question, first and foremost, "What is best for the customer?"[7]

Results

This third value has to do with results. I believe in results, not excuses.

Today, people seem to expend a lot of time and effort on excuses. It is almost as though they believe that a good explanation for failure is a legitimate replacement for the desired result. But this is not something you can build on.

---

[6] And even if there were just one, there would be conflicting priorities within that organization as well.

[7] Needless to say, this means you have to know who your customers are and what problems they face. I can't conceive of running any business, let alone a software business, without this knowledge.

The simplest way to differentiate the good from the bad is to evaluate results. Not intentions. Not effort. Not "does what he's told to do." Not "easy to work with." All these are irrelevant if results are not achieved. Note, however, that I am *not* saying "success at any cost" or "the end justifies the means." That kind of Machiavellian perversion means you are willing to act without integrity, and that is not allowed.[8]

Finally, we must realize that most goals worth achieving are not accomplished in sprint mode but in marathon fashion. Persistence counts. For those people for whom "failure is not an option,"[9] I salute you.

And the Applicability to Software Is…

I'm sometimes accused of making very general observations under the guise of talking about software development. I plead "not guilty!" It's simply that the principles I believe in are universal, and their value is not limited to the realm of software. On the other hand, I can show why the particular values I've identified are *relevant* to software—why, unless you observe them, software products and companies degrade.

Let's go back to integrity, one of our basic values: We never lie to our customers, and we never lie to ourselves. We deliver a quality product in exchange for a sum of money, and the customer has a right to expect value for that money. There is nothing specific to software in that simple equation.

Yet the production of a software product that customers will be able to use throughout an extended period requires integrity. First, the product must be sustainable in the field for many release cycles; it can't just be cobbled together for the next release and then forgotten. In order to achieve this, the product must have a maintainable underlying architecture that can be modified over time to suit new, emerging requirements. Also, the product must be supported, so that as questions and defects arise, the organization can cope with them and provide solutions for customers. It takes considerable infrastructure to support and evolve a product during many years, and making that investment requires the integrity of a long-term view. Companies that "ship it and forget it" will not be around for long.

A high-trust environment and teamwork are essential for the production of any large software product. Why? The answer is simple: Software is by nature a very complex product. Many individuals on the team make many thousands of decisions every day;

[8] This is one of the rare places where one might have to prioritize even among the small number of core values we have here. Lest there be any doubt, integrity always trumps the other two. Customer focus and results orientation rarely come into conflict with one another, so there is no need to look for prioritization there.

[9] Attributed to Gene Krantz of NASA, during the Apollo 13 rescue mission.

some are large, some are small, and all may have an impact on customers. If we were to depend on a system of permissions and checks to ensure that each and every decision was "correct," progress would grind to a halt. What we need instead is everyone making good decisions on one's own most of the time. Large, critical decisions need to be reviewed, of course, but the majority should be made promptly and implemented effectively and efficiently. This is impossible without integrity at every level of the organization.

Now let's think a little bit more about customer focus. The quality mavens are always getting up on their soapboxes and lecturing us about the need to improve the quality of the software we ship. But it's a bit more complex than that. Quality is a very subjective objective. Some people measure it by defect counts; others talk about usability ("fitness for use" for some, performance for others); still others have different metrics entirely. But none of these can be evaluated in the abstract; there is always, *always*, a trade-off between quality and some combination of cost and timeliness.

That is why I think customer focus is the right value, and the cultural manifestation of this value is that everyone in the organization thinks about the customer: developers, testers, writers, product managers, support, field technical people, salespeople, marketing folk—yes, everyone. The customer is no single group's responsibility; it is everyone's responsibility. If you have both a high-trust environment and everyone focusing on the customers, then you have a potent combination.

And what about results? Well, systems need to be architected, coded, documented, tested along many dimensions, and then built, packaged, and shipped. Without an intense focus on results, the product just doesn't get out the door. Too many things depend on too many other things. The lesson of the old folk tale, "For the want of a nail…"[10] was never more true than for software development. Most projects slip because of an accumulation of intermediate tasks that are delayed, deferred, or simply not completed. Individually, none of these small slips seems important, but the cascade is devastating.

On the flip side, there is a hidden danger in striving for "perfect" results in all the details. Everyone needs to be clear on the most important result: timely shipment of a high-quality piece of software. Creating a perfect Software Requirements Specification along the way will be irrelevant if the customer-visible result—the product—is wanting.

Building a Strong Culture

How can we in the software world implement these three values and build a strong culture around them?

---

[10] The tale starts out with a missing nail leading to a missing horseshoe, then a missing horse, and so on—all the way up to losing the battle and the kingdom, "all for want of a horseshoe nail."

Three Leadership Needs

First, we need *leadership by example*. As a leader, it is part of your job to reinforce and propagate the culture and values of the enterprise, starting with integrity. Our leaders should be held to an even higher standard of integrity than the one to which we hold everyone else. And here I mean all our leaders, not just the folks at the very top. Leadership is part of the company culture, and regardless of where you are in the corporate hierarchy, being a leader means heightened responsibility. The only way to demonstrate integrity as a leader is to act with integrity in everything you do.

It's shocking that the United States Congress has felt the need to pass legislation[11] requiring American CEOs to swear to the veracity of their financial statements. Shouldn't we just expect these statements to be accurate? "Cooking the books" is the moral equivalent of counterfeiting, and Dante in *The Inferno* put counterfeiters in the bottom of the eighth circle of Hell for good reason. His conception of Hell consisted of nine concentric circles, so being at the bottom of the eighth was almost as low as you could go.

Second, to develop a customer-focused culture, our leaders need to *spend time with customers* to gain an acute sense of what the customers need. Only then can they translate that into direction for the rest of the organization.

Finally, we need leadership in the area of *pay for performance*. Managers at software companies need to be able to objectively evaluate performance and compensate people for their contribution to the organization—and nothing else.[12]

Continuity

In addition to meeting these three needs, we need *continuity*. Cultural propagation of values is meaningful only if it survives all the varieties of change that occur in the business world. Let's have a look at some of the phenomena that threaten continuity in software companies.

That Old Devil, Growth

Inevitably, successful companies grow, however small they are at first. Their culture needs to be nurtured so that these organizations do not abandon the very values and traditions[13] that made them successful in the first place. But it is not easy to do this right.

If your company grows slowly enough, there is hope. You can recruit very selectively, working hard to find people who are "good cultural fits" for the existing organization.

---

[11] The Sarbanes-Oxley Act of 2002.

[12] See Chapter 16, "Compensation."

[13] A tradition is a cultural artifact that becomes ingrained, so that people observe the tradition without even remembering the underlying value that created it.

Rapid growth, on the other hand, is a double whammy. In the scramble to fill open positions,[14] it is easy to lose discipline and get sloppy. On the margin, we hire people we probably wouldn't if we weren't in such a hurry. Then, to make matters worse, we don't explain to them the cultural milieu into which they are about to be thrust because we are too busy hiring the next batch of folks.

Notice that we are not necessarily recruiting people with the wrong values. No, what typically happens is an overall weakening of the culture as the organization expands. For example, occasionally forgetting to put the customer first may not draw sharp criticism any more. Over time, Gresham's Law takes over: The bad money drives the good money out of circulation.[15] Those living by the old values become the minority, viewed at first with curiosity, then with derision, and finally ignored.

What replaces the strong culture is often a bureaucratic system designed to check on and enforce a wide range of policies and procedures that never quite capture the previous spirit of "do the right thing." In the absence of cultural strength, organizations fall back on meticulous attention to detail, as if we could recapture the spirit of the law by increasing the number of its letters. Leaders assume that everyone else will make the wrong default decisions, so they impose lots of rules to guide and correct them. It's a sure sign that bureaucracy has set in when the Ten Commandments are replaced by a 247-page handbook that sits on a shelf gathering dust.

Mergers and Acquisitions

After growth, the second most destructive force for a strong culture is a merger or acquisition. The software industry periodically goes through cycles of consolidation; many companies, Rational Software among them, grow "organically" for many years and then use mergers and acquisitions as a way of continuing or accelerating growth. Unfortunately, software companies seem to be much worse at this than other industries, perhaps because software companies have such a wide spectrum of cultures and values. The largest single reason for failure when two software companies combine is cultural incompatibility. Even if the two cultures are similar, merging them can be difficult for a vast variety of technical reasons. Plus, if the two companies are located some distance from one another, there is insularity because of the separation. Whatever the root

---

[14] One of my least-favorite expressions in the business world.

[15] This needs some explanation. Sir Thomas Gresham, advisor to Queen Elizabeth I, noted that when a new currency is introduced to replace an older, debased one, people tend to hoard the new currency while trying to spend as much as possible of the old. This is the origin of the expression, "Bad money drives out good." In a business context, though, we can borrow this old saw to describe what happens when a small company with a strong culture undergoes the transition to becoming a large company with a weak culture. The newer, weaker, more diffuse and less desirable culture is shared by many more people so that, over time, the older, stronger, more valuable culture is marginalized to a smaller and smaller number of adherents, eventually dying out. The "tyranny of numbers," unfortunately, wins out.

cause, in the face of fundamental incompatibility most software mergers fail, plain and simple.[16]

There is a solution. When our pioneer great-grandmothers crossed the prairie in their Conestoga wagons, they always carried a lump of "starter dough" so they could bake the same kind of bread in their new home that they did in their old location. The starter dough contained a yeast culture[17] that could spawn new loaves; every time they baked, they saved a bit of that dough to mix with new dough later.

Similarly, by transferring one or more people, preferably senior people, to the new location, software companies can provide "starter dough" to transmit the company culture and values to the newly merged or acquired company. Any merger or acquisition that forgets to transmit cultural messages early and often is a disaster waiting to happen.[18]

The Single Big Customer or Partner

Another interesting threat comes from having a single large customer or partner with a very strong culture. In this case, both subtle and not-so-subtle influences can permeate your organization. For example, the customer's or partner's style of reporting results—nature, frequency, and so on—may be imposed upon certain projects; gradually, it may spread through the ranks, so that all internal divisions start reporting in the same way.

Sometimes this can be good; we can always learn from others. On the other hand, we do need to be careful that the customer or partner shares our values and that what morphs is the cultural manifestation of those shared values, not the values themselves.

Finally, it is an unfortunate fact of life that partnerships in the software business world are complicated. Today's partner may be tomorrow's competitor, and vice versa. Figuring out the implications of that one is an exercise left to the reader.

New Efforts

Yet another threat to a strong culture is the startup of a new effort, such as a new product line or a facility in an overseas country. Here the "starter dough" principle is crucial. I have personally witnessed a new organization built from the ground up halfway around

---

[16] Wall Street confirms this almost every time a software merger is announced. The typical response is a decline in the share price of both companies prior to the accomplishment of the merger. Only after the merger has proven its value does the share price of the combined company recover. While this phenomenon is also observed in other mergers (even non-technical ones), it seems to be more severe in the case of software companies.

[17] According to the dictionary, the word culture is used for both "the customs, institutions, and achievements of a particular nation, people, or group" and "the cultivation of plants, breeding of animals, or production of cells or tissues." I leave it to you to decide whether this linguistic overloading is a mere coincidence, or whether it belies something deeper.

[18] In a stunning bit of irony, as this was being written in late 2002, Rational Software was itself being acquired by IBM. The acquisition was announced almost simultaneously with the original publication. So far, it seems to have gone very, very well. I'm keeping my fingers crossed.

the world that faithfully reproduced the "mother culture," simply because it started with one person who thoroughly understood the original recipe. He hired and trained every single addition. Ten years later, through slow but steady growth, this organization was one of the strongest in the company, both culturally and in terms of productivity, even though they were geographically farthest of all from the home office.

Be especially wary of efforts to start new groups whose express purpose is to launch a radical cultural change; these are almost always doomed to failure. Here's why: If the change is that important to make, hitch up your pants and do the hard work to make it across the entire organization. If you don't, the new organization will always be on the outside, resented by the rest of the company. If they are successful, they will be resented even more. As they grow in power and influence, civil war will loom, and the only solution may be to spin them off. In so doing, all the benefit to the original organization will be lost. On the other hand, if the experiment fails, it will likely be because the splinter group felt (or was) orphaned.

When You're Looking for a Job...

The last item on my agenda is advice about what to do when you are looking for a job. I believe, strongly, that the biggest single factor contributing to your happiness and success in any company is how comfortable you feel with its culture and values. Almost every other variable in the equation can and will change over time: your role, your responsibilities, your direct supervisor, your organization, and your compensation. Problems in any of these areas can be addressed and fixed over time. But if there is a fundamental incompatibility between the existing culture and your idea of what constitutes a good culture and healthy values, you will be working against something that will nag at you every day in good times and totally sink you in bad times. Remember that cultures and values change very, very slowly. The odds are better that you will gradually adapt to the culture than that the culture will change in a direction to your liking. So unless you really enjoy swimming against the tide, look for compatibility.

How do you discover a company's true culture and values? The best way is to talk with current employees and recent ex-employees.[19] Ask them to speak candidly about what they like and don't like. And during your formal interviewing process with the company, do two things. First, calibrate how important culture and values are by seeing whether your interviewers ask questions to determine the fit between you and their organization. If they never ask you one question in this area, beware. It means that either they are sloppy in their recruiting, or the corporate culture is extremely weak.

---

[19] You may have to discount for certain opinions, based on the circumstances. Some current employees may be overly zealous; some recent ex-employees may be bitter without legitimate cause. But the raw data is always useful.

Second, when it is your turn to ask questions, spend as much time as you can getting them to talk about culture and values. Don't be afraid to put them on the spot; for example, ask them flat-out what is the single most important value in the company, or what is the defining attribute of the most successful employee in the company. If they have the right culture and values, they will understand why you are asking and will interpret your efforts as "serious buying" questions. If you get a consistent, coherent story from almost all the people you talk to, there is reason to believe that the culture is strong: The "code" is visible to all and understood in the same way by most. Once you have established that there is a strong culture, seeing whether your own values align with it should be somewhat easier.

If you are hired, it's a good idea to begin the process of gaining an in-depth understanding of your new company's culture and values immediately. Ask lots of questions. The more quickly you can assimilate the default behaviors that represent the cultural norms of your new company, the fewer blunders you will make, and the more productive you will be. This advice also applies if you are in a company that merges with another or is acquired.

The Bottom Line

I believe in a culture that strongly transmits the values of integrity, customer focus, and results. Software can best be produced and supported by talented, creative, competent individuals who collectively function as true teams in such a context. Strong cultures are maintained over time through both leadership by example and careful attention to transmitting values in the face of growth, mergers and acquisitions, requirements imposed by large customers and partners, and new startup efforts. Just as education is what remains after all else has been forgotten, culture and values are what govern when no one else is looking. Better get them right.

Recap

It's difficult to write about culture and values without coming across as somewhat "preachy." For example, people who have integrity don't need to be told about it, and those who don't won't be swayed by this book, so what's the point? My aim here is to illustrate how important integrity is for people who want to practice it but often feel pressured to cut corners. Don't yield; be obstinate—because it is important.

The same idea carries over to customer focus and results orientation. It's not that "things were better in the good old days." We had ignorance of the basics back then, too! Continuity and consistency across space and time require that we hew to a small number of basic principles. All I have tried to do here is tell you which ones have worked for me.

We've come to almost the end of our journey. The final chapter attempts to tie it all together for you.

CHAPTER 24

Putting It All Together

One of life's great fascinations is watching people evolve over time. Some people grow and develop, while others seem to be stuck in patterns that limit their happiness and well-being. Others excel in certain areas of their lives while failing miserably in others. A small few are spectacularly successful by conventional measures, yet are perpetually dissatisfied. Is there a simple model we can use to make sense of these observations?

Many years of watching and thinking have led me to believe that we can further our understanding by simplifying the problem. The model I use consists of three fundamental states, characterized by the Yiddish words *schlepper, macher,* and *mensch.* First I will describe the states, and how people move from one state to the next. Then I will explain how people can get stuck in one of the earlier states, and how to address that failure mode. In addition, I'll talk about people in different states in different parts of their lives at a given time. Finally, I'll address the issue of the distribution of the population in the various states and the implications for getting along in the real world.

I want to be a little precise with words here. I call the three states "phases," because I believe that there is a natural progression that is accessible to all people. The phases become available as people grow, mature, and come to terms with the real world, learning how to make appropriate compromises between their belief systems and the exigencies of everyday life. Unfortunately, sometimes people get stuck in a phase and don't move on. That leads to thinking of them as a "class" of people. But the word *class* is overloaded with lots of other implications, social and otherwise. Hence, I avoid the use of that term.

Why is this important? We have a tendency to believe that life is complex, and there is a wealth of academic research on the interactions of social groups in many different contexts: family, business, teams, and so on. Most of it is inaccessible to the average person. What I have come to believe is that this very simple model explains a wide variety of real-world data and has predictive power. A simple model that people can understand and apply and that works 80 percent of the time is more useful than a complex and hard-to-use model that works 95 percent of the time.

Schlepper

Let us begin with the first state. People in this phase are collectively known as *schleppers*. This term comes from the Yiddish verb "schlep," which means "to drag." Colloquially, it also means to carry something around, as in "schlepping those bags through the airport." In most common parlance, a *schlepper* is thought of as a lazy, sloppy person, but this is not the connotation that I wish to apply here. For me, a schlepper is someone who is in the first stage of his or her development.

Literally, a schlepper is a carrier. In the good old days, a perfect example of a schlepper was a caddie, a kid who carried golf bags. You are not doing a lot of heavy thinking when you are schlepping; you are performing useful but perhaps menial labor, usually in the service of someone else. Schlepping is not very glorious, but nonetheless one should not underestimate its importance.

First of all, just because you are schlepping does not mean you are forbidden to think. In fact, just the opposite is true: Because the work content of schlepping includes little thinking, you can use this time to think and learn while you schlep. Many creative ideas occur during schlepping. For instance, how can I schlep this stuff with less effort? One of the very first caveman (or perhaps I should say "caveperson") schleppers invented the wheel as a result. The act of routinely repeating a boring, uninteresting task, or having to expend what seems like an inordinate amount of labor to achieve a mundane goal, often causes even the dullest schlepper to have an idea—necessity (made most obvious by pain or fatigue) being the mother of invention. My experience is that people who have schlepped often see new and interesting ways to avoid schlepping, even when the schlepping is associated with a new domain. They develop instincts for when something is going to turn into a big schlep and head off that eventuality at the pass. Ex-schleppers make great engineers, for example.

In general, we all need to schlep. It builds character, as trite as that may sound. It teaches us humility—humility of the sort, "If I don't get smarter about this, I'm going to have to schlep the rest of my life." There are some interesting aspects of this phenomenon.

Schleppers quickly perceive the great injustice of life. Here you are—young, smart, good looking, and so on—and you have to schlep for some old, fat, dull idiot who just happens to be your boss. How did *that* happen?

Sometimes these bosses can be downright stupid, to the point of making you schlep more than you should have to. Other times, they can increase your grief through deliberate cruelty. And because you are the designated schlepper, you have two choices: schlep in silence, or go schlep somewhere else. The third option, making a ruckus, is usually counterproductive, as schleppers are basically interchangeable by definition, and noisy ones are quickly replaced.

Some amazing truths reveal themselves to observant schleppers. For example, schlepping in silence causes erosion of the stomach lining, so the learning schlepper will attempt to deal creatively with his work or social situation in such a way as to minimize grief. Quitting and schlepping somewhere else (option two) is most often found to not be a solution at all, for just as all schleppers are interchangeable, all schlepping jobs are basically the same. Most of the time, it's out of the frying pan and into the towering inferno.

Skipping over the schlepper phase is dangerous, even if you could do it. Actually, some people do—those who are born rich. They never get to experience the benefits of schlepping—for instance, the joy of creative schlepping, or the pride one takes in a load well-schlepped. As a result, they never understand what most of the world is going through. They take too much for granted and are not well grounded in reality. And, it is almost impossible to become a schlepper later in life if you never were one to start with.

But more important, you miss out on important lessons—humility, the value of a dollar earned through a hard day's work, the intrinsic unfairness of the world, and how screwed up things are down in the trenches. The other irreplaceable lesson comes through contact with the enormous variety of people the real world presents the schlepper—the gonifs,[1] the liars, the cheats, and what used to be called in less politically correct times, "the common people." Most important, there are those wonderful others who see something special in you and say to themselves, "Why is this kid schlepping? Surely he can do more," and then act on it. They become our mentors, coaches, and champions, and that is one of the ways we move beyond the schlepper phase.

Sooner or later, every schlepper must come to understand that in order to make progress, you have to move beyond the schlepper phase. This involves investment. You can schlep forever and blame it on the evils of the class system, free-market capitalism, or whatever, but the system is there. To stop schlepping, you have to be able to do something that gets someone to say, "Hey, I'm not paying you to schlep that

---

[1] A *gonif* is a common thief.

stuff; get someone else to do it!" Often this takes the form of actually making the effort to get more education or training, thinking, or doing something that makes you stand out in a positive way. It requires, in Churchill's words, blood, sweat, tears, and toil.[2] You must show that you can add value at the next level. This is a two-part proposition. First you have to get the training, acquire the skills, get the result, do the deed. Then you have to get someone influential to recognize that something has changed and that you are ready to graduate from the schlepper phase. These are the mentors I described previously.

So, we all start out as schleppers. Kids are the schleppers in every family. Think of being a schlepper as being an apprentice. Kids are apprentice adults. If they are watchful, can avoid getting killed, and listen from time to time, they can graduate to adulthood. If not, they remain kids forever.

Resign yourself that in everything you do—every new job, every new sport, every new relationship—you start out as a schlepper. How long you remain one is up to you. And remember, while you are a schlepper, to maintain your dignity.

Macher

The second phase of life is that of the *macher.* I believe the origin of "macher" is related to the verb "to do" or "to make." Phase two is the longest and, in some ways, the most enjoyable phase of life. A macher is someone who gets things done, who makes things happen, who gets results. When you are a macher, you are "putting points on the board." This phase is incredibly productive, and most machers get a real sense of satisfaction from doing what they do. Some machers enjoy it so much that they stay machers forever—and this is not a totally bad thing. If it weren't for the machers of the world, we'd all still be schlepping.

Machers are not just the inventors, the entrepreneurs, the craftsmen, and the geniuses—although those folks generally are machers. What distinguishes a macher is that he or she adds value and makes a difference. Being a macher is usually equated with high performance, not the ordinary or mundane. Those who put in their eight hours and don't mess up too often aren't machers; they're sort of advanced schleppers. No, to be a macher, you have to be in that category that is often characterized by the exclamation, "We need a real macher to fix this!" In many firms, machers are the "rainmakers," the folks who generate business. The litmus test is this—if you take away the macher, the organization not only suffers greatly, it's just not the same.

---

[2] If you want to leave footprints in the sands of time, I suggest you wear work boots. Also, the more accurate quotation of Churchill is, "I have nothing to offer but blood, toil, tears, and sweat," in his May 13, 1940 speech. It has been misquoted so often as to become part of the language. Note, for example, the rock band "Blood Sweat and Tears."

Machers have the following interesting characteristics:

- They are usually very focused, to the point of being driven.

- They are intense.

- They are results-oriented.

- They understand the goal and can get it in the crosshairs. It is usually a bad thing to get between a macher and the macher's desired result.

- Machers are charismatic, in both the good and bad sense. It is unusual for a macher to not be charismatic, because this trait is so often linked with leadership. There are exceptions, but not enough of them to warrant more space here.

There is a dark side. Machers will err on the side of believing that the end justifies the means because, to them, it does. They can be absolutely ruthless. People who are squeamish about hurting other people's feelings themselves will often employ machers, who have no such compunctions. The macher has no illusions about what he's getting paid for—it's to get a result. But, if the truth be known, the macher would almost always do it for free—achievement is a very potent drug.

Machers can be self-limiting. The really good machers discover early in their careers that you have to be careful about breaking too much glass. Annoy enough people and you won't be able to get others to help you—even other machers! There are a lot of obnoxious young machers, but very few obnoxious old machers. The reason is obvious: It's hard for machers to progress if they can't build groups consisting (incidentally) of other machers. The scope of the problems they are asked to solve increases and gets to the point where fielding a team is the only answer. If the macher is incapable of developing the interpersonal skills necessary to get others to play, he will eventually wind up isolated and be overtaken by even more clever machers.

Machers enjoy a side benefit that is not insignificant. To some extent, they can be *prima donnas* and make their own rules. Why? Because many people and organizations will tolerate some pretty outrageous behavior if the problem to be solved is serious enough or the gain is big enough. So the macher can avoid much of the petty tyranny of organizations and bureaucracies by explicitly placing himself outside the normal system. Many machers choose this path simply because this is the only way they can function: by setting up a context in which they can get the job done by their rules. In any other context, they will fail because they have to obey constraints that they judge to be too onerous. But, live by the sword, die by the sword. When a macher fails, there is never an insufficiency of people waiting to bury him—his enemies tend to accumulate and have long memories. To survive outside the system, you have to be really good and have real integrity. If you don't, your first mistake will be your last.

Sometimes machers can become intoxicated by the power they wield and can really get out of control. In the end, an overly aggressive macher will self-destruct, but not before creating a pretty big mess. Machers rarely fade away quietly; rather, they go out in a blaze of fireworks. Hubris just catches up, and because machers do everything on a grand scale—they do have vision—they generally fail spectacularly.

Can you be a macher without having been a schlepper? Yes, but it is rare. Machers who have not served some kind of apprenticeship usually have a piece missing. It is tough to be a macher if you are not grounded in reality, and schlepping is the quintessential training ground in reality.

Machers tend to stay in the macher phase because they are an elite. They enjoy lots of tangible and intangible rewards in the business world in exchange for the results they achieve for their organizations. They are constantly being recruited for bigger and better challenges. It's a great life, and the risks are few—organizational backlash from time to time, and perhaps a premature coronary from excessive Type-A behavior. But most machers can deal with it.

In other areas of life, being a macher means being competent; actually, it means performing at the highest level of competence. There's a tendency to aspire to be a macher in all parts of one's life. Once one has become a macher in one part, it can be frustrating, as competency can be highly domain-specific. Ergo, many machers become one-dimensional, focusing their energies in their area of dominance. Because they tend to be competitive by nature, this is a natural stalling-out point for them. Once you are better than most of your peers, what is there left to strive for?

As exalted as machers are, there is a higher state. The Yiddish word for it—*mensch*— is pretty much untranslatable into English.

Mensch

A *mensch* is a gentleman, a "fine person." But that doesn't quite capture the feeling of "He's a real mensch!" The essence of being a mensch is to have a global perspective, to be somewhat introspective and philosophical, and to be kind. A mensch is good at listening and very good at seeing the other person's point of view.

We should remark here that the word mensch in German means human, and secondarily, man. While that makes this phase of life accessible to both genders, it is much more inclusive than the Yiddish usage. In Yiddish, not all humans are mensches.

There's a big difference between machers and mensches. First, machers usually have a very hard edge to them; mensches are mellower, softer, and more patient. Machers have a sense of urgency; mensches have a sense of inevitability. The mensch really believes that it all comes out in the wash. The schlepper is often viewed as dull or stupid, when in fact all he may be guilty of is ignorance; the macher is viewed as being smart or clever; the mensch is always viewed as being wise. You go to the macher when you want a problem solved now; you go to the mensch when you are looking for a long-term solution. In some sense, the schlepper can't do anything, the macher is the tactician par excellence, and the mensch is the strategist.

Before I let you think that the mensch is just a Yiddish incarnation of Yoda, I should point out that the mensch is not just a dispenser of advice, but also a doer of deeds. The thing that sets the mensch apart is that he not only knows the right thing to do, but he acts on it, even at great personal cost. Unlike the macher, the mensch is not at all interested in getting the credit for the result. He is vitally interested in the result for its own sake and doesn't really care if anyone ever knows he was the facilitator. A typical mensch-like thing to do is to make a large, anonymous donation to charity, for example.

Machers sometimes make good mentors, but only as an almost accidental side effect of their primary objective, which is to get results. Machers more often mentor more junior machers, as opposed to schleppers. Mensches, on the other hand, make superb coaches and mentors, because they are so highly attuned to the needs of others; they help everyone because they empathize with everyone. They also have a quintessential long-term perspective, so they understand the leverage of developing others and building infrastructure. They understand the Zen-like beauty of injecting energy into the system, unaware of when or where the positive consequences of that act will appear—yet confident that they certainly will.

The mensch also provides a lot of lubrication in any organization. He's above the fray, committed to the organization and its goals, but without a personal agenda, unlike the macher, who always has one. The macher is territorial, whereas the mensch is extra-territorial. The mensch will endeavor to be a peacemaker, a mediator, and someone who is creative in trying to find a solution when there appears to be none. Appearances notwithstanding, the mensch is a highly effective person. His strength comes from his ability to work well with everyone and from the respect everyone has for him.

Can you become a mensch without having been a macher? There are two points of view.

The first is that the schlepper-to-mensch transition is sort of like going from apprentice to master craftsman without ever having been a competent journeyman in between. In this point of view, the wisdom the mensch exhibits is accumulated from years of being a macher; the really good machers age well and eventually become mensches.

The problem with this point of view is that there seem to be some clear exceptions. Just as we have noted that many machers never graduate to menschhood, it is also the case that we find a few people displaying the characteristics of mensches who have not been machers. They have schlepped for extended periods of time but have not become bitter. They have accumulated wisdom, are kind, and are secure in themselves. They universally understand people and the human drama, and they exhibit lots of empathy. Their judgment is impeccable. The mystery is where their wisdom came from.

More on Mensches

The Swiss physicist and ecologist Olivier Guisan told me 30 years ago that the key to growing up was to have one's eyes opened without having one's heart hardened. A maturing process that enables us to cope with the sometimes daunting realities of life, without becoming cynical, is essential. The schlepper is typically a pessimist, the macher a cynic. The mensch is an optimist. He believes in the goodness of people and in civilization's ability to find solutions to complex problems. His own humanity is of course part of this, but he ignores that.

The noted psychologist Mihaly Csikszentmihalyi[3] has described a model in his book, *Flow: The Psychology of Optimal Experience*.[4] In this theory, there is a tension between knowledge and skill set versus the task worked on. If the task is too easy, boredom sets in, and people are unhappy. If the task is—relatively speaking—very challenging compared to competence, then people are stretched, but tense and anxious as a result. When there is a reasonable match—not too easy, not too hard—then a "flow state" is achieved. Csikszentmihalyi calls the achievement of the flow state the *flow channel*, because it spans a broad range of competency and task difficulty. Flow is a state of grace, where achievement is high and one experiences a feeling of incredible well-being; athletes call it "being in the zone."

What is interesting is that, in this model, schleppers would appear to be unhappy because they are constantly below the flow channel, working on tasks that they find boring. Machers, it would appear, are troubled because they are most frequently working above the flow channel—they are characteristically "in over their heads." And mensches, by my reckoning, are happy and effective because they are so often in the flow channel. If achieving flow is a key, then mensches would seem to have discovered it.

Surprisingly, you don't have to be old to be a mensch, although many of the traits associated with mensches can come with age. No, being a mensch is a state of mind, available to all of us with the proper perspective and attitude.

Mensches are happy people. They are surrounded by happy people. They can deal with life's worst surprises and help others to do so, too. They have extremely well integrated and balanced lives, and they are at peace.

Population Distribution

For every 100 schleppers in the world, there are 10 machers and one mensch.

Why are there so many schleppers? The easy answer is to steal from Lincoln and say, "God must have loved them, because he made so many." But even so, one would think that frustration would cause almost everyone to graduate sooner or later. Alas, it is not so. First, laziness plays a big part: Many people are just not willing to do what it takes to move up. Second, it requires maturity: An attitude adjustment is required to graduate—

---

[3] Pronounced "chick-sent-me-high."

[4] Mihaly Csikszentmihalyi, *Flow: The Psychology of Optimal Experience*. (New York: Harper Collins, 1991.) See also Chapter 16 for more details on flow.

you need to take responsibility for your own destiny. It is easier to complain about the system and your inability to advance than it is to take matters into your own hands and succeed in spite of obstacles. Finally, there is a commitment to continue to grow. Moving beyond the schlepper zone is a fundamental change, and it scares many people, because it implies a new way of life that is bereft of the simpler comforts that the schlepper enjoys. Because the "no gain" comes with "no pain," many schleppers can never quite get over the emotional barrier it takes to graduate. I think these three factors—sacrifice, maturity, and fundamental life change—explain why there are so many schleppers out there.

All this exists in the context of a real, sometimes harsh, external world. In my experience, intelligence and talent play much less a part in graduation than do hard work and a determined attitude. In today's global economy, I believe that the opportunity is there, that there are no *insurmountable* cultural, social, or other barriers. If you allow yourself to believe that external factors rule, you will consign yourself to the role of a schlepper. You can prevail over others who block the path, but no one can lift you over a barrier that you construct for yourself. That there are only 10 machers for every 100 schleppers is the greatest waste of human capital that I can imagine. It is a situation that I find untenable as we move deeper and deeper into the information economy. The schlepper jobs are going away, but the attitudes that have allowed them to persist for so long are not.

For those who graduate, a relatively short period of their lives is spent schlepping. If you are in this category, most of your life will be spent as a macher, so try to be a good one. If machers could look at this period of their lives as apprentice mensches, we might all be a little better off. I don't think it would make them much less effective, and, in the long run, we'd all live longer and be happier. But it's tough to alter the macher's behavior, because he believes his effectiveness is tied to all the characteristics that distinguish him from the mensch. It's a puzzle.

I worry that my estimate of one mensch for every 10 machers may be higher than the actual number. The world needs more mensches, as they seem to be in constantly short supply. In too many cases, their period of menschhood is short, as their spirit is more durable than the body that contains it.

Some Final Thoughts on the Model

The model makes certain assumptions. You start out as a schlepper, grow to be a macher, and hope to become a mensch. That is the usual progression, with the exceptions noted throughout this chapter. Even though the model is simple, it is not perfectly neat; anytime we deal with generalizations about people, we will have "messy" exceptions to deal with.

The problem is that while I can tell you what you need to do to become a macher, I can't give you a recipe for becoming a mensch. You can't become a mensch through hard work, the way you can become a macher. It may be that mensches are born, not made. Asking how to become a mensch is a little like asking how to become wise, or how to become enlightened.

It helps to have come under the influence of a mensch or two, especially early in life when they can serve as examples. Growing up with a macher for a father and a mensch for a grandfather—and seeing how their styles played against each other—could be very enlightening, if the schlepper child were especially aware.

Another key idea is understanding that the mensches of the world want nothing in return for their kindness but that you pass it on to the next generation.

But what do I know?

Recap

This chapter is dedicated to Roslyn Rosenthal Marasco (1921-1998).

We need to make the following progression clear to managers:

$$\text{Data} \longrightarrow \text{Information} \longrightarrow \text{Knowledge} \longrightarrow \text{Wisdom}$$

The arrows here should be read as "can lead to." Misapplication at any step along the way leads to the wrong answer. Starting out with "good data" is a must, but it is no guarantee that anything useful comes out at the other end.

There is an enormous gap between stage one and stage four. Too many technical organizations focus almost exclusively on improving data collection ("metrics"), without working on their abilities in the next three phases. I think this behavior has its roots in managers who come from an engineering or science background: they want numbers. But numbers are useless without intelligent interpretation; in fact, numbers will *at best* get you only halfway up the ladder. This approach won't lead to much overall improvement in your organization, because bad answers derived from clean data just don't do you very much good. *It's what you do with the data that counts.*

You can gather data automatically. Getting to stage two entails intelligent human analysis and synthesis. Achieving stage three requires an intellectual framework from which you can derive general principles. Finally, progressing to stage four demands, once again, human intelligence and great judgment, so that the application to the real world can be effective.

Awareness of the world around us exists at various levels of abstraction. The higher the level of abstraction, the more generally can we apply our awareness to real-world situations. *D-I-K-W* represents increasing levels of abstraction, and abstracting the right stuff grows harder at each stage. Data is concrete and specific; wisdom is abstract and universal; information and knowledge are intermediate states. It is important not to confuse information with knowledge or knowledge with wisdom. When you have a concept in hand that derives from data, ask yourself whether it is information, knowledge, or wisdom. The answer to that question is often crucial.

We can think of people in the three phases of life as being capable *agents* who perform different transformations. We can modify our chain with more generic arrows:

Data ⟶

    (is gathered and transformed by *schleppers* into) ⟶

        Information ⟶

            (which is transformed by *machers* into) ⟶

                Knowledge ⟶

                    (which is transformed by *mensches* into) ⟶

                        Wisdom

This representation explains why we swim in data, distill some of it into information, refine precious little of that into hard-earned knowledge, and extract very scarce wisdom as the ultimate product. We start out with a lot at one end of the chain and get very little at the other end. The process itself requires that as we move up the abstraction ladder, we formulate our conclusions in fewer, simpler, and more powerful ideas. More important, the number of available agents goes down by a factor of 10 at each stage of the process; the work gets harder, and there are fewer competent people to do it at each level.

The agents who do the work at each stage bring to it their particular skill set; having 10 times the agents of the wrong type at any juncture is worthless. No, it is a classical impedance-matching problem: You have "stuff" in a certain state, and you need to transform it into "stuff" of the next-higher state. Only people with requisite experience and maturity can perform the necessary transformation—and do it correctly and efficiently. Distinguishing quality from mediocrity is a moral action, requiring passion as well as intelligence and judgment.

Our job as managers of the managers is to make sure that we have the right people stationed at the right places at the right time. Only then can we hope to reap the complete benefits of the progression from data to wisdom.

Acknowledgments

How does one even *begin* to complete this task? In my case, this book represents a career that spans several decades, and, believe me, there were many, many people who influenced me during that time. I've decided to recognize them chronologically.

From Far Rockaway High School: Amelia Wexler Ashe*, who taught us all how to write.

From The Cooper Union: Clarence Sherman*, Bob Steinberger, Mary Blade*, and Charles Richard Extermann*. Each of these people was pivotal in teaching me about being a human being as well as a chemist, engineer, or physicist. Bob Steinberger, the best man at my wedding, and I have sustained a friendship that is in its 40th year.

From Stony Brook: Leonard Eisenbud and Alfred Goldhaber.

From Switzerland and France: Pierre Extermann, Olivier Guisan, Ronald Mermod, Michael Pouchon*, Michael Ispérian*, René Turlay*, and the LeMones. It is impossible to thank these people enough for helping me get through the Ph.D. process in one piece.

From Irvine: Steve Franklin, Alfred Bork, Bob Dodge, and Joe LaRosa. At UC Irvine and then at Fluor, I made the transition from the university world to the "real world." These folks were helpful guides in that process. Bob Dodge in particular showed me what it meant to be a good boss. Mike Kinsman taught me how to look at business numbers and make sense of them, and he has been a good friend and trusted advisor for more than 25 years.

From San Mateo: Bill Buchanan, who pointed me in the direction of the Silicon Valley.

From MacLeod Labs: Bill Irwin, who showed me the "start-up" ropes, and who instilled in me the notion that it was all a general management problem. Also Dennis Allison, who was always there when you needed him, and especially there when you didn't know you needed him. Not to mention Paul Hwoshinsky, who exposed me to the idea of non-financial assets.

At Rational, the founders, Mike Devlin and Paul Levy, whose combination of passion and intelligence was inspirational. Mike and Paul made a whole generation of people better than even they thought they could be.

At Rational, for teaching me about marketing: Brett Bachman, Yosi Amram, and Jerry Rudisin.

At Rational, for teaching me about customers: Bob Bond, Tom Rappath, John Lovitt, Kevin Haar, Mark Sadler, John Lambert, and Burton Goldfield. These guys were masters of all they surveyed. From John Lovitt, I took away the long-range view of what it means to build an organization. Bob Bond was perhaps the best mentor one could ever hope for. And Robert Gersten, behind the scenes, almost a brother.

At Rational, some of the most incredible software developers and managers I have had the pleasure of working with: Jim Archer, Jack Tilford, Dave Bernstein, Dave Stevenson, Rich Reitman, Howard Larsen, Ashish Vikram (now in Bangalore), Scott Johnson, Phil Garrison, Pete Steinfeld, and Tim Keith. Each of these gentlemen taught me something about software development that altered my perspective on the field. Jim introduced me somewhat derisively to the concept of "content-free management," and Jack was noteworthy in never, ever, giving up.

From Stockholm: Jaak Urmi, who educated me on the way large organizations react to technological sea changes. Also, Martin Lesser from the KTH, the original "Magnificent Six" from RatScan, and my dear colleagues from Celera.

From Rational and elsewhere, people who reviewed many of these chapters in their original form and made substantive suggestions that improved them: Philippe Kruchten, Pascal Leroy, Walker Royce, Grady Booch, Dave Bernstein, Max Wideman, Paul Campbell, Bob Steinberger, Jack Tilford, Jim Archer, Rich Reitman, David and Marc Marasco, and Kate Jones. It would be hard to go overboard in expressing my appreciation to this fine corps of reviewers who kept me honest.

At Rational, my editors at *The Rational Edge,* Mike Perrow and Marlene Ellin. Just as a gentleman has no secrets from his butler, I have no writing secrets from them. They are just a class act.

Reviewers of the manuscript by the time it got to Addison Wesley: Martin Lesser, Gary Pollice, John Walker, Steve Franklin, Boris Lublinsky, Joaquin Miller, Karl Wiegers, Don Gray, Bill Irwin, Jerry Rudisin, and Bob Bond. Not to mention Anonymous One and Anonymous Two. And, at the very end, the eagle-eyed Kate Jones, who made a final pass over everything.

At Addison-Wesley: Mary O'Brien, Chris Zahn, Chris Guzikowski, Brenda Mulligan, Michael Thurston, Amy Hassos (Specialized Composition, Inc.), and Lisa Thibault. I would like to thank Mary for having the courage to publish a somewhat unconventional book.

Marvin Hoshino, my brother-in-law and strong supporter, who edited my doctoral dissertation lo these many years ago and never was recognized or thanked for it. Tim Brennan, my faithful companion as CFO during the period at Rational when I was Senior Vice-President of Operations. Dr. Hingson Chun, who is in charge of pump maintenance. Carol Weiss, one of my oldest friends, who was so supportive of my wife and family over all these years. These are folks who helped me maintain sanity.

The following authors have inspired me through their books. Their work has affected both what I write and how I write: Ralph Palmer Agnew, Foreman S. Acton, Richard W. Hamming, Richard P. Feynman, Maurice d'Ocagne, Frederick P. Brooks, Mihaly Csikszentmihalyi, Grady Booch, Philippe Kruchten, and Walker Royce.

Billie and Lester, for providing the music. R. P. Feynman, who was living proof that a kid from Far Rockaway could make it big.

These folks all showed that you don't get there by yourself, and you should consider yourself lucky to have worked with such an amazing array of people.

Joe Marasco
Pebble Beach
December 2004

Index

A

abstraction, 66
acceleration, 127
   of a vertical ball toss, 129-130
accidental degeneracy, 231
accuracy, 109
achieving flow, 181
acquisitions, 277-278
adding
   employees, 250
   useful hours to product, consequences of naïve model, 256
algorithms, quadratic algorithms, 172
altitude variable, 94
American-born engineering students, 15
analogies, 202
   Newton's Laws of Motion, 203-205
   oil changes, 217
physics, 201-203
quantum mechanics, 207-211
relativity, 205-207
thermodynamics, 211-212
anarchy, 47
"The Animal Game," 72-74
   So What? test, 74-75
anticipating obstacles, managing teams, 35-36
applications, mission-critical applications, 4
applied learning
   iterative development, 53-54
   short vectors, 51
Archer, James E., 82
Arrow, Kenneth, 212
assumptions, naïve model, 252-253
attrition, 267
audience for this book, 6
avoiding issues, 244

B

bad science, 213
Barry, Dave, 17
bartering, 149, 151
baseball, fantasy baseball, 226-228, 230, 232-235, 239
batch processing, 19
batteries, 218
     solar power, 223
batterychip, 220-221, 223
"Being in the zone," 180
Bernstein, Dave, 55
Bilenko, Herman, 17
Boehm, Barry, 113
Bond, Bob, 78
Booch, Grady, 137
Borgenstam, Curt, 198
Brooklyn Bridge, 199
Brooks, Frederick P., 102, 118, 250
Brownian Motion, 47
build processes, 79
     difficulty of, 79-82
         organizational politics, 80-81
         tools, 83-84
     iterative development, 84
build rhythm, 125
buildmeister, 83
business implications, waterfall development versus interative development, 54-55

C

calculating, 225-226
     Leroy, Roscoe; adventures while being shipwrecked, 226-228, 230, 232-235, 239
calculators, 18
calibrating schedules, 120, 122-123
candidate releases, 78
cell phones, 217

Central Limit Theorem, 104
Cha, Sandra E., 269
Chaos Theory, 213
Churchill, 284
citizenship, 272
Clauuswitz, 83
closure, communicating with engineers, 162
code, counting lines of, 114
code reviews, 59
code rot, 216
coding, 69
cognitive dissonance, 102
commitment, 168, 174-175
     deadlines, 171-172
     definition of, 170
     elaboration and construction, 176-177
     excuses, 170-173
     high-trust environments, 175
     honoring, 174
     large project chicken, 175
     scheduling, 175-176
     Texas handshake, 169-170
communication, 158-159, 162-164
     closure, 162
     establishing ownership, 160-161
     iteration, 164-165
     not suggesting solutions, 161-162
     pseudoscientific jargon, 213
     remember who you're dealing with, 159-160
compartmentalization effect, 108
compensation, 179, 191-192, 276
     flow, 182
         Cone of Correct Compensation, 185-191
         diagonal cases, 186-187
         job-based models, 184-185
         skills-based models, 183-184
     productivity/performance, 181-182
     win-win, 190-191
competition, 29

completion, 138
compromise, 148-149
computations, 16-18
computers, engineers from 1960-1970,
    18-19
Cone of Correct Compensation, 185-191
    mapping team members, 191
Conestoga, PA, 50
consequences of naïve model, 253-255,
    257-258
    adding useful hours to product, 256
    cost, 257-259
    multipliers, 254-256
constants in the software development
    business, 5-6
constraints, 161
construction, 137, 139-140
    commitment, 176-177
continuity
    culture, 276
        growth, 276-277
        mergers and acquisitions, 277-278
        new efforts, 278-279
        single big customers or partners, 278
    of leadership, 199
contribution of new hires during transition,
    251-252
Cool Hand Luke, 119
Cooper Union, 15
core values, 272
corner cases, 227
corporate values, defining, 271-272
    customer focus, 273
    integrity, 272-273
    results, 273-274
correct compensation, 183
cost
    consequences of naïve model, 257-259
    labor cost, 260
counting lines of code, 114

crisis, 243
    avoiding issues, 244
    critical paths, 246
    dealing with, 247-248
    fish, 244-246
    fish markets, 244
    fixing problems, 245
    turning points, 245-246
crossing the chasm, 131
Cskiszenthmihalyi, Mihaly, 180, 288
cultural differences, politics, 146
culture, 270, 280
    continuity, 276
        growth, 276-277
        mergers and acquisitions, 277-278
        new efforts, 278-279
        single big customers or partners, 278
    job hunting, 279-280
    leadership by examples, 276
    strong cultures, 271, 280
    weak cultures, 271
curves. *See also* graphs
    completion curves, 138, 140
    force curves, 133-134
    human behavior, 130-131
    learning curves, 130, 138, 140
    percent completion curves, 126
    project velocity, 132
    and reality, 134-135
    S-curves, 130
customer focus, 273
customers, 276
    continuity, 278
czar of the build, 83

D

Dangerfield, Rodney, 158
Dante, 276
Darwin, Charles; Theory of Evolution, 213

Davis, Derrick, 91
deadlines, commitment, 171-172
debuggers, 210
decisiveness, 28
derivatives, 127
design, Vasa, 199
devices, 217
    buying batteries packaged with
        software, 218-223
    cell phones, 217
    upgrading, 217
diagonal cases, flow and compensation,
    186-187
dialects, 60
dice, 226
distributing software development
    projects, 96
distribution, project pyramid, 97-99
documentation, 8-9
Dr. Dobb's Journal, 126
Drabkin, Mikhail, 83
drafting, 15
drag, effect of new hires on existing
    team, 252

E

Edmonson, Amy C., 269
education, 14
educational system, 12
Einstein, Albert
    relativity, analogies, 205-207
    Special Theory of Relativity, 207
    Theory of Relativity, 207
elaboration, 137, 139-140
    commitment, 176-177
electromagnetism, 211
embedded software, refreshing, 216-217
empathizing, 7-9
empire building, 155
employees
    adding, 250

attrition, 267
new hires, 250
    contributions during transition,
        251-252
    effect on existing team, 252
    evaluating, 262
engineering, 13
engineering discipline, 4
engineering mapping, 153
engineers, 153
    1960-1970, 15-16
        computers, 18-19
        heritage of, 20
    politics, 152-153
entropy, 79, 211
error rates, 215
establishing ownership, 160-161
estimating, 107-111, 113-114, 119-120
    schedules, commitment, 175-176
estimation, 17
eternal verities, 5
Euclid, 112
evaluating new hires, 262
evolution, 213
examples
    leadership, 276
    of naïve model, 259-260
    of politics, 147-148
excuses for breaking commitments, 172-173
experience, selecting teams, 25

F

failure, common causes of, 30-31
false-positives, 3
fantasy baseball, 226-228, 230,
    232-235, 239
Faraday, Michael, 211
"Father Knows Best," 13
featuritis, 199
feedback, 9
Feynman, 18

"Field of Dreams," 78
finite horizon, 97
first-level disconnect, 69
fish
    crisis, 244
    death of, 244-246
    moral of story, 246
fish markets, 244
fixing problems, 245
flow
    achieving, 181
    compensation, 182
        Cone of Correct Compensation,
            185-191
        diagonal cases, 186-187
        job-based models, 184-185
        skills-based models, 183-184
    productivity/performance, 181-182
flow channels, 180-181, 288
focus, 29
    managing teams, 34, 37
forces curves, 133-134
FORTH, 75
FORTRAN, 19
Franklin, Dr. Stephen, 83
frugality, 93

G

Galileo, 127, 206
generating probabilities, 230
GIGO (Garbage In, Garbage Out), 19
goals, 27-29. *See also* milestones
Godel's Incompleteness Theorem, 213
Godfather offers, 37
gonifs, 283
good science, 213
Gorshkov, Sergei Georgievich, 83
Gould, Stephen Jay, 213
Grady, Booch, 113
graphics, 59-60

graphs. *See also* curves
    parabolic position graphs, 130
    project completion graphs, 130
    total forces on a project, 141-142
Gresham's Law, 277
Gresham, Sir Thomas, 277
growth, 249
    attrition, 267
    continuity, 276-277
    employees, 249-251
    mergers and acquisitions, 277
    naïve model, 251
        assumptions, 252-253
        consequences, 253-255, 257-258
        contribution of new hires during
            transition, 251-252
        drag created by new hires on existing
            team, 252
    nomographs, 264-265
    non-linearity, 260-261
    productivity, 263-264
    spreadsheets, 265, 267
    suggestions for, 261-262
guidelines, iteration estimating
    guidelines, 115
Guisan, Olivier, 287

H

Hamming, Richard, 22
Hawthorne Effect, 210
heat death, 212
Heisenberg's Uncertainty Principle, 209-210
Hello world, 71
Heppenheimer, T. A., 20
high-trust environments, 148, 153-154, 175
Highsmith, James, 24
honoring commitments, 174
horseshoes, miscalibrations, 46
human behavior, curves, 130-131
human factor, 32

human nature, 270
humility, 282
humor, managing teams, 38
Hybertsson, Henrik, 199

I

ICD (implanted cardioverter defibrillator), 3
impedance mismatch, 163
imprinting, 33
inception, 137, 140
increasing probability of success, 100-101
The Inferno, 276
input mistakes, 18
inquest, Vasa, 200
inspiration, managing teams, 35
instincts, trusting when managing teams, 39
integrity, 272-273
    and software, 274
interations, 48, 114
    communication, 164-165
    estimating guidelines, 115
    phases, 137-139
issues, avoiding, 244
iterative development, 43-44, 118
    applied learning, 53-54
    build processes, 84
    project pyramid, 103
    rhythm, 135-137
    technology, 57-58
    versus waterfall development
        business implications, 54-55
        staffing effects, 55-57

J-K

Jacobsson, Hein, 199
job-based model, compensation, 184-185
job hunting, culture and values, 279-280

K&R, 70
Kant, Immanuel, 201

Katzenbach, Jon R., 34
Kennedy, John F., 12
Kernighan, Brian W., 70
Kludge, 198
koan, 192
Krantz, Gene, 274
Kroll, Per, 44
Kruchten, Philippe, 44, 137, 222
    culture, 270
KSLOC (kilo source lines of code), 113

L

labor content, 257
labor cost, 260
Laika, 12
large project chicken, 175
Larsen, Howard, 180
Laws of Motion, analogies, 203-205
leaders, 35, 147
leadership
    continuity of, 199
    customer-focused culture, 276
    by example, 276
    pay for performance, 276
learning
    new programming languages, 70-71
        standard problems, 71-74, 76
    Rational Unified Process, 138
learning and completion curves, 140
learning curves, 130
Lencione, Patrick, 269
Leroy, Pascal, 97, 220
Leroy, Roscoe, 44-45
    calculating, 226-228, 230, 232-235, 239
    calendars, 110-111
    commitment, 168-169, 174-175
        deadlines, 171-172
        definition of, 170
        excuses, 170-173
        honoring, 174

large project chicken, 175
Texas handshake, 169-170
communication, 158-159, 162-164
closure, 162
establishing ownership, 160-161
iteration, 164-165
not suggesting solutions, 161-162
remember who you're dealing with, 159-160
estimating, 108-111, 114, 120
long vectors, 48-49
short vectors, 47
square roots, 111
life of software, 215-216
life outside of work, managing teams, 38-39
lifetime meal tickets, 14
light, 213
speed of lights, 206
limitations of project pyramid, 101-105
listening, 7-8
managing teams, 36
lognormal, 97
lognormal distribution, 101, 104
long vectors, 48-49
lots of rules and no mercy, 82
Lovitt, John, 192

M

machers, 281, 284-286, 289
malice, avoiding when managing teams, 37-38
managers
audience for this book, 6
learning new programming languages, 70-71
standard problems, 71-74, 76
managing teams, 34
anticipating obstacles, 35-36
avoiding malice, 37-38
focus, 34

focus on facts, 37
humor, 38
inspiration, 35
life outside of work, 38-39
listening, 36
stability, 37
trust your instincts, 39
mapping
politics, 152-153
team members, 191
Marasco, Andrew, 20
Maxwell, James Clerk, 211
Mayo, Elton; Hawthorne Effect, 210
measurements, 209
mechanical drawing, 16
menschs, 281, 286-288
Meretsky, Wayne, 40
mergers, 277-278
milestones, 26-27
miscalibrations, horseshoes, 46
missile gap, 12
mission-critical applications, 4
mistakes, learning from others, 34
modeling UML, 60-61
abstraction, 66
first example, 61
relevance to software, 65-66
second example, 61-63
third example, 63-65
models
naïve model. *See* naïve model
non-linear relationships, 260-261
momentum, 133
Monday, 226
solution to fantasy baseball probabilities, 234-236, 238-239
monitoring, 27
Moore, Geoffrey, 131
motion, Newton's Laws of Motion (analogies), 203-205
mountain climbing, 23

multipliers, consequences of naïve model, 254-256

The Mythical Man-Month, 250

N

naïve model, 251
    assumptions, 252-253
    consequences of, 253-255, 257-258
        adding useful hours to products, 256
        cost, 257-259
        nailing the multiplier, 254-256
    contribution of new hires during
        transition, 251-252
    drag created by new hires on existing
        team, 252
    example of, 259-260
Nagasaki bomb, 12
negative payoff, 97
negotiating, 157
net force, 127
new efforts, continuity, 278-279
new hires, 250
    contributions during transition, 251-252
    effect on existing teams, 252
    evaluating, 262
    growth, 263
Newton, Sir Isaac, 127
    Laws of Motion, analogies, 203-205
Newton's Second Law, 126-127
nomographs, 264-265
non-linear relationships, 260-261
non-linearity, 260-261
notation, abstraction, 66

O

observation, 7-8
OD (organizational development), 249
"off by a factor of ten," 17
Ohm's Law, 65

Ohms, 64
oil changes, 217
organizational politics, difficulty of build
    processes, 80-81
organizing teams, 25-26
overpaid, 182
ownership, 160-161

P

parabolic position graphs, 130
Parkinson's Law, 53
partners, continuity, 278
paths in crisis, 246
paying for software upgrades, 218
    batteries packaged with software,
        218-223
people
    machers, 284-286
    menschs, 286-288
    population distribution, 288-290
    schleppers, 282-284
percent completion curve, 126
performance, 181-182
period of transition, 251
Perrow, Mike, 147
personality, 270
Peter Principle, 187
phases, 281
    iterations, 137-139
    machers, 284-286
    menschs, 286-288
    schleppers, 282-284
physics
    acceleration of a vertical ball toss,
        129-130
    analogies, 201-203
    electromagnetism, 211
    entropy, 211
    Newton's Laws of Motion, analogies,
        203-205

Netwon's Second Law, 126-127

quantum mechanics, 207-211

thermodynamics, 211-212

trajectory of a vertical ball toss, 129

velocity of a vertical ball toss, 128-129

piracy, 223

planck, 208-209

planning

decisiveness, 28

goals, 29

handling risk, 27-28

milestones, 27

monitoring and recordkeeping, 27

scheduling, 26-27

scope, 24

plateaus, 131

PM (project management), 249

political process, definition of, 147

politics, 145, 150

bad politics, 152, 154-155

compromise, 148-149

context of, 146

good politics, 150-151

high-trust environments, 153-154

mapping, 152-153

neutral politics, 151

scenarios, 147-148

population distribution, 288-290

position, 127

potential, 182

precision, 109

predictability, 123

scheduling, 119

primacy of time, 90

prioritizing risks, 52-53

probabilities, 226, 228-229, 232-235, 239

generating more, 230

probability of success, 94

project pyramid, 99-100

increasing, 100-101

problem-solving, 21

problem-solving clock, 6-9

problems, fixing, 245

product versus prototype, 200

productivity. See also growth

flow, 181-182

growth, 263-264

new hires, 263

programming languages, managers learning

new languages, 70-71

standard problems, 71-74, 76

project completion graphs, 130

project management (PM), 249

project managers, adjusting schedules for, 122-123

project pyramid, 90-91, 93

altitude variable, 94

distribution, 97-99

iterative development, 103

limitations of, 101-105

probability of success, 99-101

risk, 92, 105

scaling, 95-97

volume, 94-95

project velocity curves, 132

projects

failure, common causes of, 30-31

human factor, 32

success of, 31-32

prototype versus product, 200

prototyping, 51

pseudoscientific jargon, 213

pyramid model, results of, 101

Q-R

quadratic algorithms, 172

quality, 92-93

of software, 4-5

quantum mechanics, analogies, 207-211

Queen Elizabeth I, 277

quick studies, 131

ramps, 130

random number generators, 226

random numbers, 228, 234. *See also*
    probabilities

Raskin, Jef, 220

rates of change, 127

Rational Software, 5-6
    acquisition, 278

Rational Unified Process, 137

reality and curves, 134-135

recordkeeping, 27

refreshing embedded software, 216-217

registers, 272

relativity, analogies, 205-207

religion, culture, 271

repeatable build process, 78

resources, 92

respect, 158

results
    iterations and phases, 138-140
    values, 273-274

rhythm
    build rhythm, 125
    curves of human behavior, 131
    iterataive development, 135-137

risk, 27-28, 92
    prioritizing, 52-53
    project pyramid, 105

risk targeting, 51-52

Ritchie, Dennis M., 70

Roebling, John, 199

Royce, Walker, 44, 113, 137

S

S-curves, 130

Sadler, Mark, 214

sandbaggers, 120

sandbagging, 176

sandboxes, 79

Sandstro, Anders, 198

Sarbanes-Oxley Act of 2002, 276

scaling, 250
    project pyramid, 95-97

scarcity premiums, 183

scenarios of politics, 147-148

scheduling, 26-27, 117-118, 120-121
    adjusting schedules for different
        managers, 122-123
    calibrating, 120, 122-123
    commitments, 175-176
    estimates, 119
    final week, 123
    predictability, 119, 123
    Roscoe's graph, 122
    square root, 120
    "two-schedule" game, 117

schleppers, 281-284, 289

schrodinger, 208

science, 13, 213
    physics. *See* physics

scope, 92-93
    prelude to planning, 24

scope creep, 127

scope management, 90

searching for a job, values and culture,
    279-280

selecting teams, 25

shipping the product, 77-78
    build processes, difficulty of, 79-84

Shooman, Martin L., 251

short vectors, 47, 49
    applied learning, 51
    software development, 50

signing up. *See* commitment, 167

skill levels, 180

skills-based model, compensation, 183-184

slide rules, 16-17

slope, 127

Smith, Douglas K., 34

So What? Test, The Animal Game, 74-75

software
    importance of good software, 4-5
    life of, 215-216
    packaged with batteries, 218-223
    upgrading, 218
        packaging batteries with software,
            218-223
    and values, 274-275
software developmenet managers, 6
software development, short vectors, 50
software development projects,
    developing, 96
software piracy, 223
solar power, 223
sound, 206
space race, 12
Special Theory of Relativity, 207
speed, 93, 129
speed of light, 206
speed of sound, 206
spreadsheets, growth, 265-267
Sputnik, 12
Sputnik II, 12
square roots
    estimating, 114
    Leroy, Roscoe, 111
    scheduling, 120
stability, managing teams, 37
staffing effects, waterfall development
    versus interative development, 55-57
standard problems, learning new
    programming languages, 71-74, 76
starter dough, 278
states. *See* phases
stogies, 50
strong cultures, 271, 280
subscriptions, 218
success
    definition of, 101-102
    of projects, ingredients for, 31-32

sunk cost, 215
synthesizing, 8-9

T
tables
    Mapping Politics, 153
    Learning and Completion Metrics for
        Phases in the Rational Unified
        Process, 138
    Product of Total Force Peak Value and
        Time Interval Length, 141
    Results of Using the Pyramid Model and
        Lognormal Distribution, 101
tangents, slope of, 127
team members, mapping, 191
teams
    competition, 29
    managing, 34
        anticipating obstacles, 35-36
        avoiding malice, 37-38
        focus, 34
        focus on facts, 37
        humor, 38
        inspiration, 35
        life outside of work, 38-39
        listening, 36
        stability, 37
        trust instincts, 39
    organizing, 25-26
    selecting, 25
testing, 8-9, 200
tetrahedron model, 92
Texas handshake, 169-170
Theory of Relativity, 207
Thermodynamics, analogies, 211-212
"throwing money at the problem," 12
time, 92
tools, difficulty of build processes, 83-84
trade-offs, project pyramid. *See* project
    pyramid

traditions, 276
trajectory of a vertical ball toss, 128
transition, 137, 140
trusting instincts, managing teams, 39
Turing's Machine, 213
turning points, in crisis, 245-246
"two-schedule" game, 117
Tzu, Sun, 152

U

UCM (Unified Change Management), 82
UML (Unified Modeling Language), 60-61
    abstraction, 66
    first example, 61
    relevance to software, 65-66
    second example, 61-63
    third example, 63-65
undecideability, 213
underpaid, 183
update releases, 77
upgrading
    devices, 217
    software, 218
        packaging software with batteries,
        218-223
Urmi, Jaak, 197

V

values
    core values, 272
    corporate values, defining, 271-274
    customer focus, 273
    integrity, 272-273
    job hunting, 279-280
    results, 273-274
    and software, 274-275
Vasa, 197-199
    design, 199

    inquest, 200
    leadership, 199
    product versus prototype, 200
    testing, 200
Vasa Museum, 197
vectors, 49
    long vectors, 48-49
    short vectors, 47, 49
        applied learning, 51
        software development, 50
velocity, 127
    percent completion curves, 132
    of a vertical ball toss, 128
Voltaire, 83
volume, project pyramid, 94-95

W

Walker, John, 52
waterfall approach, 46
waterfall development versus iterative
    development
        business implications, 54-55
        staffing effects, 55-57
weak cultures, 271
Westheimer, F. H., 52
Wideman, Max, 105
    iron triangle, 90
Williams, Ted, 240
win-win, compensation, 190
Woods, Tiger, 122

Get
The
Rational
Edge